VENANTIUS FORTUNATUS

Poems to Friends

VENANTIUS FORTUNATUS

Poems to Friends

Translated, with Introduction
and Commentary, by

JOSEPH PUCCI

Hackett Publishing Company, Inc.
Indianapolis/Cambridge

Printed in the United States of America

14 13 12 11 10   1 2 3 4 5 6 7

For further information, please address
   Hackett Publishing Company, Inc.
   P.O. Box 44937
   Indianapolis, Indiana 46244-0937

www.hackettpublishing.com

Cover design by Abigail Coyle
Interior design by Elizabeth L. Wilson
Composition by William Hartman
Printed at Sheridan Books, Inc.

Library of Congress Cataloging-in-Publication Data
Fortunatus, Venantius Honorius Clementianus, ca. 540–ca. 600.
   [Poems. English. Selections]
   Poems to friends : a translation with commentary /
Venantius Fortunatus ; translated, with introduction and
commentary, by Joseph Pucci.
     p. cm.
   Includes bibliographical references and index.
   ISBN 978-1-60384-187-0 — ISBN 978-1-60384-186-3 (pbk.)
   1. Fortunatus, Venantius Honorius Clementianus, ca.
540–ca. 600—Translations into English. I. Pucci, Joseph
Michael, 1957– II. Title.
PA8310.F7A2 2010
871'.02—dc22   2010011507

Contents

For my Mother, who taught me to love books—and for my Father, who made the home in which I read them.

Preface

The reputation of Venantius Fortunatus has always been measured against the perspective one brings to the age in which he lived. Romanists will see him as a late antique figure and emphasize the strains of a lingering classicism that abide in his poetry, while medievalists will see especially in the Christianity of his large output the move toward something more aptly belonging to the Middle Ages. Historians of Rome or of the so-called Dark Ages have mined the poetry for all manner of information, finding it to be a prosopographical storehouse and a check on Gregory of Tours' (No. 15) vast *Histories*. Yet Fortunatus knew nothing of our periodization and saw himself only as a man of his day. He surely took life as it came, understanding his time and place neither as an end of something grand nor the beginning of something momentous, seeing it instead simply as a time of rapid change—of which he was always an eager student and to which he was many times an assiduous eyewitness. That the forms his poetry takes look backward and forward in time is natural—that is part and parcel of living in a particular time and place and attests both to Fortunatus' training and to his interest in advancing Latin poetry formally for his audience. That he makes foundational to his poetry the feelings of life and their ambiguities, on the other hand, is not to be taken for granted and distinguishes him from poets who grapple in their verse with experience in more workaday and, therefore, less appealing ways.

Readers of French, Swedish, Catalan, and Italian who lack the ability to read Latin have been able to wander in Fortunatus' poetic riches for some time—in the case of French, since the late nineteenth century—but English readers remain at a disadvantage.[1] Geoffrey Cook's *A Basket of Chestnuts*, published over a quarter of a century ago and long out of print, couples versions of twenty-one personal poems with renderings of four of the acrostics. The translations are free verse and aim to make the reader forget that she or he is reading something written in another language, but they often are hard to follow on that score. Judith George's translations, to which I refer from time to time, published in 1995 but now also out of print,[2] cover about one quarter of the poet's output in literal versions that sometimes place at

---

1. See Abbreviations for a guide to those used in what follows. Nisard, Reydellet (French); DB (Italian), who notes that there are also partial translations in Catalan and Swedish (40); there is no full translation into German of which I am aware, though individual poems have been rendered in scholarly studies.

2. George, *Poems*.

a remove those qualities of expression that show Fortuantus' talents to best advantage.[3]

Given the ever-growing interest in late antiquity and in light of the dearth of English translations of Fortunatus' works, the time seems right to bring this poet to a wider audience. In the Introduction I address the principles of selection and translation that inform the pages that follow. Here I need to say a word or two about my intended audiences. I have two in mind. First, I hope to have rendered translations that can be of use to Latinless readers who wish to know something of the vision and voice of the most prolific poet writing between the fourth and the eighth centuries. I envision this translation and commentary to be of use, therefore, in opening up the literary remains of late antiquity to wide audiences without specialized language training or historical knowledge.

The inclusion of a commentary with my translations may seem to run at cross-purposes to the goal of reaching such an audience, but the relative obscurity of Fortunatus (and his friends) made assistance for readers essential. That, coupled with the fact that no commentary on the poetry exists in any language, convinced me that I had an opportunity, in bringing these poems to light, to reach a quite different audience at the same time, one literate in Latin yet requiring some assistance in contextualizing and interpreting Fortunatus' words. In the essays that introduce individual poems, therefore, in addition to the normal prosopographical information, I have included discussions of earlier scholarly views while paying attention also to Fortunatus' prosody. The necessity of doing this was perhaps furthered by the ease with which it could be done, for the number of works that address the poetry interpretively can still be counted on two hands (with fingers to spare). And so, while I have not included the sort of full scholarly citation one would expect in a commentary per se, I have paid attention to issues quite apart from the purely historical. My hope is that this translation can be of some use to students of Latin reading Fortunatus for the first time, not as a crib to facilitate translation so much as a source of scholarly context for a large body of poetry not easily understood.

Pondering friendship in Fortunatus' life has reminded me that I owe much to it in my own as I bring this book to publication. Kenneth Haynes and Bryn Canner read a first draft barely deserving of comment, but their tempered

---

3. Only twenty-five of the seventy-two poems translated by George are duplicated in my translation since her focus is on the political poems. The promised volume by Brian Brennan in the same series that would have covered the public and religious pieces has never, to my knowledge, appeared, though George mentions it in her Introduction (xxii). English translations of some of the poems are also found in Rogers and, less completely, in Macchiarulo.

criticism encouraged a second version that Christopher Geadrities vetted. His unmerited attention to those gossamer adaptations was met by Lesley Jacobs, whose control over English lingers here, and John Jacobs, whose incomparable Latinity helped me to recognize that it's best to inhabit the middle. The poets Alexandra Zelman-Döring and Joshua Bocher (once students; always friends) offered word-by-word alternatives. Colleagues were unstinting: Jeri DeBrohun helped with elegy while providing a model of friendship that Fortunatus would recognize; Geoffrey Russom explained the prosody of what I had done after I had done it; David Warner warned me of the shoals of Merovingian history; Andrew Romig read the final manuscript with an historian's eye but a poet's heart. The Dean of the College at Brown provided support to Morgan Palmer, Jennella Sambour, and Michael Jacobs in their roles as summer research assistants. In Deborah Wilkes I have had an editor willing to work against market pressures in order to bring Fortunatus' words to a wider public. That she was indulgent of deadlines but recognized when to push makes my debt all the greater. Joel Relihan, a reader in a million (many millions, really) knows what he did and why my gratitude is so great. Lome Aseron, Nancy Evans, Michael Gleason, Jarrett Lobell, Dan Pearson, Dave Vernaglia, Catherine Ware, and Jim Whitta are in my earliest memories of teaching and have my enduring thanks for making a place for me when they didn't have to. I hope my more recent students know they share in that gratitude, even if they remain unnamed here (you know who you are). To my teachers František Svejkovksý, Françoise Meltzer, Winthrop Wetherbee, and W. R. Johnson, and to Kitty and Joey, go my last and best thanks—joined by the two to whom this book is dedicated—my first friends—with a son's gratitude and love.

Abbreviations

carm.   *Carmen/carmina* = "poem" or "poems" in Fortunatus' collection, followed by book number, then poem number within the book, e.g., *carm.* 9.1 is the first poem of the ninth book of the collection. Sometimes line numbers for individual poems are included, e.g., *carm.* 9.1.1 is the first line of the first poem of the ninth book. When a book number is followed by two numbers separated by a dash, it indicates a range of poems, e.g., *carm.* 9.1–3 is the first, second, and third poems of the ninth book. "App." is equivalent to a book number and indicates that the poem in question is found in the Appendix to the collection.

DB   S. Di Brazzano, ed. and trans. *Venanzio Fortunato Opere I.* Aquileia, 2001.

Duchesne   L. Duchesne, ed. *Fastes épiscopaux de l'ancienne Gaule.* 3 vols. Paris, 1907–1915.

Ep. Aust.   See *MGH,* Epist.

George   J. George. *Venantius Fortunatus: A Latin Poet in Merovingian Gaul.* Oxford, 1992.

George, *Poems* J. George, trans. *Venantius Fortunatus: Personal and Political Poems.* Liverpool, 1995.

HF   Gregory of Tours, *Historiae Francorum.* Vol. 1.1. in *Monumenta Germaniae Historica, Scriptores rerum merovingicarum,* edited by B. Krusch and W. Levison. Hanover, 1937–1951.

Koebner   R. Koebner. *Venantius Fortunatus. Seine Persönlichkeit und seine Stellung in der geistigen Kultur des Merowinger-Reiches.* Leipzig and Berlin, 1915.

Meyer   W. Meyer, *Der Gelegensheitsdichter Venantius Fortunatus* in *Abhandlungen der königlichen Gesellschaft der Wissenschaften zu Göttingen.* n.f. IV. Berlin, 1901.

MGH   F. Leo, ed. *Venanti Honori Clementiani Fortunati Presbyteri Italici Opera Poetica.* Vol. 4.1 in *Monumenta Germaniae Historica,* Auctores Antiquissimi. Berlin, 1881.

MGH, AA   B. Krusch, ed. *Venanti Honori Clementiani Fortunati Presbyteri Italici Opera Pedestria.* Vol. 4.2 in *Monumenta Germaniae Historica,* Auctores Antiquissimi. Berlin, 1885.

MGH, Epist.	W. Gundlach, ed. *Epistolae Austrasicae.* Vol. 3 in *Monumenta Germaniae Historica,* Epistolae Merovingici et Karolini Aevi. Berlin, 1892.
MGH, SRM	B. Krusch, ed. *Monumenta Germaniae Historica,* Scriptores rerum Merovingicarum. Hanover, 1885.
Nisard	M. C. Nisard with M. E. Rittier. *Venance Fortunat. Poésies mêlées traduites en Français pour la première fois.* Paris, 1887.
OLD	P. G. W. Glare, ed. *Oxford Latin Dictionary.* Oxford, 1982.
PL	J-P. Migne, ed. *Patrologiae cursus completus, series Latina.* Vol. 88, *Venantii Fortunati Opera Omnia.* Ed. D. Luchi. Paris, 1862.
PLRE	J. R. Martindale, ed. *The Prosopography of the Later Roman Empire,* Vol. III: A, B: AD 257–641. Cambridge, 1992.
Praef.	*Preface,* in *MGH.*
Reydellet	M. Reydellet, ed. and trans. *Venance Fortunat Poèmes.* 3 vols. Paris, 1994–2004.
Roberts	M. Roberts. *The Humblest Sparrow: The Poetry of Venantius Fortunatus.* Michigan, 2009.
Tardi	D. Tardi. *Fortunat. Étude sur un dernier représentant de la poésie latine dans la gaule mérovingienne.* Paris, 1927.
Vit. Mart.	*Life of St. Martin,* in *MGH*
v./vv.	verse/verses of a poem.

Introduction

1. From Roman to Frankish Gaul

In 565, when Venantius Fortunatus saw it for the first time, Gaul had transmogrified from a Roman province into a powerful kingdom ruled by the Franks. Linked perhaps by language and a sense of shared origins but otherwise heterogeneous,[1] the Franks first appear in extant Roman memory in the third century C.E. as raiders across the Rhine-Danube frontier. By the word *Franci* the Romans designated without distinction the dozen or so Frankish tribes situated north and east of the lower Rhine,[2] including the most important of these, the Salian Franks. In the calamitous third century, the Franks overran the northwestern part of Roman Gaul until the emperor Postumus pacified the area, not least through the use of Frankish mercenaries, and throughout the fourth century the Franks continued to be simultaneously a thorn in the empire's side and an ally, depending on the tribe involved and Roman military necessity. Not the least of the emperors who found himself dealing with the Franks were Constantine, at the beginning of the century, and Julian, at its midpoint.

In the great invasions of the early fifth century, however, the Franks seem not to have played a significant role. Gaul was invaded by the Visigoths, who, with Roman assent, took control of the southwestern part of the province; and by the Burgundians, to whom the southeast was ceded. By the middle of the century, an accommodation seems to have been reached whereby, on behalf of the Romans, portions of the Rhine-Danube frontier were defended by the Franks. At about the same time, in the first burst of Salian power, the Franks attacked the Roman stronghold of Arras. Defeated by Aetius, representing Roman interests in Gaul, the battle brought to notice the Salian leader Clodio, a figure Gregory of Tours considers a forbear of Merovech (d. 456), the legendary founder of the Merovingians, the dynasty that bears his name, whose heirs dominated Gaul in the decades in which Fortunatus lived there. The Salian Franks, joined by the Visigoths and Burgundians, fought alongside Aetius in 451 when he led the Roman army against Attila's invading hordes.

---

1. See also McKitterick (193–231, 371–96). Given the necessity of relying almost exclusively on Gregory of Tours' *Histories* to reconstruct it, Merovingian history remains a controverted field, with an unwieldy bibliography. What follows is a narrative of bare fact intended to situate Fortunatus in his time and place; more specific issues are treated, such as they can be, in the introductory essays throughout.

2. James (36); Musset (72).

But in Gaul this was more or less Rome's last stand. Aetius was assassinated not long afterward, and imperial power in the west quickly began to fade.

As the Roman presence waned as the fifth century wore on, the Salian Franks, under two powerful kings, came increasingly to dominate Gaul in the century's last decades. The first, Childeric (d. 481), possibly the son of Merovech, fought under the Roman general Aegidius against the Visigoths in 463 at the battle of Orléans. Then, according to Gregory of Tours, Childeric was exiled to Thuringia (or possibly Tournai) but eventually returned with a wife about a decade later. Increasingly isolated in northern Gaul once the emperor who had sponsored his Visigothic campaign was assassinated, Aegidius seems in the meantime to have founded his own kingdom, with its capital at Soissons, that he passed on to his son, Syagrius, in 464, who was elected, according to Gregory of Tours, *rex Romanorum,* "king of the Romans."[3]

In the meantime, Childeric was consolidating his power in northern Gaul as the leader of the Salian Franks, with his capital at, or near to, Tournai. He managed to stay on good terms with the Visigoths in Burgundy, the most powerful kingdom in the west, into whose ruling family Childeric's sister had married. He was also on excellent terms with the local Gallo-Roman nobility, which brought him the support of the bishops in Gaul. He seems to have cooperated, too, with Aegidus and, in due course, Syagrius, but when Childeric died in 481 his son and successor, Clovis, was not so accommodating. Five years after his accession, Clovis initiated a campaign against Syagrius, defeated him at a battle near Soissons, and eventually saw to his murder. He then consolidated his power with the Gallo-Roman nobility and the bishops before taking on the other Frankish, Celtic, and Germanic tribes in Gaul, on either side of the Rhine-Danube frontier. In short order a series of small wars resulted in victories over the Thuringians, the Alemanni, and, early in the sixth century, the Burgundians.

In 506, on the cusp of an important military victory against the Alemanni and in circumstances that remain controverted, Clovis converted to Christianity. Around the same time, he began planning a campaign against the Visigoths in southern Gaul, whom he conquered in 507 at the battle of Vouillé. Clovis' alliance with Anastasius I, the Byzantine emperor, who was already in conflict in Italy with Theodoric, the king of the Ostrogoths, gave Clovis free rein in this southern campaign against the Visigothic king, Alaric II, whom Theodoric considered a kinsman. After his victory at Vouillé, in

---

3. James (71) notes that Gregory of Tours may have misunderstood the evidence he culled in postulating this kingdom, perhaps willfully, in order to ennoble Clovis' victory over Syagrius, but Geary (81) reflects the general acceptance of Gregory's view.

which Alaric was killed, Clovis was named by Anastasius an honorary consul of the Roman empire, a title whose prestige Clovis was able to leverage as a means to augment his power in northern Gaul, where he ruled until his death in 511.

Clovis married Clotild, a Burgundian princess and Catholic Christian, a union that strengthened his hand within the kingdom once led by Clotild's father, Chilperic. They had two daughters, Ingomer, who died young, and Clotild, who married the Visigothic king Amalaric, and three sons, Chlodomer (d. 524), Childebert I (d. 558), and Lothar I (d. 561). By a concubine Clovis also fathered Theuderic I (d. 534). Clovis' kingdom was divided after he died among his four sons, whose combined rule stretched for half a century across Gaul, ending with the death of Lothar I. In between, Clovis' sons made the Franks the dominant successors to Rome in the west, not least by managing, when they weren't scheming against each other, to act in tandem in order to consolidate their power over much of western Europe.

The Burgundian kingdom of their mother was brought into the Frankish realm in 534. Provence was ceded by the Ostrogoths not much later, in part to effect a Frankish alliance against the Byzantine empire, which was determined at the time to reconquer Italy. The Visigothic presence in Gaul, already diminished by the wars of Clovis, was reduced even further toward the middle of the decade. Theuderic I took much of Italy from the Ostrogoths as they struggled against Justinian's wars of reconquest. Theuderic's son, Theudebert I (d. 548) went one step further, subduing the Thuringians and parts of Saxony while conquering the remnants of the Alemanni still present east of Burgundy. He also exploited the chaos initiated by the Byzantine-sponsored incursion of the Lombards into northern Italy and managed eventually to bring this large swath of territory, including Bavaria and Raetia, under Frankish control. With Aquitaine already under Frankish rule, and with northern Gaul as their homeland, by the middle of the sixth century Clovis' sons ruled a realm, conceived of as a unity—the *regnum Francorum,* "the kingdom of the Franks"—that included virtually all of modern-day France, Belgium, the Netherlands, substantial parts of western and southern Germany, Switzerland, much of Austria, and northern Italy.

When, in 561, Clovis' last surviving son, Lothar I, died, the Frankish kingdom was divided among Lothar's four sons, Charibert I (d. 567), Guntram (d. 592), Sigibert I (d. 575), and Chilperic I (d. 584). Charibert died not long after his father, however, and his inheritance was absorbed into his brothers' holdings.[4] The three remaining siblings did not get on nearly as well as their father

---

4. While Charibert lived, his inheritance included Paris and environs, Aquitaine, Bordeaux, and Toulouse.

had with his brothers. Part of the difficulty may have derived from the fact that Guntram and Sigibert shared a mother, Ingund, while Chilperic's mother was Aregund. The discord effected by these brothers, in any case, shaped the Frankish kingdom to which Fortunatus journeyed in the spring of 566.

The sons of Lothar I each ruled discrete parts of the kingdom of the Franks. The so-called Austrasian realm included, as befits its name, not only the eastern parts of the kingdom, but also Champagne and large portions of central and southern Gaul. This became Sigibert's domain, whose capitals were at Reims and Metz. Guntram inherited parts of Neustria and all of Burgundy, whose capital was at Orléans (and, eventually, Chalon) and found himself king of the most Romanized of the three realms. Those parts of Neustria not granted to Guntram were inherited by Chilperic and included the lands surrounding the cities of Paris, Tours, and Rouen. Chilperic's kingdom was considerably smaller than that of his brothers, a fact not lost on Chilperic, who spent much of his reign waging campaigns to conquer his brothers' holdings.

Not too long after the death of Lothar I, for example, Chilperic seized the royal treasury at Berny-Rivière and took Paris, an outcome eventually reversed by the combined forces of his brothers. In 567 he seized Tours and Poitiers, cities that Sigibert had recently acquired, which caused Guntram and Sigibert to unite under the general, Mummolus, who thereupon won the cities back for his sponsors. More ominously, in 575, Chilperic's son, Theudebert, pillaged a large swath of Sigibert's realm, including the Touraine and Poitou. Sigibert routed Theudebert and nearly defeated and captured Chilperic, but at just this moment he was assassinated, most likely on the orders of Chilperic's queen, Fredegund.

At this point Brunhilde stepped into the political void created by her husband's murder. To be sure, Chilperic tried to play his advantage by taking Paris and Soissons and confiscating Sigibert's considerable treasury. But he was hardly a popular figure, perhaps least of all within his own family, for his son, Merovech, chose this moment to marry Brunhilde, Sigibert's widow. Thereafter battles for control of the Frankish realm waxed and waned on all sides. Guntram joined Chilperic, for example, in order to gain Aquitaine, and in an attack on the church in 581, Chilperic accused Gregory, bishop of Tours, of having seduced Fredegund, an event in which Fortunatus was much involved as witness and eventual conciliator.

When the young heirs to Chilperic's throne died in 581, however, affairs took a different turn. Gestures were made respecting a rapprochement between Chilperic and Brunhilde, acting on behalf of her son, Childebert II (d. 595), but Chilperic's murder in 584 made Guntram the sole surviving heir of Lothar I. He therefore sought an alliance with Brunhilde and Childebert II, presumably under considerable pressure from the nobility and bishops, and in 587 all parties agreed to the terms of the treaty of Andelot. By them, each king became the other's heir and Guntram promised to protect Childebert's young sons, Theudebert II (d. 612) and Theuderic II (d. 613). Importantly for Fortunatus, Poitiers passed to the control of Childebert, presumably ushering in an era of greater peace and stability for the city that he was to lead as bishop in the coming decade.

But such peace as the treaty brought was by all accounts short-lived. Guntram died in 592, and by the terms of Andelot, Childebert acquired Burgundy. Childebert died soon thereafter, however, at which point Brunhilde attempted to hold both Austrasia and the newly-inherited Burgundy for her minor grandsons, the sons of Childebert, and, eventually for her great-grandson, Sigibert, the eldest son of Theuderic. In time, however, events caught up with the aged queen, who was tortured then murdered in 613, at the hands of Chilperic's son, Lothar II (d. 629). But by this time Fortunatus had been dead for several decades, and the world that he had known was already rapidly changing. It is no coincidence that one of the important figures who supported Lothar II against Brunhilde was Pippin the Elder (d. 640), the grandfather of a figure also named Pippin (d. 714), whose great-grandson would complete the usurpation of the Merovingian kings begun by his forbears and go on to be called by posterity Charlemagne.

2. Fortunatus in Italy—and Gaul

Fortunatus began life far from the confines of Clovis' *regnum Francorum*, in Italy where he was born, in Venetia near Treviso at Duplavis (modern Valdobbiadene), between 530 and 540 C.E.[5] His father's family had lived in Duplavis for several generations[6] and as landowners may have been of the aristocracy.[7] The poet calls himself Fortunatus in his poetry, while the full name recorded in the manuscripts, *Venantius Honorius Clementianus Fortunatus,* provides little information about ancestry, since Roman nomenclature had fallen out of regular use by the sixth century. Of his immediate family Fortunatus mentions his parents, a brother, a sister, Titiana, and nephews.[8] Some have understood certain lines in the *Life of St. Martin* to indicate that the poet and his family left Duplavis for Aquileia to escape the civil

---

5. George (19 with n. 93) and Reydellet (vol. 1, vii-viii with n. 2) summarize conjectures as to possible dates; Koebner (11, n. 3) argues for 540 based on his (idiosyncratic) reading of *carm.* 9.7.50.

6. *Vit. Mart.* 4.668 in *MGH* (293–370).

7. Tardi (26–28); Reydellet (vol. 1, viii).

8. *Vit. Mart.* 4.670–71 in *MGH* (293–370); *carm.* 11.6.8, with George (19).

unrest surrounding the death, in 526, of the Ostrogothic king, Theodoric.[9] But all that can be said with certainty is that after a childhood in Duplavis Fortunatus moved to Ravenna to complete his education.[10]

At Duplavis Fortunatus' training included readings in the classical Latin canon: Cicero, Sallust, Virgil, and Terence. At Ravenna, he was exposed to a wider array of authors, both pagan and Christian, with the aim of becoming rhetorically accomplished, including study of the Christian Bible. Given Ravenna's prominence as both a Gothic and Byzantine capital, its location at the crossroads of east and west, and the competing Christian cultures established there, part of Fortunatus' education, too, must have derived from the rich urban environment the city provided, unlike any other in the West in the sixth century, shaping the poet in multiple ways as he completed a training intended to secure a career in the law or in government. Yet there exists in his writing no indication that the poet sought to exploit the advantages his education gave him for civil or legal preferment.[11]

Perhaps the allurements of Ravenna induced Fortunatus to begin his poetic career, for the first two pieces of his collection, *carm.* 1.1 and 1.2, seem to date from the years in which he resided there. But he did not stay in the illustrious city in which he had gained his training, claiming instead, as he reports in the *Life of St. Martin,* that temporary blindness, cured through the intercession of this saint, led him to make an arduous pilgrimage—over the Alps and through Frankish Gaul—to St. Martin's tomb in western France.[12] Nor is this the only reason he gives for leaving Italy. In the *Preface* to his collection, written a few years later, it is no longer blindness but an inclination to endure the trials and tribulations of the life of a wandering poet that, he says, prompted the journey.[13] The two rationales are not incompatible, given the venues in which these brief autobiographical vignettes fall. For the *Life of St. Martin* is a sensible place for Fortunatus to insinuate his life into the fabric of this saint's miraculous cures, while the *Preface* to the collection, written by a patronized poet wandering from one sponsor to the next, seeks to glorify through poetry the rising fortunes of Frankish Gaul in the figures of its most illustrious leaders.[14]

---

9. Tardi (26–37), based on *Vit. Mart* 4.658–62 in *MGH* (293–370); George (19–20) and Reydellet (vol. 1, viii) have Fortunatus move from Duplavis directly to Ravenna.

10. See also Brennan ("Career," 78).

11. Reydellet (vol. 1, viii).

12. *Vit. Mart.* 1.40–45; 4.665–67; 684–85; 692–701 in *MGH* (293–370).

13. *Praef.* 4.

14. On Fortunatus' motivations for leaving, see also George (25–27 with n. 125); Tardi (58–68); Koebner (14–16); Reydellet (vol. 1, xv–xvi); and Brennan ("Career," 54–56).

Whatever his reasons, Fortunatus left Italy in the late summer or early autumn of 565. In the *Preface* to his collection, by naming the rivers and regions he crossed, he offers an itinerary of his journey north and west:

> Proceeding from Ravenna, I crossed the Po, Adige, Brenta, Piave, Livenza, and Tagliamento rivers, proceeding through the highest summits of the Julian Alps, then crossing the Drave River in Noricum, the Inn River in the region of the Breunii, the Lech River in Bavaria, the Danube among the Alemanni, the Rhine in Germany, then the Moselle, the Meuse, the Aisne, the Seine, the Loire and the Garonne—these powerful rivers of Aquitaine— before advancing to the Pyrenees, covered with snow in July![15]

To this bare-bones frame can be added the details the poet provides in his *Life of St. Martin,* which relates at vv. 630–80 a more precise journey told in reverse chronology.[16] After several stops in Italy, including Padua, Treviso, Aquileia, and a final trip to his hometown at Duplavis, Fortunatus began his long journey, crossing the Carnic Alps at Plöchen Pass, then tacking west, making his way through present-day Carinthia and eventually reaching Augsburg. This is likely the place where Fortunatus was met by Sigoald, the guide sent by King Sigibert to ease the poet's journey into Gaul. From Augsburg, poet and guide would have been required by protocol to report directly to the king in Metz.[17]

Fortunatus arrived in Metz in the spring of 566 on the cusp of Sigibert's marriage to Brunhilde, daughter of Athanagild, king of the Visigothic kingdom in Spain. Given the difficulties, not to mention the expense, of traveling from Ravenna to Metz, the fact that Sigibert sent an emissary to escort him, and his arrival at Metz coincident to the royal wedding, it seems likely that Fortunatus was invited to this signal event. If, on the other hand, the poet fortuitously arrived in Metz, he either arrived early enough to be able to compose a wedding poem or already had such a poem prepared.[18]

---

15. *Praef.* 4; my translation.

16. See also Quesnal (xi–lxii) on the literary background of this itinerary; Cartellier describes various routes over the Alps with detailed maps.

17. Thus argues Koebner (17–18), but Meyer (9–11) has the poet travel to Metz after visiting various Austrasian cities; Reydellet (vol. 1, x) places the poet in Metz first and wonders if the poet accompanied Sigibert and Brunhilde on a tour of Austrasia meant to introduce the new queen to the country.

18. Brennan ("Career," 56–57 with n. 33) rightly notes that if Fortunatus' trip had been planned only as a pilgrimage, his route to Tours is unnecessarily circuitous.

This poem, *carm.* 6.1, exploits classical imagery and diction, not least the figures of Cupid and Venus, in order to frame the "love" shared by Sigibert and Brunhilde. Recited by Fortunatus at the wedding, its words made the poet a celebrant in the royal festivities. As this wedding was a national event, with courtiers, nobles, and churchmen from all across Gaul in attendance, Fortunatus essentially auditioned before an audience brimming with those who could further his stay among them. Many of these figures, destined to become the addressees of his poems, provide the organizing principle for the translations collected here, which are grouped by addressee. Not the least of the friends he made at this time were Gogo (No. 19), Dynamius (No. 18), and Jovinus (No. 22), to whom he wrote multiple poems in token of friendship and respect. A second poem written at this time, *carm.* 6.1a,[19] celebrates the conversion of Brunhilde from Arian to Catholic Christianity.

As much as Fortunatus needed the patronage of powerful people in order to further his stay in a foreign land, Sigibert, too, needed someone of Fortunatus' training and background to further his own dynastic aspirations. For the king had searched for and found a queen outside of Gaul precisely to brace his position within the Frankish realm, securing an alliance with the Visigoths and affirming his own royal worth over that of his brothers and fellow kings, Guntram, Chilperic, and Charibert, whose marriages contracted from among the Franks came, according to Gregory of Tours, with intrigue and acrimony. Fortunatus thus brought to a national ceremony international prestige that confirmed Sigibert's extra-Frankish dynastic hopes.[20]

Fortunatus took full advantage of his time in Metz. In addition to composing and reciting *carm.* 6.1, and apart from meeting a variety of influential nobles and churchmen with whom he remained on friendly terms for the rest of his life, he seems likely to have taken up a quasi-official post at Sigibert's court. Gogo says as much in a letter written to Traseric, in which he mentions, though not by name, a foreign poet present at Sigibert's court at this time, playing the part of teacher.[21] The responsibilities of such a post may also explain Fortunatus' extended sojourn in Metz, where he remained well into the summer of 566.[22] Whatever such a posting required Fortunatus to do, however, it also allowed him time to visit other cities in Austrasia, including Trier, Cologne, and Mainz.

---

19. Translated by George, *Poems* (25–31, *carm.* 6.1; 31–33, *carm.* 6.1.a).

20. Sigibert's dynastic hopes are made explicit by Gregory of Tours at *HF* 4.27 apropos of Charibert's marriage to Theudechilde, the daughter of a shepherd.

21. *Ep. Aust.* 16 in *MGH,* Epist. (128). Traseric is also perhaps the recipient of *carm.* 2.13; George (28–29) doubts that the poet mentioned is Fortunatus.

22. *Carm.* 6.9, to Dynamius, places Fortunatus in Metz a year after Sigibert's wedding.

In Trier the poet met the venerable Bishop Nicetius,[23] whose wide network of associations both within and outside of Gaul likely facilitated Fortunatus' initial contact with King Sigibert. Nicetius also likely placed Fortunatus in touch with bishops, courtiers, and kings the poet had yet to meet. While it is unclear how long Fortunatus remained in Trier, *carm.* 3.11, a praise piece, and 3.12, celebrating Nicetius' castle overlooking the Moselle,[24] give evidence of a more than cursory friendship.

In Mainz, Fortunatus met Bishop Sidonius, whose Gallo-Roman pedigree may have provided the initial basis for a friendship reflected in three poems.[25] The first, *carm.* 2.11, celebrates the baptistery of Mainz and praises King Theudebert I and his daughter, Berthoara, both of whom, along with Sidonius, were involved in its building; the second, *carm.* 2.12, commemorates Sidonius' efforts in establishing the church of St. George at Castel; and the third, *carm.* 9.9, praises the presence of an incumbent in the long-vacant Episcopal seat at Mainz, focusing on the especial spiritual and political skills that make Sidonius successful. In Cologne, finally, Fortunatus met Bishop Carentinus[26] and composed *carm.* 3.14 to praise him for restoring and enriching the churches of his bishopric, singling out the founding of the church of St. Gereon for special notice.

In this season Fortunatus also visited Ageric,[27] bishop of Verdun, composing *carm.* 3.23 and 3.23a in his honor; and Igidius, bishop of Reims,[28] the recipient of *carm.* 3.15. At Soissons the poet met Duke Mummolenus, who figures in *carm.* 7.14 as a fellow celebrant at a banquet at which Fortunatus overindulged;[29] and he also visited the tomb of St. Medard, bishop of Noyon, to whom *carm.* 2.16 is dedicated.[30] Continuing on his slow pilgrimage to venerate St. Martin, Fortunatus left Sigibert's Austrasian kingdom in the spring of 567. Traveling west, he entered Neustria, ruled by Sigibert's brother,

---

23. See also Duchesne (vol. 3, 37–38); Gauthier (172–81); and Reydellet (vol. 1, 106, n. 67).

24. See also Roberts (85–93) on this complex poem.

25. Duchesne (vol. 3, 157) with Reydellet (vol. 1, 189, n. 87).

26. Duchesne (vol. 3, 179, s.v. *Carentinus*) with Reydellet (vol. 1, 113, n. 96).

27. Duchesne (vol. 3, 70, s.v. *Agericus*) with *HF* 9.8; Ageric died in 588.

28. Igidius later involved himself in intrigues against nobles and kings that resulted eventually in his deposition and exile, long after this poem was written; see *HF* 7.33, 10.9; Reydellet (vol. 1, 196–97, n. 97).

29. *PLRE* (898–99, s.v. *Mummolenus* 2) with Reydellet (vol. 2, 109, n. 83).

30. Mentioned by Fortunatus also at *Vit. Mart.* 4.639 in *MGH* (293–370); and by Gregory at *HF* 4.19, 4.21, and 4.51, he died in 560. Fortunatus' prose life of Medard is in *MGH, AA,* but see Roberts (181 and n. 47) for reasons to worry about his authorship.

Charibert,[31] and arrived at the capital, Paris, perhaps after passing through Meaux. Charibert may already have been ailing at the time, since the king died later in the year, but Fortunatus was at his court long enough to compose a praise piece to him, *carm.* 6.2,[32] which speaks of the king's singularity from multiple angles while seeking to alleviate divisions between secular and ecclesiastical concerns. The poem was likely recited by Fortunatus as part of a ceremony celebrating the king's entry into Paris.

During his stay in Paris, Fortunatus also met Queen Ultrogotha, the widow of Childebert I, who, along with her two daughters, had been exiled by Childebert's brother, Lothar I, after Childebert's death in 558. Charibert I offered her and her daughters a safe haven in Paris, and Fortunatus composed *carm.* 6.6 to commemorate a garden planted by Childebert but tended now by his widow. While in Paris the poet also met Rucco, destined to become bishop of Paris, for whom he wrote *carm.* 3.26; and Germanus, the city's current bishop, whose life Fortuantus would eventually write[33] and who figures prominently in *carm.* 2.9 as a builder of churches and a spiritual leader of the first rank.

In order to make good on his vow to visit St. Martin's tomb, Fortunatus left Paris in the spring of 567. Upon his arrival in Tours, the poet met Bishop Eufronius,[34] to whom he wrote 3.1 and 3.2, prose letters that stand in praise of the bishop's especial spiritual qualities; and *carm.* 3.3, a poem that holds up Eufronius' piety as an example to his flock. Having thus fulfilled his vow, Fortunatus was now free to return to Italy. Instead, he pushed on to Poitiers to pay homage to St. Hilary, resulting in *carm.* 2.15, a piece that praises this fourth-century bishop for his theological acumen.[35] There may have been a double attraction in visiting Poitiers, too, for it seems hard to imagine that the wandering poet would have been unknown to the nuns living there at the Convent of the Holy Cross. Given the poet's connections with the sons of her former husband, Lothar I, Radegund, the founder of the convent, would clearly have been known to Fortunatus. It seems difficult to imagine, in any case, that they did not meet on this initial visit to the city that was to remain the poet's home for the rest of his life, an encounter at which Agnes, as the abbess of Holy Cross, would also likely have been present.

---

31. *PLRE* (283–84, s.v. *Charibertus 1*), with Reydellet (vol. 2, 53, n. 18).

32. George (43–48) with Roberts (54–55), who translates vv. 7–8, 55–58.

33. *HF* 4.19, 4.36, 5.5, 8.33, with Duchesne (vol. 2, 470–71, s.v. *Germanus*); Fortunatus' *Life of Germanus* is in *MGH, AA.*

34. Duchesne (vol. 2, 307, s.v. *Eufronius*); Stroheker (170, n. 130); Reydellet (vol. 1, 192, n. 81).

35. Fortunatus also wrote a prose life of Hilary, in *MGH, AA.*

Whether or not this trio met in the summer of 567, the poet was off again on a journey not long thereafter in order to visit cities in the south of Gaul. In Bordeaux, Fortunatus cultivated a warm friendship with Leontius II, that city's bishop, and his wife, Placidina (No. 1), commemorated in more than a few poems devoted to them. Almost certainly at this time, too, Fortunatus visited the southern cities of Toulouse and Limoges.[36] He composed two poems that pertain to Toulouse: one, *carm.* 2.7, to celebrate the dedication of the church of St. Saturninus,[37] and another, *carm.* 2.8, to honor the church's benefactor, Duke Launebod. Fortunatus' role in inscribing this signal event in the life of Toulouse may indicate that he was invited to the city for the purpose of celebrating it.[38] At Limoges, finally, Fortunatus may have composed *carm.* 5.19, to abbot Aredius, though the piece may belong to a later visit.[39]

By late 567 or early 568, Fortunatus had returned to Poitiers, where Radegund and Agnes provided a home for him at the Convent of the Holy Cross. He may have been lured back as part of an arrangement to serve the convent in an official capacity, for, in a poem that contrasts his own role with that of Agnes' position as abbess (*carm.* 11.4), Fortunatus styles himself an *agens,* that is, a "manager" or "overseer." It seems unlikely, in any case, that Fortunatus could have settled at Holy Cross absent some sort of official function to perform. Since he was not in holy orders when he arrived,[40] propriety would require a role for him to play, but the poet would hardly have found the sedentary life of monastic retreat appealing unless it came with the

---

36. Fortunatus likely visited Agen, near to Toulouse and Limoges, at this time, since he wrote *carm.* 2.14 to honor Agen's saints, although this poem could reflect a later journey.

37. On which see Vieillard-Troiekouroff (298–300, no. 303).

38. George (31–32) locates the visit in the early 570s, but Reydellet (vol. 1, xxx) dates it to 567, and (in vol. 1, 59, n. 45) he understands *carm.* 2.7 and 2.8 to reflect Fortunatus' participation in the dedication of the church of St. Saturnin and in the subsequent feast, at which some or all of *carm.* 2.8 would have been recited.

39. Tardi (76) believes that Fortunatus also took at this time a trip to Braga, in Spain, to visit that city's celebrated bishop, Martin. Wording in the *Preface* to the collection may be understood to support such a view, though Brennan ("Career," 64), in arguing against such a journey, suggests why this does not have to be the case; Reydellet (vol. 1, xiv) does not rule it out.

40. George (212–14); Brennan ("Career," 67–68); and Raby (vol. 1, 135): "He was still a layman . . ." The details of daily life revealed in his poetry suggest to me that Fortunatus remained a layman up until the 590s, when he was named bishop of Poitiers and had to proceed quickly through orders so as to take up a post that I presume he accepted as much in honor of Radegund and Agnes as out of any singular devotion to Episcopal service.

opportunity to have contact with the figures great and small that arrived in Poitiers in order to pay their respects to Radegund and Agnes. What better way to be of use while cultivating a continued taste for contacts with new people than to serve Holy Cross as an *agens*? Whatever such a role entailed, from this time on, in the monastic setting provided by Radegund and Agnes, Fortunatus pursued the poetic career for which his talents well suited him with enormous productivity and variety. He never returned to Italy.

When Fortunatus settled there Holy Cross was a new establishment, having been founded in the previous decade by Radegund. A daughter of Berthar, king of Thuringia, she was born c. 510 but lost her family and homeland in 530, when the Franks, under Lothar I, conquered Thuringia. Spirited off to Gaul as Lothar's war prize, she trained to become queen, a role presumably played, when she eventually assumed it, with great reluctance. At the same time, she already was practicing a severely ascetic form of Christianity. When Lothar murdered her brother, who had traveled west with her in defeat, Radegund left her husband, fled to Noyon, and submitted herself to the protection of Medard, the bishop of that city, who in due course consecrated her a deaconess. Gaining the protection of Pientius, bishop in Poitiers, she soon decided to found a religious community there and established the Convent of the Holy Cross. Not the least of Radegund's accomplishments at this point involved garnering support for her fledgling convent from important bishops. She died in 587, an international figure of piety and spiritual power who also became, in their twenty-year association, one of Fortunatus' intimate friends.

Radegund refused the position of abbess for herself and instead named Agnes to this office, a woman whom she had adopted and raised in her own unique brand of ascetic Christianity. Agnes' birth and death dates are unknown, but a birth year of c. 525 can be conjectured based on details found in the poems Fortunatus wrote to her. It is surmised that Agnes died no later than 589, since, according to Gregory of Tours, a new abbess was in office in that year.[41] Radegund and Agnes brought to Holy Cross the monastic rule of Caesarius of Arles, one of the more stringent then available to women religious. Along with Radegund, Agnes also became Fortunatus' intimate friend. The rich history of their years together is told in the dozens of poems the poet wrote to both women. The worldly poet kept his friends' memories alive after their deaths by allowing himself to be named bishop of Poitiers, a post he held until the end of his life, surmised to have occurred in the first decade of the seventh century.

---

41. *HF* 9.39.

3. The Poems

Fortunatus seems to have given up writing poetry after the deaths of Radegund and Agnes. The publication of his work, on the other hand, came in stages. The complete collection comprises eleven books of poetry, an appendix of poems not recorded in these books, and a metrical life of St. Martin. Books 1–7 of the collection were published, with a preface and a dedication to Gregory of Tours, no earlier than 576, a terminus a quo provided by *carm.* 5.5, which recounts the conversion of the Jews of Clermont-Ferrand datable to that year. With the exception of *carm.* 1.1 and 1.2, which seem to have been written in Italy, the poems contained in these books date from after 565. On the other hand, *carm.* 7.25 places Gundegiselus in the bishop's seat in Bordeaux and thus dates from no earlier than 585, the year in which he assumed that city's Episcopal seat. *Carm.* 7.25 must therefore have fallen out of its original place in its own later collection, to be tacked on in the copying of manuscripts to Book 7—certainly a feasible explanation given that this is the final poem of that book.[42]

This first collection takes in all manner of poems. Book 1 focuses on Leontius II, bishop of Bordeaux, and his wife, Placidina (No. 1), for whom thirteen of the book's twenty-one poems were composed (*carm.* 1.6, 1.8–12, 1.14–20), including three celebrating the couple's palatial villas (*carm.* 1.18–20). In addition, there are poems devoted to churches not associated with Leontius (*carm.* 1.3–5, 1.7, 1.13) and a humorous piece on the Gers River (*carm.* 1.21). Book 2 opens with six poems devoted to the holy cross: two complicated acrostics (*carm.* 2.4–5), two hymns (*carm.* 2.2, 2.6), and two pieces (*carm.* 2.1, 2.3) on the cross generally—all inspired by the arrival at Holy Cross of a relic of the true cross sent to Radegund by the Byzantine emperor. Two poems deal with St. Saturninus (*carm.* 2.7–8) and two others with the church at Paris (*carm.* 2.9–10). Three poems pertain to religious architecture (*carm.* 2.11–13), while the final three poems treat the saints of Agen, St. Hilary and St. Medard (*carm.* 2.14–16).

The first two pieces of Book 3 are in prose, addressed to Eufronius, bishop of Tours, followed by a poem to this bishop (*carm.* 3.3), then another prose piece written to Bishop Felix of Nantes (No. 2), to whom the next cluster of poems is addressed (*carm.* 3.5–10). A handful of poems honor bishops—Nicetius of Trier (*carm.* 3.11–12); Vilicus of Metz (No. 3, *carm.* 3.13, 3.13a–d); Carentinus of Cologne (*carm.* 3.14) and Igidius of Reims (*carm.* 3.15). Other figures to whom poems are addressed include Hilary (No. 4, *carm.* 3.16);

---

42. Meyer (28–29); George (209); Reydellet (vol. 1, lxix); this strengthens the idea, too, that an original collection ended with Book 7.

Bertrand of Bordeaux (No. 5, *carm.* 3.17–18); Agricola (No. 6, *carm.* 3.19); Felix of Bourges (*carm.* 3.20); Avitus (No. 7), who merits three poems (*carm.* 3.21–22, 3.22a); Ageric of Verdun (*carm.* 23, 23a); Anfion (No. 8, *carm.* 3.24); Paternus (No. 9, *carm.* 3.25); Rucco of Paris (No. 10, *carm.* 3.26); and, finally, a cluster of deacons: John (No. 12), Anthimius (No. 13), and Sindulf (No. 14, *carm.* 3.27–30).

The poems gathered in Book 4 are epitaphs written on bishops (*carm.* 4.1–10), abbots, priests, deacons, and some nonreligious figures (*carm.* 4.11–28). Bishops reappear in Book 5, which opens with a prose piece to Martin of Braga, followed by a poem to him (*carm.* 5.2); a piece to Syagrius of Autun, partly in prose, that describes an acrostic that forms the poetic portion of *carm.* 5.6; and a poem to Felix of Nantes (No. 2, *carm.* 5.7). *Carm.* 5.3–5 are written to, or about, Gregory of Tours (No. 15), who is the addressee of most of the remaining poems of the book (*carm.* 5.8–17). The final pieces are to Aredius (No. 16, *carm.* 5.19) and to a group of unnamed leaders of the church in Gaul (*carm.* 5.18).

Book 6 contains only ten poems, but of greater length than those found in the earlier books. The addressees are political figures associated with Fortunatus' arrival in Gaul and his sojourn in Metz in 566–567. *Carm.* 6.1 and 6.1a celebrate the marriage of Sigibert and Brunhilde, and 6.2 is a panegyric on King Charibert. Four poems (*carm.* 6.3–6) are about, or written to, women—Theudechilde, Berthchilde, Gelesuintha, and Ultrogotha (No. 17). One piece attends to a villa associated with Aredius (No. 16, *carm.* 6.7), and another is a comical piece on Coco, a cook who once stole Fortunatus' boat (*carm.* 6.8). Two poems to Dynamius of Marseilles (No. 18) round out the book (*carm.* 6.9–10).

Book 7 contains poems to nobles and friends, including Gogo (No. 19, *carm.* 7.1–4); Bodegisilus (*carm.* 7.5–6); Lupus (No. 20, *carm.* 7.7–9); and Magnulf (No. 21, *carm.* 7.10). Two poems to Jovinus (No. 22, *carm.* 7.11–12) are joined by a brief piece written to Fortunatus' boyhood friend, Felix of Treviso (No. 23, *carm.* 7.13). There follow pieces written to other Frankish figures: Mummolenus; Berulf (No. 24); Conda; Gunduarius (No. 25); Flavus (No. 26); Evodius (No. 27); Sigimund (No. 28); Alagisilus (No. 29); Boso (No. 30); Paternus (No. 9); and Galactorius (No. 31, *carm.* 7.14–25).

Fortunatus published a second group of poems, Books 8–9, after 589, since *carm.* 8.12 and letter 8.12a seem to refer to a revolt at Holy Cross among the nuns that occurred in that year, thus providing a terminus a quo.[43] Meyer's

---

43. Reydellet (vol. 1, lxx); Roberts (285–86) understands the poems in Book 8 to offer a saintly, ascetic depiction of Radegund meant in part to restore the reputation of Holy Cross, badly tarnished in this revolt.

view, that Book 8 was published along with Books 1–7, is no longer accepted,[44] given Tardi's argument that *carm.* 8.1 supplies an introductory piece to a second collection comprising Books 8–9.[45] Tardi's view, however, strengthens another of Meyer's contentions respecting the final three poems of Book 7 (7.23–25), which, on various grounds, are out of place, not least *carm.* 7.25, which could have been written no earlier than 585. Meyer felt these poems were originally published in Book 10 but fell out of the manuscript tradition and were simply added to the end of Book 7 later.[46] Such a view furthers the idea that Book 7 marks the end of a collection, providing an easy place for these misplaced poems to be included.

Book 8 is comprised of poems focused on the Convent of the Holy Cross in the figures of Agnes and Radegund, but it also contains some pieces written to Gregory of Tours. *Carm.* 8.1 invites its readers to provide books to Holy Cross, while *carm.* 8.3 and 8.4 attend to the topic of virginity in celebration of Agnes' consecration as abbess. *Carm.* 8.2 and 8.5–10 are addressed to, and paint an ascetic and spiritually rich picture of, Radegund (No. 40), while *carm.* 8.11–21 are pieces addressed to Gregory (No. 15) and reveal him in various lights. Book 9 contains poems to Chilperic, Fredegund (No. 32), and their two sons (*carm.* 9.1–5); two poems to Gregory of Tours, one of which is written in the sapphic meter (*carm.* 9.6–7); and individual poems to a diverse group of figures, including Baudoald (*carm.* 9.8); Sidonius of Mainz (*carm.* 9.9); Rucco of Paris (No. 10, *carm.* 9.10); the religious figures Droctoveus (No. 33), Lupus (No. 35), Waldo (No. 35, *carm.* 9.11, 9.13); and Faramod (No. 34), a secular official (*carm.* 9.12). Rounding out the book is a poem on the miracle associated with a beam used to build a church (*carm.* 9.14), a piece on a wooden house (*carm.* 9.15), and a poem written to Chrodinus (No. 36, *carm.* 9.16).

The gathering and publishing of Books 10–11 likely occurred after Fortunatus' death, while the poems of the so-called Appendix, which appear only in manuscript Σ, *Parisinus lat.* 13048, seem either to have fallen out of the manuscript tradition or to represent poems (perhaps unfinished) found with the poet's papers and otherwise not included in those collections published in his lifetime. The latest datable poem of Book 10 is written to Plato, bishop of Poitiers, who took his Episcopal seat in 592. The poems of Book 11 can only be dated within the lifetimes of Radegund, who died in 587, and Agnes, who died not long after that. Koebner felt that the poems of Books 10 and 11 cohered, especially if the introductory prose pieces in

---

44. Meyer (25–29).

45. Tardi (92–96).

46. Meyer (28–29).

both were removed, leading him to argue that these books were gathered and published by Fortunatus himself.[47] George agrees with this view, noting that the deaths of Radegund and Agnes made publication of the bulk of the poems possible.[48] This view places these books in circulation as a published collection at some point in the last decade of the sixth century, certainly after 592.

Whether Fortunatus published Books 10–11 himself or not, he writes in them primarily to Agnes and Radegund, although both books begin with prose pieces, and Book 10 with a likely incomplete discussion of the Lord's Prayer, along with three further prose works. *Carm.* 10.5 and 10.10 treat the oratory of Artanne, while *carm.* 10.6 recollects the restoration of the cathedral of Tours datable to 590. Two poems are addressed to Brunhilde and Childebert II (*carm.* 10.7–8), and a third concerns the poet's trip to Austrasia (*carm.* 10.9), all of them dating from 588. *Carm.* 10.11 describes a visit to Tours by the preceptors of Childebert in 589, while *carm.* 10.12, addressed to Gregory of Tours and the secular leaders Romulf, Gallienus, and Florentinus, is concerned with a maligned man seeking to be reunited with his daughter. Bishops are addressed en masse in *carm.* 10.13, a poem of recommendation, while Bishop Plato of Poitiers is the topic of *carm.* 10.14. Gregory of Tours' mother, Armentaria (No. 37), is the addressee of *carm.* 10.15, followed by four poems written to, or about, Sigoald (No. 38, *carm.* 10.16–18) and Galactorius (No. 31, *carm.* 10.19).

Book 11 begins with a prose discussion of the Credo, with the remaining poems, *carm.* 11.2–26, addressed to Radegund and/or Agnes (No. 40) or otherwise pertaining to them in their respective roles at Holy Cross. The focus on Radegund and Agnes continues in the Appendix, though its first poem, written in Radegund's voice, laments being separated from her cousin, Amalfred, as a result of the Franks' conquest of her homeland. App. 2 is written to the Byzantine emperor and empress, Justin and Sophia, while App. 3–5 are to, respectively, Artachis, Sigimund, and Childebert II. App. 6 is written to Brunhilde; App. 7 to Agiulfus; App. 8 is an epitaph for Nectarius; and App. 9 remembers a gift of fruit. App. 10–31, finally, are poems to Radegund and/or Agnes (No. 40) that detail life from a variety of angles in and around Holy Cross.

---

47. Koebner (125–128).

48. George (211); George ("End Game," 32–43); but Roberts (286 with n. 97) remains unconvinced.

4. Elegy

With rare exceptions, Fortunatus writes in elegiac couplets, a meter he inherited from Greco-Roman antiquity.[49] It is difficult to determine how much of the genre's history he knew, but its greatest Latin practitioners are surely in his mind in some way: Gallus, Catullus, Tibullus, Propertius, and Ovid—most certainly the last three. These poets inherited the meter and its generic assumptions from the Greeks, but the origins of elegy as a literary form are obscure. In fifth-century B.C.E. usage the term *elegos* seems usually to have meant "song of mourning," yet the earliest extant examples of elegy have nothing to do with mourning. Thus it is safer to say that Greek elegy is defined by its rhythms rather than its moods, which can be various—martial, convivial, personal, erotic, hortatory—while also taking in the grief associated with loss.[50]

The classical Latin elegists that Fortunatus knew adhere to a number of features in their poetry. Not least, they make their own subjective erotic or amorous experiences a primary, though by no means exclusive, topic, exploiting shared conventions in order to articulate them. These qualities of elegiac composition form, so to speak, a world unique to the elegist,[51] and Fortunatus insinuates his poems into that world not least by drawing on the diction of his predecessors while adhering by and large to the metrical rules established by them.[52] He departs from his models, on the other hand, in using the elegiac meter to offer praise, leading Reydellet to assert that Fortunatus effectively invented a new genre, the elegiac poem of praise. In Fortunatus' hands such poems can be short pieces, presumably composed in gratitude or to memorialize an event, or longer pieces, written to royal figures, nobles, and bishops.[53]

The elegiac meter is written in couplets, the first line of which is in dactylic hexameter, the meter of epic poetry, and has, as its name suggests, six metrical feet, with each foot either a dactyl (long—short—short) or a spondee (long—long). The two are interchangeable in the first four feet, whereas the

---

49. See also on the elegiac meter Halporn, Ostwald, and Rosenmeyer; Reydellet (vol. 1, lxiii–lxviii; and "Tradition," 81–98) also offers full treatments of Fortunatus' specific elegiac habits.

50. Luck (17–18), with Conte (321–23).

51. Conte (321).

52. Consolino explores in more detail these affiliations but refuses to see interpretive connections; Roberts (283–319 passim) touches on the connections in short discussions of the Agnes/Radegund poems.

53. Reydellet (305).

fifth foot is normally a dactyl and the sixth is always a spondee whose last syllable can be long or short. There is normally one primary caesura in the hexameter, that is, a point at which a word ends within a foot, usually the third but sometimes the fourth foot.

The second line of the couplet is a pentameter, a line that is identical to the hexameter except that it omits the last half of the third and sixth feet. In the first two feet, dactyl and spondee are interchangeable, with the half-foot that follows always long; but only dactyls are allowed in the last two feet, with, again, a long half-foot concluding the verse. In classical practice, the third foot (the first half-foot) always corresponds to the end of a word, forming a diaeresis. In the first four feet of the hexameter sixteen combinations of dactyl and spondee are possible, while in the first two feet of the pentameter, just four can occur. The remaining feet in either line must be dactylic.

The power of the elegiac couplet inheres in the ways it exploits metrical expectations. As the most common of meters, the dactylic hexameter of the couplet's first line invites little metrical surprise, whereas the pentameter initially sounds like a hexameter but then suddenly stops short in the third foot. That abruptness is then more or less repeated in the second half of the pentameter, but the required dactyls of this half of the line anticipate the familiarity of the hexameter that follows, returning readers to their metrical bearings—with the process repeating itself until the end of the poem. Thus it might be said that the epic flow of the hexameter is broken in the first half of the pentameter, then picked up again in the second half.[54]

Fortunatus more or less accords with his elegiac predecessors in the ways he constructs his lines metrically, aligning most closely with Ovid. Like them, he is sensitive to the metrical symmetry that encourages rhyme between the two halves of the pentameter, but he reverses the preference of the earlier poets for the rhyming words in question to be connected grammatically.[55] But this goes to more general habits of elegiac composition that mark Fortunatus off from his predecessors, too, and speak to what Roberts calls his "tendency to the epigrammatic," that is, to constructing lines that are "carefully turned forms of expression."[56] These include a consistent use of short clauses reinforced by rhyme, assonance, antithesis, and paronomasia, features that will be examined more closely in the essays introducing individual poems.

---

54. Thus Luck (22).
55. Reydellet (vol. 1, lxiii–lxviii).
56. Roberts (322).

5. Friendship

The term "friendship" is fraught with complication, not least because it may not designate the same phenomenon over time. Some have argued, for example, that the current notion of what it means to be a friend was invented in the Renaissance or later, thus making it anachronistic to think about friendship in our own terms in the centuries preceding the rise of humanism. From the ancient side of the equation comes the argument that the terms normally associated with friendship designate bonds of reciprocal obligations rather than affection, emotional warmth, or intimacy. On this view, "friendship" (*amicitia*) means to the Romans something like "clientship," whereas "friend" (*amicus/a*), a term used more than a few times by Fortuantus, designates nothing more than a "political follower."[57] This more sterile notion of friendship is predicated on the idea that the qualities of disinterestedness and intimacy peculiar to modern friendship exist now only because individual bonds occupy the space freed up by the emergence of an economy governed by market relations.[58]

This is not the place to interrogate such views nor even to attempt to situate Fortunatus' notions of friendship within a wider context. Here I will limit myself simply to describing some features of those poems written by the poet to dozens of friends over the course of several decades. I should say at once that I take these poems at face value, seeing them as emblems of personal devotion rather than mere rhetorical productions composed out of political necessity or calculation. Fortunatus was a patronized poet, to be sure, and he frequently wrote for kings and high officials in formal capacities. Such poems are not poems of friendship, per se, even if the figure involved is described in intimate terms or we know from other evidence that the recipient was, in fact, a friend in a modern sense. Circumstances regularly required Fortunatus to write pieces to serve formal civic, political, or religious ends.

But the poems with which I am concerned were not written in these contexts, and such pieces, composed away from the energies provided by patronage and power, express personal devotion rather than public acclaim. By dint of the variety of friendships they describe, it is difficult to generalize about them, but an emblem of their complexity is *carm.* 11.16, written to Agnes to apologize for an unintended slight. This poem is intriguing for many reasons, but if my understanding of it is correct, perhaps most notably in the way it depicts Fortunatus, in a moment of intimacy, calling Agnes, "my soul's delight" (*delicias animae*, v. 6), a phrase that evokes Catullus' Lesbia cycle.

---

57. Konstan (2).
58. Konstan (5).

Presuming Fortunatus' purpose in using such a phrase inheres in Agnes' ability to understand its Catullan resonances, we are thus led to believe that Agnes herself knew something of Catullus' poetry or at the least, in this instance, that ancient diction provided some of friendship's currency.

Whether or not Agnes could hear, or even appreciate, classical quantities, it should not go unremarked that many of the friends whom Fortunatus addresses in his poetry were themselves trained in the Greco-Roman literary tradition. Gogo, for example, was a practicing poet and Dynamius a poet and hagiographer. Extant letters from both men demonstrate their ability to write in the opaque, allusive prose of which Fortunatus also was a master. Lupus, the courtier of Sigibert, was not only learned but also a shrewd judge of intellect, as Gregory of Tours reports. And, of course, Radegund is presumed to have written poetry, though none of it survives. There were, in other words, more than a few figures in Gaul who had been raised in literary traditions of Greece and Rome. In the poems to these friends, therefore, Fortunatus could rely more aggressively on allusion to his classical models while exploiting other features of ancient elegy—diction, rhyme, assonance, and the like—to communicate.

But in several ways it is difference rather than conformity that marks the poems Fortunatus wrote to his friends. One difference involves diction, for Fortunatus relies on a stock set of words to address his friends, thereby setting those friends and their poems apart. A group of words derived from the act of loving, such as "loved" (*amatus/amata/amate*) and "lover" (*amator*) are used by the poet, either of his friends or of himself, more than a few times. Equally intimate, in addressing his friends, the word "dear" (*carus/cara/care*) is found nearly two dozen times in the vocative case and more than a few times in adjectival forms. Perhaps most important, however, are those words denoting sweetness: "sweet"(*dulcis*), "sweetness" (*dulcedo*), "sweetly" (*dulciter*).[59] *Dulcedo,* for example, is found in poems addressed to no fewer than twenty-one friends, not least, Gregory of Tours.[60] It is also consistently used of Agnes, though with the rare exception provided by the Appendix, never of Radegund. Moreover, of the fifty-eight times I count *dulcedo* or its cognates in the poems translated here, over half feature these words in epithets in the vocative case—"sweet father," "sweet friend," "sweet head of the city," and so forth.

---

59. Koebner (30–39) notices *dulcedo* in a larger discussion of friendship poetry.

60. But also Felix of Nantes, Hilary, Agricola, Avitus, Anfion, Rucco, Anthimius, Aredius, Gogo, Lupus, Gunduarius, Flavus, Sigimund, Alagisilus, Boso, Galactorius, Faramod, Waldo, Sigoald, and Agiulfus.

This sort of expressiveness may mark a notion of friendship more akin to Romantic than classical models,[61] yet however Fortunatus' words fit into a history of western friendship, the presence of *dulcedo* and its cognates points up another feature prevalent in the poems composed by the poet to his friends, that is, his use of epithets. To contemporary ears, the deployment of what amounts to formulaic phrases to express private sentiment sounds stilted. But epithets provided Fortunatus with an idiom of friendship in part demanded by metrical constraints but also owed to a desire to say more with less. That he could indeed say less with more should not be doubted, given the elaborations of praise that fill Fortunatus' prose works. But especially because he sometimes repeats epithets verbatim but more often recombines words into similar phrases in them, Fortunatus clearly intends for his epithets to be understood on their own terms, within their own contexts, even when the same epithet is applied to multiple friends.

This is especially the case with the poems written to his closest friend, Gregory of Tours, where different contexts clearly call for individual understandings of epithets repeated across poems. Contemporary readers might gain from the repetition nothing more than monotony, but it seems difficult to believe that Fortunatus, or his friends, heard his epithets monovocally even in repetition. To call someone "sweet head" (*dulce caput*), for example, demands a context in order to be understood cogently. A nobleman will be the head of a city or a dukedom, a bishop the head of a church, an abbot the head of a body of monks, and so forth. The "sweetness" thus involved will differ, too, for surely no one can quibble with the idea that the "sweetness" associated with civic leadership is substantially different from that attending to the abbacy of a monastery.

Instead of standing as rigid, formulaic markers of rote praise, therefore, in Fortunatus' handling, epithets provide an opportunity for readers to articulate in their own terms details adumbrated but left unstated. For example, the phrasing at *carm.* 5.12.2, "towering in your honor, a beacon in my love" (*culmen honore tuo, lumen amore meo*), is similar to *carm.* 5.8.1, "tower of honor, kindly glorious, rich beacon" (*culmen honoratum, decus almum, lumen opimum*). Both phrases describe Gregory of Tours, and one might be tempted to elide their differences in favor of privileging their obvious similarities. Yet the differences controlling how one must read these epithets are stark.

The first occurs in a poem in which Fortunatus hopes that Gregory remembers him in moments of intimate prayer. That intimacy therefore calls for a less abstract, more concretized, understanding of Gregory. The Latin noun *culmen,* literally, "tower," can therefore be understood to mean something

---

61. Konstan (173).

like "towering," a word that brings Gregory into (albeit imposing) physical proximity to Fortunatus and makes the poet's longed-for hope at the poem's conclusion that much more dramatic. The second epithet, on the other hand, falls in a poem that celebrates Gregory's return to Tours. The poet speaks in propria persona but clearly articulates the joy of Gregory's flock, which has felt lost without its bishop's good presence. Here Gregory more literally is a "tower," a taller-than-life figure whose return, as Fortunatus goes on to say, has relumed city and citizen with light.

The ways in which epithets comprised of similar or identical words can mean in different ways points up a final quality I wish to consider in the poems Fortunatus wrote to his friends, that is, the use of ambiguity. In his handling, ambiguity almost always hinges on a single word, whose resonances then infect the ways that the poem might be profitably understood. Many times these words fall in a poem's final distich and force the reader to resist or rethink the conclusion anticipated only a line earlier. In every instance, they become ways for the poet to honor recipients, either by equating them with incomparable figures or allowing a more private sentiment to be heard, or both.

In *carm.* 3.26, for example, written to Rucco, Fortunatus is somewhere off the French coast while Rucco is holed up in Paris. A contrast between storms and safety leads the poet to think of love as a force that can overcome separation, especially if, as Fortunatus hopes, Rucco returns the favor that the words of this poem betoken. Yet in the poem's final couplets, the expected call to sublimate friendship's devotion to God's eternal love is undercut by an emphasis on the humanity, rather than the divinity, of God as Christ and on Christ's grace as something that enriches the humanity of both friends. In this view, the final line of the poem can be read in three discrete ways:

> Requite my wish, Rucco: think of me,
> share the thought that God gave to us both,
> to let Christ's grace make us more fully human,
> to speak, to think only of who commands us.

The dominant image of the poem's final line, "who commands us" (*domino*, v. 18) applies to Christ, to be sure, the figure held up in prior lines as full of a grace that renders the friends "more fully human." But this command-ing figure could also be Rucco himself, who demands Fortunatus' love, or even Fortunatus, who orders his friend to write back to him to prove his devotion.

Another example comes in *carm.* 8.5, in which Radegund, on Lenten retreat, is envisioned as a figure of earthly and heavenly majesty, a former queen now regal in her service to God. This bifurcation between worldly and otherworldly concerns is reflected in an acrostic that the poem's first lines form, spelling out the name of Radegund on the horizontal axis and including that name also prominently on the vertical axis supplied in the poem's first line. The figure of the cross that results from the intersection of her names on each axis thus points up Radegund's incomparability while symbolizing the worlds she straddles:

> **R**oyally born, powerful in the world, **RADEGUNDES**,
> **A**waiting heaven, despising the world,
> **D**ue to earn Christ,
> **E**ternity glimmering in your cave,
> **G**rasping the universe, crushing Satan   5
> **U**nderfoot as you walk the happy stars,
> **N**estled in a cave become heaven,
> **D**ripping tears on ground that blooms joy,
> **E**mptying, cutting, fatten the soul
> **S**ingularly loved by its own lord.

In the poem's last line, however, Fortunatus seemingly claims that Radegund's soul has its "own lord" (*Dominus . . . suus,* v. 10), which might be God but could be the poet himself. Especially since the poem trumpets the opposition between worldliness and eternity, the ambiguity points up both the worldly love the poet feels for Radegund and the eternity of God's love that Radegund herself desires.

A different sort of ambiguity inhabits App. 16:

> I coveted what the shadows dispersed,
> but that darkness didn't steal you entirely from me:
> the soul sees lovers even vanished from view,
> my soul was there—where I could not be.
> Incomparable the place that lovers never leave,   5
> who light their eyes on those they covet,
> with Christ, prince of goodness, in their midst,
> his love a sacred ligature that binds the heart.
> Let more poems be ordered down the years:
> take them away from here—and there I will say worthy
>   things to you.   10

Separation occasions this poem, which imagines the good presence of Radegund and Agnes through its words that become, in the poem's final distich, a means by which the poet can be with his friends even in absence. The verb "say" (*loquar,* v. 10), however, presents a grammatical ambiguity that complicates the poem's conclusion, for it can be present subjunctive or future indicative. If it is present, then the idea is purposive, that is, "take [the poems that I've been ordered to write] with you from this place, so that I might say only worthy things to you." The poet is thus inspired by the fact that Radegund and Agnes command him to write while their acceptance of his poetry inspires him to produce more. If the verb is future, on the other hand, then the idea is that in taking Fortunatus' poems with them, Radegund and Agnes will be able to hear the poet's voice, even in absence. The ambiguity heightens the ways in which Fortunatus honors his friends by managing to say in one line both that they are an inspiration to him and that his poetry can in his absence bring him into their presence.

A final example of ambiguity comes in *carm.* 8.7, written to Agnes and Radegund to praise the decoration of the cross and altar at Holy Cross. The poem offers vivid descriptions of a natural world used to honor a sacral space. Yet at poem's end, Fortunatus turns his attention from nature and altar to think about Agnes and Radegund, who have caused this beautiful tableau to take shape:

> You have dressed festive altars in colored wreaths,
> painted them fresh with flowery threads.   10
> A golden, crocusy line goes forth, and here a purple row
> of violets, flushed scarlet meets milky white.
> The Blues and the Greens take their stand, colors wage a
>   flowery war,
> imagine—in this place of peace, plants drawing up battle lines:
> the lily, pleasantly white, the rose with ruddy allure,   15
> the lily teasing fragrantly, the rose prettier in pink,
> flowers arrayed for a various war whose colors are brighter
> than any jewel, nor incense more fragrant than they;
> Agnes, Radegund, this is what you built.
> May your fragrances breathlessly mingle with eternity's
>   flowers.   20

Here, the word "fragrances" (*odor,* v. 20) in the poem's final line can refer to the odors of the flowers with which Agnes and Radegund have bedecked the altar at Holy Cross. But it may also be understood to refer to the incomparable fragrance of the women themselves, a fresh instance of their excellence, and a means by which Fortunatus can link his good friends to the bounties of nature and the perfections of Paradise simultaneously.

Lending to the poems written to friends a complication and subtlety that augments their intimacy, Fortunatus' penchant for ambiguity can be understood to derive from his larger view of experience. Especially in these more private pieces, he seems almost haunted by a bifurcated vision of human action. This is perhaps owed to the explicit way in which Christianity insists on the binarism of this world in measurement against the next. Or, it may be owed to his social status, for whatever his pedigree in Italy, it mattered not at all in Gaul, where Fortunatus was always an emigrant and outsider, a "Roman" and Italian, and an emblem of the old Greco-Roman tradition set amid the sometimes brutal power wielded in the Frankish ascendancy. It was a brave new world that the poet spied as he made a life for himself in Gaul. To one used to the old imperial conflicts roiling Italy and the Byzantine east, Gaul must have seemed the wave of a future very much being made outside the Roman mold.

Although it seems logical to assume that an artist of Fortunatus' sensibilities would perceive the world in manifold ways, Radegund, in her own presence in Fortunatus' life, must have also provided a vivid example of ambiguity. For the poet found himself on intimate terms with a woman of striking contradictions: a Thuringian princess who also happened to have been the queen to Lothar, son of Clovis, who despite her ascendancy renounced these royal affiliations in favor of pursuing God's embrace. At the same time, Radegund retained the bearing of a queen, and in her mien the poet would have been reminded of the new Germanic world in which he resided, not to mention the old world he had left behind, while her rejection of temporal allurements offered the possibility of achieving an even greater world apart from Roman tradition and Germanic power.

6. Translating Fortunatus

Though I began by composing versions of the poems collected here that attempted to replicate the elegiac couplet in English, I abandoned them in the belief that hewing to it would simply replace one stultified form with another without furthering the goal of making Fortunatus accessible to a wider audience. From that decision derived an opposite tack, that is, to produce renderings in free verse that hewed to large themes and ideas but sounded more contemporary. But these versions seemed to err too much in the opposite direction. There was no one-to-one correspondence between the Latin and English lines, vitiating the usefulness of the translations to those who might come to them with some knowledge of Latin and skewing the sense of symmetry that even the Latinless reader senses in poems written in couplets. I finally settled in the versions here on a compromise between something rigidly transliteral and something breezily free. Each line is a stand-alone version of its Latin counterpart.

In creating a poetic idiom that could hew line-by-line to the Latin while communicating the poetry of Fortunatus' words, I have two goals in mind.

First, I replicate where possible, and as closely as possible, the formal features of Fortuantus' Latin. For example, the poet likes to rhyme the two halves of a line, as at *carm.* 7.9.13, *pagina blanda* **tuo** *sub nomine missa* **benigno** (7.9.13), and I have replicated this tendency where the English would allow. To achieve this idiom, I sometimes bend Latin morphology to shape versions in English that communicate the richness of the poet's language. For example, at *carm.* 3.22a.12, *vel memorare tuum nomen, opime, sacrum,* I render the vocative *opime*, "rich one," as an adjective, "to echo your rich and sacred name"; similarly, at *carm.* 3.28.1 and 3.29.1, the noun *pignus*, "pledge," becomes in both instances the verb "pledged."

Further, while I adhere to the tenses Fortunatus chose—variation of tenses is a powerful feature of the poet's prosody—occasionally I have changed the historical present and/or future, which sounds stilted in English, to the perfect, which sounds more dramatic to contemporary ears. Thus, at 3.29.6–7, *sic mea culpa tui causa soporis* **erit** / **discedo** *tacitus, veluti fur* . . . , the future *erit* and the present *discedo* both become simple past in English: "my guilt left you undisturbed [not "will be the cause of your sleep"]. / I crawled [not "crawl"] away, a thief in the night. . . ." Occasionally I have translated the pentameter of a couplet before its hexameter, as at *carm.* 1.17.3–4; and, more rarely still, parts of the pentameter and hexameter in two separate lines, as at *carm.* 5.19.5–6, but moments such as these are duly noted.

The second way of creating this idiom is rhythmical, although my decision not to translate the elegiac form in English meant I could only gesture toward rather than replicate this aspect of Fortunatus' prosody.[62] To achieve it I exploit the effects of prose rhythms in English. These include constructing adjacent or alternating lines, or adjacent phrases or clauses, with the same syntax, and outfitting adjoining or alternating lines, phrases, or clauses with the same rhythms.

Carm. 6.9, to Dynamius, can be used as an example:

> I'm waiting, my love, revered Dynamius,
> you're absent, though beheld in my poem.
> I ask the wafting breeze where you might be,
> gone from my eyes, unfled from my soul.
> Metz is pleasant enough for me, Marseilles and environs
>   satisfy you,   5
> vanished, except in the junctures of my heart,

---

62. I pondered but ultimately resisted the temptation to indent the pentameter of each couplet, as is normally done in Latin, to suggest visually that it is a foot shorter than its hexametrical partner. Since my translations are not elegiac this seemed unnecessarily intrusive, even if my versions are line-for-line renderings.

where some part of you (apart from you) forgotten until now
remained: do you not recall in your heart the part of you
                        left behind?
If sleep has sneaked in, may your dreams tell on me,
where sundered souls are sometimes joined;   10
if you're awake, I confess, there's no forgiving
a friend sprawled in unjustified silence.
Twice now the zodiac's ambit of months has
wearied the horses' breathless race across the sun
that you snatched from me when you left;   15
lacking you I'm blind to the unfolding day.
Send a poem whose words flow like your voice,
so that to read it is to speak with you.
But, friend, still, I dearly want you here,
come at last—make me see again.   20

My translation opens with adjacent lines (vv. 1–2) whose phrasing is identical in stress and word boundary, followed in v. 3 by an English pentameter, then a line (v. 4) that splits into two syntactically and metrically parallel halves, followed by the lengthy v. 5, comprised of four-stress half-lines with parallel syntax. The next three lines, vv. 6–8, exploit rhyme (part/heart/apart) and gradually increasing metrical stress—from three in v. 6, to four in v. 7, to six in v. 8—in order to emphasize the importance of what is said in them. The next four lines, vv. 9–12, are (rough) English pentameters alternating with tetrameters, while enjambment connects vv. 13–14, followed by a short, three-beat line (v. 15) and a longer line of two (rough) trimeters (v. 16). Finally, vv. 17–20 are English pentameters.

    Carm. 9.13, to Lupus and Waldo, offers a different set of gestures:

A ceaseless piety, a parent's heart, demand that
you be cherished: Lupus, they're the source of your charm,
Waldo, they make you holy; ministers equal in goodness
and grace, always fixed, a side-by-side love in my heart.
From afar I try to pay the greeting I owe,   5
if I can't see you I can seek you with this trifle.
Commend me to the lofty bishop (I pray),
take my best wishes to courtiers and kings,
tell sweet Droctoveus, tell citizens and clergy,
what I would do if I were there.   10
My best to excellent Mummolus and Caesarius,
don't let me slip from my Constantine's mind.

Here, vv. 1–4 feature syntactically parallel phrases with nonparallel rhythm in nonparallel parts of the line ("Lupus . . . charm / Waldo . . . holy"); vv. 3–4 are a cluster of dactyls, beginning with "ministers" in v. 3. Verses 5–6 have parallel rhythm, with iamb followed by anapest in adjacent but nonparallel positions ("From afar I try to pay the greeting I owe, / if I can't see you I can seek you with this trifle"). Verses 7–8 are a pair of four-beat lines with parallel syntax, with alliteration on parallel nouns, while vv. 9 and 11 end in heavy conjuncts and vv. 10 and 12 are shorter and more colloquial, as befits (so I believe) Fortunatus' tone.

More than a few times, my English renderings exceed the number of words—between six and nine—expected in lines written in traditional meters. This is due to my insistence that the English correspond line-for-line with the Latin but is also the result of Latin's superior concision. But in every instance I have tried to make such lines divisible metrically by two, as is the case in *carm.* 6.9.5 above, though to print each half separately would jumble the line-for-line correspondence. I have not adhered to any preordained metrical scheme but have allowed the Latin to express itself in English before working the English into something that might gesture toward poetry. My goal was for the English to sound good, with each line achieving its own rhythmic integrity that, as much as possible, carries over in terms of sound and sense to the next line. Finally, I have tried to construct lines whose rhythms support, by drawing attention to, Fortuantus' tendency to shift suddenly in theme or tone at the end of his pentameters and, especially, in the final couplets of his poems.

7. The Text—and Using This Translation

Numerous extant manuscripts record the eleven books of Fortunatus' poetry, providing a stable witness to what he wrote, while separate witnesses to individual poems are found in florilegia. All extant manuscripts come from the same archetype except Σ, discovered by Guérard in 1831, which adds another thirty-four poems to the collection while also preserving many poems recorded elsewhere. Leo thought these additional poems derived from a more complete and now lost version of the collection but, rather than placing them back into it, chose to publish them in the so-called Appendix.[63] Meyer thought that App. 10–31 formed the final part of Book 11 and located poems 1–9 in specific places in the other books.[64] Koebner felt that Σ in toto was the work of an anthologist who gathered and circulated specific pieces by

---

63. Leo (*MGH*, viii), with Reydellet (vol. 1, lxxvi).

64. Meyer (131).

dint of personal interest, but with clear principles of selection and ordering.[65] Reydellet believes that Σ represents the work of an anthologist, but he does not consider Σ a better witness to those poems also recorded in other manuscripts. Moreover, because those pieces that occur only in Σ have no other witness, Reydellet finds it impossible to believe in a more complete but now lost version of the collection that they presumably represent. Neither would he meld the poems that only occur in Σ back into the collection.[66]

The witness of the manuscripts suggests two families,[67] from which derive the editions printed since the Renaissance. The editio princeps was produced by Solanus in Venice in 1578. There followed in 1603 Brower's edition, published at Mainz and subsequently reedited in 1617 and 1630. In Rome in 1786–1787, Luchi published his edition, which in 1862 Migne reprinted as *PL,* vol. 88. Leo's *MGH* text appeared in 1881 and stood as the only modern edition until Reydellet published his text in the Budé series between 1994 and 2004.[68] Editorially important, too, are studies by Blomgren, published over the course of many decades, that have furthered the establishment of the most reliable Latin text.[69]

I translate 122 of the 249 poems of the collection—just about half.[70] According with the breakdown of the complete collection, in which a third of the poems are written to Gregory, Agnes, and Radegund, Gregory of Tours is the recipient of 22 of the 122 pieces translated here, while Radegund and Agnes are the recipients of 49. The remaining 51 translations are addressed to 40 recipients, ranging from kings and queens to figures, such as the archdeacon of Meaux, who lack even a name.

The poems I have selected range across the eleven books of the collection and the Appendix, except Book 2, which contains only one poem, *carm.* 2.8, that might be considered a poem to a friend, and Book 4, comprised entirely of epitaphs. Many poems were ruled out by their function, such as the praise pieces to kings and queens, the poems written to celebrate the arrival of

---

65. Koebner (128–38).

66. Reydellet (vol. 1, lxxviii–lxxxiii).

67. Reydellet (lxxxiii–lxxxv).

68. DB is not an editorial project but rather a reprinting for Italian readers of Reydellet's text for Books 1–8 and Leo's for Books 9–11 and the Appendix, with facing Italian translation. His notes for Books 1–8 are essentially translations of Reydellet, but he has original things to say throughout, especially respecting Books 9–11 and the Appendix.

69. Blomgren (*Studia,* 1933; *Eranos* 42; and *Eranos* 69). There are also more specialized treatments of the diction of Ovid, Virgil, Statius, and the elegists in separate articles by Blomgren.

70. Of the collection's poems, 218 are in Books 1–11, and 31 are in the Appendix.

various figures, the acrostics, the hymns, and pieces written to commemorate churches, castles, rivers, or inanimate objects. The epitaphs were omitted not because they cannot be read as poems of friendship—*carm.* 4.10 to Bishop Leontius of Bordeaux clearly can be so read—but because they commemorate friendship rather than bear witness to it as a present, lived, experience. I privileged pieces that focus on recipients as individuals and ruled out those poems that linked individuals to larger political or ecclesiastical contexts, such as the building or renovation of a church. In the probably false (and clearly arbitrary) belief that less is more in such a project, I also omitted poems longer than forty lines. Finally, the desirability of including all the poems one would expect in a collection of this sort had to be balanced by the necessity of producing a volume of reasonable length. I perforce had to leave out a cluster of poems that could rightly have found a place here.[71]

I translate the poems in the order in which they fall in the collection, except where poems to a recipient are found in more than one place. In those cases, the poems from across the collection are grouped together. Because this occurs more than a few times, for each poem I cross-reference the Latin texts of *PL, MGH,* Reydellet, and DB and the translations of George. The numbering of poems according to book, then poem is conventional and identical in *MGH,* Reydellet, and DB; divergences from this convention in *PL* are noted.

Because I have organized the translations according to addressee, none of whom are well-known figures to twenty-first century readers, I offer the introductory essays with several goals in mind. Most importantly, they provide biographical detail, to the extent such can be determined. They also raise issues of interpretation, normally through an examination of earlier views by way of offering my own positions. Finally, they examine, where appropriate, Fortunatus' use of language, treating his penchant for wordplay, repetition, rhyme, and the like, in the belief that the Latinless reader can profit in learning about the ways the poet manipulates the language in which he wrote. These essays pretend neither to the learning nor to the thoroughness that one expects in a full-length commentary, though they do rely heavily on the standard treatments of Fortunatus' poetry, written across more than a century in Latin, German, French, Italian, and English, including names that will become familiar to those who read what follows—Luchi, Nisard, Meyer, Koebner, Tardi, Leo, George, and Roberts.

---

71. These include *carm.* 3.3 to Eufronius; 3.11 to Nicetius; 3.14 to Carentinus; 3.15 to Igidius; 3.23 and 3.23a to Ageric; 7.14 to Mummolenus; 9.6 to Gregory of Tours; 9.8 to Childebert II and Brunhilde; 9.9 to Sidonius; 9.14 to Plato; App. 5 to Childebert II; and App. 6, to Brunhilde.

Finally, the "contents" of Fortunatus' poetry are lists of the individual poems, with titles, appended to the beginning of the manuscripts, whereas titles found there are sometimes at variance with the superscriptions that separate individual poems in the manuscripts. Both are later additions of copyists that sometimes fail accurately to reflect the poems to which they are attached, and though I often refer to them in the essays to follow, they should not be understood to have the weight of Fortunatus' hand behind them.[72]

I translate Leo's *MGH* text except in the instances cited, where I follow Reydellet or, in one case, Brower; at *carm.* 11.3.14, against Leo and Reydellet, I return to the reading of the manuscripts.

5.14.7	an incomplete line = Brower as reported by Luchi: *fletibus adfuit huc genitor genetrixque puellae.*
7.3.3	*remus* (false form for *remur?*) = *Remus,* locative for Reims.
7.9.13	*benigne* Σ^2 = *benigno* codd. rell.
7.10.10	*novis* F = *novus* rell.
7.25.1	*nauta* = *nautam* codd.
7.25.8	*qui* codd. = *quo.*
7.25.13	*aestibus ille* = *et himus ille* codd.
8.6.6	*vicias* = *violas* codd.
8.6.6	*ferret* rell. = *fert et* A.
8.6.11	*hae . . . gerunt* = *haec . . . gerit* codd.
8.8.3	*ipsa* Σ L = *ipse* rell.
8.15.9	*huic* = *vir* codd.
8.21.14	*inde* = *unde* codd.
9.16.17	*gravis* = *gratus* codd.
11.3.14	*opes* = Pucci *opus* codd.
11.11.6	*fragrat* = *flagrat* codd.
App. 7.9	lacunose final metrical foot = DB *ipsis.*
App. 10.1	*aure* = *ore* Σ.
App. 18.6	*mora ioti* Σ = *mora loci.*
App. 21.12	*ago* = *agor* Σ.
App. 22.11	*surcula* = *sarcula* Σ.
App. 26.5	*fano* Σ with modifying *tali* = *fano* with modifying *talis.*

---

72. Meyer (87–88) with Koebner (123).

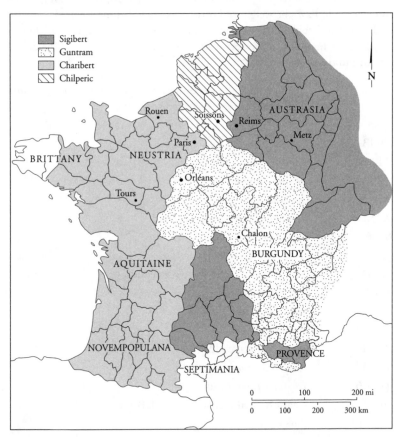

Gaul at the death of Lothar I (561)

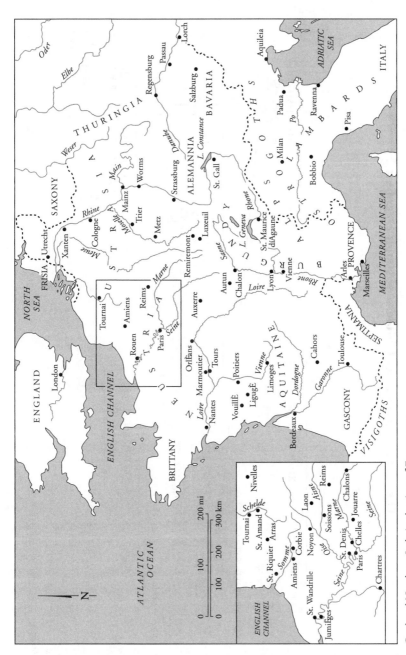

Gaul and Northern Italy in the time of Fortunatus

The Merovingians from Childeric through Dagobert I

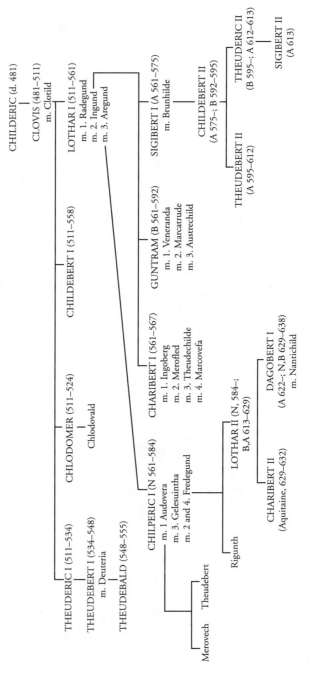

KEY:

A: Austrasia   B: Burgundy   N: Neustria

Poems to Friends

1. To Placidina (fl. 550)

Except for *carm.* 4.10, the epitaph on Leontius II, bishop of Bordeaux (fl. 550), commissioned by his wife, Placidina, this noblewoman and her husband appear only in the first book of Fortunatus' collection, where they figure in thirteen of the book's twenty-one poems. Of the many illustrious friends cultivated by Fortunatus, perhaps none were more distinguished. The *Leontii*, one of the older and more eminent families in Aquitaine, traced their lineage to Pontius Leontius (fl. c. 450), and could, perhaps, also claim collateral kinship with the Italian *Ruricii* and *Anicii* families.[1] Leontius' career included military service with Childebert I (d. 558), not to mention the civil and ecclesiastical activities attending to high church office.[2] Placidina numbered the emperor Avitus (r. 455–456) among her distinguished forebears.[3]

Along with an ancient pedigree came extensive wealth, betokened by Fortunatus in three poems, *carm.* 1.18, 1.19, and 1.20, that celebrate villas at Besson, Vérégine, and Preignac;[4] and Episcopal accomplishment, the focus of *carm.* 1.15, in which Fortunatus praises Leontius for balancing political power, personal virtue, and spiritual achievement. This combination of talents is also extolled in *carm.* 1.8 and 1.9, which, respectively, praise Leontius' restoration of a basilica devoted to St. Vincent and his founding of a martyrium to hold this saint's relics. A corollary of Leontius' attention to St. Vincent is his interest in church-building, as *carm.* 1.10 and 1.11 demonstrate, whose lines depict, respectively, his dedication of a shrine to St. Nazarius and his renovation of the Church of St. Denis. Placidina appears regularly in these poems as Leontius' helpmate. In *carm.* 1.6, she decorates and maintains the basilica of St. Martin that Leontius sponsored, while, in *carm.* 1.12, a poem celebrating the basilica of St. Vivien, she adorns the saint's shrine in silver.[5] She joins her husband in gift-giving, too, as *carm.* 1.14 suggests, whose four lines are presumed to represent an inscription on a chalice given by the couple to an unnamed church.

Yet if many of the poems written to Leontius celebrate him in terms drawn from the Latin panegyrical tradition, the words Fortunatus sends to Placidina in *carm.* 1.17 open up the private space of friendship. The poem has been variously interpreted. Luchi thought it signaled the poet's intention to gather relics stored on an island by holy men, an aim stymied by a storm that sent him instead to one of Placidina's estates.[6] Building on this reading, Nisard conjectured that Fortunatus' destination was Cordouan, an island off the Gaulish coast that for some time had attracted religious figures seeking a place of retreat.[7] On the other hand, Reydellet, following Meyer, thinks that the poet, having departed for a trip on a boat, was swept to an island by a storm, where accidentally he discovered seashells that he subsequently sent to Placidina.[8]

That the poet's destination was Cordouan cannot be proven, but it makes good sense of the word "island" (*insula*, v. 3 = "Cordouan," v. 4 in the translation), while its location at the mouth of the Gironde as it empties into the Atlantic accords with the ocean-borne swells mentioned in v. 4 (*tumidas . . . aquas*, v. 3 in the translation). That Cordouan lies within fifty miles of the three estates known to have been owned by Placidina and Leontius strengthens the case to be made in its favor. Cordouan also makes sense in the context of the northerly wave the poet mentions in v. 6, for a north wind would push a boat attempting to land at Cordouan back to the French coast—precisely what happens in the poem.

In any case, because Placidina would have known these details of geography, the poet has no need to mention them. The lack of precision thus adds to the poem's intimacy, a closeness the poem's final couplet confirms. For in it, Placidina's "bounty" (*prosperitas*, v. 7) provides the trifles Fortunatus sends, making her a figure who competes with nature's fullness. She is thus "rich" (*plena*, v. 7) in the same sense that nature contains all things and freely gives them, whether we understand her estate to be the source of the poet's gift or view her as the gift itself, better than anything Cordouan might have given.[9]

Verses 3–4 of the translation reverse the order of the Latin for ease of reading.

1.17
[*PL*, col. 83; *MGH*, 21;
Reydellet, vol. 1, 42–43; DB, 136–37]

A gift, too small—Pia, take it willingly, please—
more nearly a gift in yourself, you gleam, decent in the world.
The ocean whispered the swells to sleep,
from midchannel Cordouan was poised to offer gifts;
as I hurried—I wished to know this place in the sea—   5
a wave ravening from the north tossed me back to shore.
Your bounty still proved itself rich:[10]
what I sought in the brine I found in your field.

2. To Felix (d. 582)

Felix, bishop of Nantes, hailed from an illustrious Aquitainian family, though of it we know nothing beyond the names of his nephew, Burgundio; his father, Eumerius, who preceded him as bishop; and the presence of an otherwise unnamed niece.[1] Of his controverted episcopate we know much more. He had a notorious falling out with his superior bishop, Gregory of Tours, accusing Gregory's brother of murder and supporting the charge of treason leveled against Gregory by the noblemen Leudast and Riculf.[2] Nor did he lessen animosity toward himself when, shortly before his death in 582, Felix attempted to name Burgundio his successor, a move that Gregory, as Felix's superior, refused to approve.[3] Given Gregory's intimacy with Fortunatus, these events must have strained the poet's friendship with Felix. Nonetheless, nearly a quarter of the poems collected in Book 3 concern Felix. *Carm.* 3.4 is a lengthy reply written in prose and poetry that mimics the letter from Felix that prompted it; *carm.* 3.6 celebrates the dedication of the cathedral of Nantes; *carm.* 3.7 concerns the relics founds therein; *carm.* 3.8, dated to 567–573, was written as part of the celebration attending to the completion and dedication of the cathedral of Nantes sponsored by Felix; and *carm.* 3.9 is a lengthy Easter poem written to Felix.[4]

Felix's run-ins with Gregory of Tours may have eventually led to a falling out with Fortunatus, but in those poems in which the poet speaks as a friend, he emerges as a man of energy, skill, and action. One reason for this is practical: Felix's bishopric included lands in Brittany whose Celtic inhabitants had migrated from England in the previous century but whose assimilation into Frankish culture, outside the key cities of Nantes, Vannes, and Rennes, was marginal.[5] Felix thus found himself the leader of a church constantly threatened by indigenous Bretons, not to mention wandering groups of Bretons and Saxons moving south from England and the continent. Apart from these external threats, Felix also had to mediate civil disputes among the Breton nobility while attending also to the rote of duties implied in his office.[6]

While sustaining the seriousness that informs many of the poems written to Felix, *carm.* 3.5 frames his qualities, and the poet's stake in them, in more personal terms, offering praise for Felix's adroit handling of the latest incursions of the Bretons into Brittany.[7] After an initial couplet that places Felix in an appropriate ecclesiastical context (vv. 1–2), Fortunatus turns to the public outrage felt by the aggrieved homeland and affiliates Felix's martial triumphs with the political, social, and military successes of antiquity (vv. 3–4). By dint of his strength, Felix was able to act as a safe haven, preventing Brittany's metaphorical shipwreck (vv. 5–6). A couplet that links worldly with otherworldly attainments (vv. 7–8) precedes the closing lines, in which the poet enjoins Felix to live on as a splendid example to Brittany and the world (vv. 9–10). Throughout, there is an emphasis on the civil and spiritual roles Felix plays, just as Felix's worldly acumen and noble lineage contrast with the brilliancy of his example to the church and the humble way in which he willingly serves all people.

While the brevity and concision of the poem lend to it a more personal tone, Fortunatus makes his boldest claim of intimacy, as he will do elsewhere, by exploiting the acrostic form.[8] He does this by placing Felix's name in the center of v. 1, surrounded on either side by an equal number of words (in the Latin, three; in the translation, six), thus playing also on a triune design. Contrasted to the normal horizontal axis of reading is the poet's own name, spelled out on the vertical axis in the first letters of each line. The names thus create a cross, providing a visual means for Fortunatus to affirm his respect for Felix's work. There is a playfulness to the poem, too, for the poet puns on Felix's name and his own, both of which in Latin are adjectives meaning "lucky," "happy," "fortunate." That lightheartedness ramifies the intimacy of poet and addressee: both are fortunate to share a friendship that their names commend.[9]

3.5
[*PL* col. 124; *MGH*, 54;
Reydellet, vol. 1, 91–92; DB, 194–95]

Faith-filled savior of the hearth, **Felix** in name, hope, and
heart, the
order of priests gleams in your diamond-light,
reluming the land, as outrage demanded,
trundling ancient joys to our time;
voice of princes, a people's defender, beacon of nobility,   5
no shipwreck in the safe haven you make,
apostle-like, crushing the Bretons' might, you
trammeled brawn with a cross, strapping against adversities:
valiant to the hearth, fiery of faith, honor's founder, live on—a
source of brilliancy for the priests—my love for you is as big
as the world.   10

3.10
[*PL* col. 134; *MGH*, 62–63;
Reydellet, vol. 1, 104–105; DB, 208–11]

Carm. 3.10 balances images of epic boldness with more intimate assessments of Felix's humanity. The ancient poets are told to step aside, and readers learn that, had Homer witnessed Felix's latest project, the epic poet would have written only of Felix, abandoning all interest in Achilles (vv. 1–4). Then come the specifics of that project: the shoring up of a deteriorating river bank. There follow descriptions of a dam being built, the removal of the mud that lined the now-dry river bed, and the construction of a channel to hold the rerouted water (vv. 5–16). Felix is thus able to prevail upon this river to flow in a new direction by dint of building up its once-breached channel so that it flows calmly now rather than coursing over the break (vv. 17–20). At the same time, there are social benefits to Felix's accomplishment. The waters formerly in the marshland now irrigate fields downstream, producing fresh harvests that feed a people always in need of sustenance (vv. 21–24). Such competence leads Fortunatus to ruminate on the affiliation of great accomplishment and human discernment. If Felix is able to command a river, how much more is it the case that the bishop can bend to his will the doubtful motives of his flock and its enemies (vv. 25–26).

Luchi identified the river in question as the Loire, a view shared by Aupest-Conduché, who thinks that Felix dammed up at least one of its branches and built a road on it.[10] Reydellet qualifies this view by suggesting that the river in question could be the Erdre. It is hard to think, as Aupest-Conduché goes on to argue, that vv. 9–10 depict Felix cutting a path to the sea by building a dam. As Reydellet notes, Felix didn't make an artificial lake but rather rerouted the course of a river.[11] Given the fact that it is, even today, much wider upstream, the Erdre likely is the river involved, whose diminished flow as it joins the Loire at Nantes was remedied by Felix in order to increase the water supply to his Episcopal city.

> Let bygone poets, epical yarns, recant:
> deeds, long done, yield to innovation.
> If Homer in his time had seen this river blockaded
> he would have filled his own sweet poem from its flow:
> Achilles would now be lost to time—everyone would read
>   of Felix   5
> and Homer's skill would swell his name.
> Brimming with genius, altering, turning things for the better,
> you make an old river run a new course,
> building a bank, hauling sludge fallen into the flow,
> you chisel a channel where Nature demurred and   10
> level a marsh with a mountain of earth.
> Now swamp and mound are akin,
> to see one is to see the other,
> convex valley, concave hill.
> Where water once ran a mound staunches the flow,   15
> now carts meander where prows once sailed.
> You bend put-upon waves to unwilling hills,
> force a river to make peace with hesitant heights:

coursing quickly, headlong, it stayed its course
where rapids once fell—its path altered by a newborn hill.   20
Water used to cascade as if to no good end,
but now, like a servant, it nourishes people,
who reap a harvest, water-sown, man-made
through you, since their feasts are birthed by waves.
What prowess: to bend the doubtful motives of men   25
like the river, swift, bridled at your command.
May your life go down through time, pious, unstained.
Felix: your power shifted a river's course.

5.7

[*PL,* col. 197 (= 5.8); *MGH,* 118;
Reydellet, vol. 2, 34; DB, 316–17]

Carm. 5.7 expands on Felix's affiliation with nature explored in the previous
poem. As one of five pieces in Fortunatus' collection written in hexameters,
the poem is set apart by meter.[12] Meyer conjectured that it might be the
beginning of a much longer but now lost piece, but, as Reydellet notes, the
poem can be read as a response to an invitation, while the shift to hexameters
might be a way to charm Felix, who is perhaps inured to the elegiac couplet
in which Fortunatus normally composes.[13]

Instead of seeing in the poem hints of Fortunatus' compositional habits, I
focus on the phrase, "to sing pastoral with you in your idyll" (*tecum modularer
in illis,* v. 6), which would seem to announce Fortunatus' pastoral intentions—
not coincidentally, at the poem's midpoint. For the verb *modulari,* "to sing," is
used by Virgil of his own pastoral compositions[14] and, as a structural marker,
indicates that all to follow will be a pastoral piece. On this view the meter of
the poem makes good sense. A similar marker falls at the end of the poem,
in v. 12, where *amoenum,* "pleasant" (translated as "idyll" below), designates
natural fecundity and beauty, the obvious topics of pastoral poetry betokened
by a word also associated with the genre.

That *Cariacus* designates a villa is clear from the poem's context, but its
location remains controverted. Reydellet, following Luchi, hears *Cares* in the
word *Cariacus,* the Latin name of the Cher River, and conjectures that the
villa may have been situated at the confluence of the Cher and the Loire.[15]
I read the poem in tandem with *carm.* 3.10, bearing witness from another
angle to Felix's grand engineering feat, in which, for purposes of bringing
more water to Nantes, he rerouted the Erdre at a point where its bank had
been breached upstream. Since Fortunatus mentions the Loire explicitly in the

poem, *Cariacus* would be located at or near the point where the Erdre flows into it. From this vantage point Felix is able to witness directly the results of his efforts, since the increased supply of water running downstream has augmented the fecundity of the countryside surrounding his villa.

The poem thus forms a response to Felix's invitation, recalled in vv. 5–6, to share the bounties of *Cariacus,* whose increased prosperity Felix rightly would have wished to celebrate with a poet who had already honored in verse the feat that made it possible. At the same time, the chance to ponder nature affords Fortunatus a venue in which to render the new bounties of the downstream landscape in a brief pastoral that becomes in its conclusion a poem celebrating the friendship the two men share, wherein the beauty of the land is transferred to the beauty of Felix's countenance.

In v. 12, the phrase "fortunate friend" (*fortunato*) puns on the poet's name while reminding readers of its synonym, *felix,* returning readers to the second line of the poem, where Fortunatus admits that Felix's name makes him smile precisely because it means "happy." The intimacy of the pun is perhaps reinforced by the poem's abrupt beginning ("I know . . . ," *sentio,* v. 1), but if this declaration is meant to reflect colloquial discourse, the poet thinks better of his recipient, stopping himself short in vv. 1–3 in order to address Felix with the respect due to him. Only then, in v. 4, does he pick up the narrative thread begun with the poem's breezy first word.[16]

> I know—father, Godlike, revered, beacon to all,
> sweet leader of the city, whose name makes me smile, Felix:
> clasping you, bearing you, in my heart, in the arms of piety—
> my burden is sweet (of a sort that doesn't oppress a lover).
> Highness, why summon me—lowly me—to this agreeable
>   place to see, dear,   5
> the allurements that hold you back? To sing pastoral with
>   you in your idyll:
> the Loire, chilly, glassy, soaks your fields
> as Cariacus, with its handsome lawn, ambles down to
>   river's edge,
> where a stream restores its flow, or a shoot revives in shade
> and the crackling north wind nags the pinewood's leaves.   10
> Fertile this land, truly so, beautiful with its fish-tossed shore
> as your idyll-face returns to a fortunate friend.

3. To Vilicus (fl. c. 566)

Apart from a reference to him at *carm.* 6.8.22, Vilicus appears only in *carm.* 3.13, a poem of forty-four verses that praises this important bishop against the natural backdrops of the Moselle River and of Metz, his Episcopal city. These praises tell us little beyond the typical attributes of a successful bishop, and two extant letters written to him provide no further details.[1] The four brief poems appended to *carm.* 3.13 are in their own way more forthcoming. Presumably composed in the context of meals the poet attended, these pieces seem little more than extemporaneous recitations. Di Brazzano notices the temperaments of Martial and Ausonius in them and, in the mention of Falernian wine (3.13c.4), senses a compliment meant to bring Vilicus into the orbit of *Romanitas* while perhaps also suggesting his Gallo-Roman lineage.[2] Whatever the circumstances of their creation, Fortunatus' words affirm a world of clever banter and civilized compliment befitting warm hospitality and the poetic talent used to praise it. The poem may date from the spring of 566, when Fortunatus was in Metz as a celebrant at the wedding of Sigibert and Brunhilde, though a later date cannot be ruled out.

3.13 a–d
[*PL*, col. 139–40 (= 3.15–18); *MGH*, 66–67;
Reydellet, vol. 1, 111–12; DB, 216–19; George, *Poems,* 3]

a.

Rich shepherd of a flock (your fodder benefits all sheep):
you satisfy souls—how well you pamper bodies:
restoring banqueters with milk like nectar
drunk straight from the bowl—no ladle.

b.

A sheep runs in, demanding its own pasturage, pastor:
you're accustomed to being a meal—give me the power of bread.

c.

A bird in tangled vines blooms under the sprigs,
its beak nimbly pecking a painted feast;
a banqueter beheld a double meal:
sees grapes on a wall, drinks Falernian they give.

d.

Father, your nets overflow with a burden of fish:
it appears you've deserved to trade places with Peter.

4. To Hilary (fl. c. 570)

The identity of Hilary is unclear. He cannot be the bishop present at the council of Auvergne in 535, since his successor, Evanthius, is active as early as 541, long before Fortunatus arrived in Gaul. He may be the bishop of Digne, who took office in 554,[1] but he need not be a bishop at all. The contents of Book 3 and the title to *carm.* 3.16 simply call him by name. The figure by this name mentioned by Gregory of Tours is already dead in Gregory's day,[2] while the Hilary who traveled from Rome to Gaul in 599 with letters from Pope Gregory is too late to have known Fortunatus.[3] The poet refers to a Hilary at *carm.* 3.28.7 (No. 12) and memorializes him in *carm.* 4.12, where he is identified, not very helpfully, in the contents of Book 4 and by title as a "priest" (*presbyter*) and member of the Gaulish nobility. Stroheker thinks *carm.* 3.16 is addressed to this figure, esteemed here as a close friend, and barring the discovery of further evidence, his view makes best sense. [4]

3.16
[*PL,* col. 142 (= 3.21); *MGH,* 69;
Reydellet, vol. 1, 115; DB, 222–23]

My soul's pure light, always sweet to me, Hilary:
absent now, though my care still sees you through;
your worthy love has so filled my heart
that I cannot speak, my mind is blank, when you're away.
Meager lines pray you to safety;   5
love gave them—let them be dear to you, please.

5. To Bertrand (d. 585)

The contents of Book 3 and the title of *carm.* 3.18 identify Bertrand as a bishop (*episcopus*). Ruling out Bertrand of Le Mans, Meyer shows that Fortunatus must have composed this piece for Bertrand of Bordeaux, the successor of Leontius II.[1] The date of Bertrand's accession is not known, though his many appearances in the pages of Gregory of Tours' *Histories* commence with the year 577; he died in 585.[2]

Gregory reports that King Guntram and Bertrand were maternal kinsmen, leading Meyer to conclude that the bishop was related through his mother to Ingund, the second wife of Lothar I and the mother of Kings Charibert I, Guntram, and Sigibert I.[3] An impressive lineage failed to keep Bertrand from the center of controversy. He was accused by Leudast of being the lover of Queen Fredegund and eventually testified against Gregory of Tours when the author of the *Histories* was accused of having spread the rumor on which Leudast based his charge. He also involved himself with Gundovald, a pretender to Lothar's throne, which placed him in a poor light with Guntram, Lothar's son (and presumably Bertrand's first cousin); openly fought with Bishop Palladius of Saintes; and was forced to pay an indemnity to Bishop Faustianus of Dax.[4]

In addition to *carm.* 3.18, Bertrand is the addressee of *carm.* 3.17, which takes as its focus a ride that the bishop gave to the poet in his wagon, while *carm.* 3.18 demonstrates Bertrand's literary interests, which, if this poem is any indication, included composing in imitation of the ancient poets. Fortunatus seems not always to approve of Bertrand's verses, however, for the added "foot" mentioned in vv. 15–16 refers to false quantities found in some of Bertand's lines. Nonetheless, the poet hopes poetry swapping will continue.

3.18
[*PL,* col. 143 (= 3.23); *MGH,* 70;
Reydellet, vol. 1, 116–17; DB, 224–25]

I've taken up tough poems in a pile of letters:
words turned on a Greek lathe.
Running through frothy songs, swollen lines,
it seemed I made sail in a breaking sea:
a flat page belched stormy waves,   5
as if the ocean recoiled from its source.
In Trajan's forum[5] now old Rome rarely hears
poems so worthy, with such elegant gleam.
If you had declaimed them to the ears of the Senate,
it would have lavished gold carpets under your feet;   10
through provinces, populations, at crossroads, you would see
the empire run to your little verses—everyone a fan
of your words—even those, ancient and purloined
(so I've noticed)—that pretend to be new
but crash on the shoal of an added foot,   15
the groan of their wounds clopping a beat.
Now, father, revered, I say *hello* every way I can,
kneeling to you, commending my heart, my soul.
May your life continue on longer still as your Muse, with
                                                her modulations,
forces me to pay back some words, bantering the way we
                                                like to do.   20

6. To Agricola (d. 580)

Three bishops contemporary to Fortunatus are named Agricola. The first, warmly remembered in the *Histories* of Gregory of Tours, is the bishop of Chalon-sur-Saône, who died, at the age of 83, in 580.[1] Duchesne doubts that he is the addressee of *carm.* 3.19 but does not say why.[2] The second is the bishop of Nevers, who is listed as a signatory to a letter concerning the revolt at the Convent of the Holy Cross written to Bishop Gundegisilus in 590.[3] Luchi and Nisard think he is the recipient of *carm.* 3.19, since, for reasons of age, Fortunatus would not have been able to know the father of Agricola of Chalon-sur-Saône, who is, on a literal reading of the poem, a key figure in it.[4] The third Agricola, active c. 565, is styled by Marius of Avenches as bishop of the church of Valais, a city whose Latin name could be *Cavillonensem*, vulgarized from *civ(itatis) vallensium*.[5] This accords with the title found in the contents to Book 3, where Agricola is styled *episcopus Cavillonensem*. But, as *Cavillonensem* can also designate Chalon or Cavaillon, the matter remains controverted.

The evidence supplied by the poem shows Agricola to be a man of some prestige, who, if not elderly, is old enough to be considered a father figure to the poet. The five epithets that form the poem's first couplet are enough to prove Fortunatus' esteem,[6] but these attributes, which go to Agricola's public roles, are balanced in subsequent verses by the bishop's incomparable spirituality. Playfully, Fortunatus draws on images of sowing and reaping that pun on the bishop's name, which in Latin means "farmer."

Gregory of Tours' descriptions of Agricola of Chalon-sur-Saône accord well with the epithets Fortunatus uses in *carm.* 3.19, perhaps strengthening the case to be made for identifying him as the poem's recipient. Gregory tells us that Agricola was from a Gallo–Roman senatorial family, that he was wise and refined, that he was responsible for many building projects in his city both private and ecclesiastical, that he practiced extreme abstinence, and that he was eloquent.[7] Especially in the epithets that speak of Agricola as a source of honor and as the acme of nobility and faith, readers hear a clear evocation of lineage and social standing that allowed this bishop to be also a protector and an effective pastor to his flock. That he was more than this to Fortunatus this poem also proves.

3.19
[*PL*, col. 144 (= 3.24); *MGH*, 70–71;
Reydellet, vol. 1, 117–18; DB, 224–25]

Protector, honor's pinnacle, summit of nobility, of faith,
mighty sower of fields, rich pastor of flocks:
since my plot earned furrows by a father's hand,
let it come back tilled by the plow of his son.
For Father, whose sweet devotion is unforgettable to the world,   5
cherished me, also you—two souls, one love, of a son
for a father (also nurse and teacher) who
gave an honesty, diligent, deep, strong.
That man scored new furrows with godly zeal:
cherish that seed father poured for me.   10

7. To Avitus (d. post 591)

After Gallus, Gregory of Tours' uncle and guardian, died in 551, Gregory
was raised by Avitus, who became bishop of Clermont-Ferrand in 571. Given
the high esteem in which Sigibert held Avitus, the bishop was consecrated
to office in Metz in the royal presence.[1] In Gaulish affairs Avitus was best
known for his conversion, in 576, of the large Jewish population of Clermont-
Ferrand,[2] an event recalled by Fortunatus in a lengthy tribute to the bishop
that comprises *carm.* 5.5.[3] Since Gregory does not report Avitus' death, it is
assumed that he was still alive in 591, the year in which Gregory completed
his *Histories.*

Apart from *carm.* 5.5, which is technically addressed to Gregory of Tours,
Fortunatus composed *carm.* 3.21, 3.22, and 3.22a to Avitus. The first of these
praises Avitus' spirituality, while the other two, translated here, are more inti-
mate. *Carm.* 3.22 takes as its conceit the poet's inability to write, due to some
disability that has rendered his poetic Muses unresponsive. Fortunatus calls
Avitus "father" (*pater,* v. 1) but *Avite,* the vocative of Avitus' name in Latin,
puns on the adjective meaning "grandfatherly," suggesting more specifically
the ways in which Avitus is a father figure to Fortunatus. *Carm.* 3.22a, more
directly a praise piece, offers its admiration to Avitus in ways that make it one
of the poet's more personal compositions.

3.22

[*PL,* col. 145–46 (= 3.27); *MGH,* 72;
Reydellet, vol. 1, 120; DB, 228–29]

Priest, holy and adored, father,
Avitus sweet, your wishes have always been my command
but my Muse, playing a squeaky flute, would rather prattle today
than please with a clarion melody.
But, lover of goodness, forgive me still,   5
be tractable when you weigh my poem.
For a mountain of gifts I send this clump of words like the
                                                                    middling poet
whose language is rough: judge him by his heart's intention.

3.22a

[*PL,* col. 146 (= 3.28); *MGH,* 72;
Reydellet, vol. 1, 120–21; DB, 228–29]

Honor and virtue, trusted to the hilt, are redeemed
in the contours of your life, sweet Avitus, highest of priests,
whose sacred love binds every soul.
Father, dear, you captivate hearts into following you
but, still, among those whom your sweetness has filled,   5
as if I had tasted a greater share, I'm driven on, prompted
                                                                    by your love.
My sweet revelation, pillar of the hearth, nourisher to those
                                                                    in need,
refuge to wanderers, leader of fathers, and of honor,
if my voice could send a song to the vaults of heaven,
it would crack as it tried to sing your praises yet boom in
                                                    the love of you.   10
My heart's desire rises to this occasion,
to echo your rich and sacred name.
Let Agnes of the humble voice and her partner Radegund
be entrusted to your piety's love.
May you flourish in a life that safely stretches the years,   15
for mine, dear, is whatever your lot will be.

8. To Anfion (fl. c. 570)

Anfion is called a priest (*presbyter*) in the contents to Book 3 and in the title to *carm.* 3.24. Since Fortunatus refers to Leontius in v. 19, he is presumed to have been a priest in Bordeaux, Leontius' Episcopal city. The poem is among the most intimate of the collection, and focuses especially on those qualities of heart and mind that endeared Anfion to Leontius and, in turn, to Fortunatus.

3.24
[*PL,* col. 148–49 (= 3.31); *MGH,* 74–75;
Reydellet, vol. 1, 124; DB, 232–33]

A man stoked in piety, sweetly, pleasantly, blooming:
in your aspect a precious flash of soul
made me know, when I first got to see your face
aglow, that the light of God was deep in you.
Anfion, father, dear to me, revered priest,   5
your love is always held in my heart.
When you see some unrecognized face, you draw him up
                            next to you,
unmindful of any family ties, in your reckoning he becomes kin.
Your will, agreeable, reassuringly spoken, goads us
to be of one soul, always yours.   10
Bursting with genius, robust in managing your heart,
fitted out with a burden of wisdom no matter where you
                            happen to stay,
your guidance bridles action with caution,
tempers the position that honor bestows.
Alive to every worthy thing, bound by a lavish integrity,   15
no matter who comes to the city, he joins himself at once to you,
steeped in the patterns of daily life, you offer all comers decency:
you are made the only home for us.
There's no surprise that Leontius, the bishop, in his own
                            telling praises you,
nor that I believe his words—he's an impeccable judge of men. 20

9. To Paternus (fl. c. 570)

Brower confused the recipient of *carm.* 3.25 and 7.23 with the much more famous bishop of Avranches,[1] but the title of 3.25 calls Paternus an abbot (*Ad Paternum abbatem*). He is otherwise unknown. Both poems call on the imagery of exchange to honor Paternus' beneficence. In *carm.* 3.25 Fortunatus fears that, owing to less than adequate skills, the manuscript he has copied for Paternus will be filled with errors. Its salvation can therefore come only when Paternus reads and redeems his production (vv. 5–7). *Carm.* 7.23 deals more abstractly with the currency of friendship. That the initial line of the first poem nearly replicates the opening line of *carm.* 3.22, written to Avitus, suggests the affinities of these two friends rather than a poetic deficit on Fortunatus' part. Not the least of the similarities inheres in the abbot's name, which, like that of Avitus, offers Fortunatus a fresh occasion to link identity to action, *paternus* being in Latin an adjective meaning "fatherly."

3.25
[*PL,* col. 149 (= 3.32); *MGH,* 75;
Reydellet, vol. 1, 125; DB, 232–33]

Your wish was finally my command, priest, revered
Paternus, whose duty and name are as one,
whose merits adorn the altars of Christ:
praying, vowing to offer what will give pleasure to God.
Still, I humbly ask to be forgiven, if anything has tripped me up 5
by happenstance, for error is used to holding my hand.
May this humble page gain salvation now:
remember me when you read it again.

7.23
[*PL,* col. 258; *MGH,* 175;
Reydellet, vol. 2, 119–20; DB, 416–19]

Paternus, all that you've done in your gleaming life is implied
in the lilt
of your name; you make a gift of yourself in making yourself
a father.
Not unmindful that I am your servant; still, you give
every reward,

offering tender vows to those who have fallen under your spell.
So prompt—famously—to give only good things: 5
may your riches swell so that you can give more.

10. To Rucco (d. 591)

As the bishop of Paris, Ragnemod (Rucco to his friend Fortunatus) was an
active participant in Frankish affairs. He baptized Theuderic, the son of
Chilperic and Fredegund, then gave refuge to the queen after Chilperic's assas-
sination; he spoke on behalf of Praetextatus after this bishop had been found
guilty of conspiring against Chilperic; and he excommunicated the deacon
Theudulf for refusing to return to the church to which he had been assigned.
Gregory reports that Ragnemod's brother, Faramod, attempted unsuccessfully
to succeed him as bishop when Ragnemod died in 591.[1]

The poems to Rucco are complicated and intimate. The words of *carm.*
3.26 are occasioned by separation: the poet is somewhere off the French coast,
while Rucco remains safely in Paris. The contrast between ocean storms and
the protection the Seine affords leads naturally to an evocation of love as a
force that can overcome severance (vv. 1–6). The poet then demands that
Rucco return the favor that the words of the poem represent. Fortunatus
expects his friend to think of him, just as he has now proven that Rucco is
on his mind (vv. 15–16). On the other hand, in the poem's final couplets, the
seeming sublimation of human friendship to God's eternal love is undercut
by the poet's emphasis on the humanity, rather than the divinity, of God as
Christ. This emphasis thus renders ambiguous the poem's final line, whose
dominant image, that of one "who commands us" (*domino,* v. 18) can apply to
Christ as Lord; to Rucco, who commands Fortunatus' love; or to Fortunatus
himself, who commands his friend to write back to him.

By the time *carm.* 9.10 was written, poet and bishop had known each other
for many years, as the reference to a "veteran friendship" (v. 3) suggests. The
opening epithet, "father, no one higher in the land" (*summe pater patriae*), is
used also of Gregory of Tours at *carm.* 5.10.1 and thus gives a clearer sense
of the intimacy shared by Fortunatus and Rucco. The poem then goes on to
offer thanks to Rucco for two gifts sent to his spiritual "daughters," Radegund
and Agnes. The nuns see in the first gift, a dish, a durability akin to Rucco's
piety, while the second gift, gems, honors the bishop who gave them as much
as the cross to which they are affixed.

Carm. 3.26 was written early in the friendship, for the contents of Book
3 calls Rucco a "deacon" (*diaconum*), while the poem's title adds "priest"
(*presbyter*), offices Rucco held prior to his installation as bishop of Paris in

576. Fortunatus made his way to, and through, Paris in 567, so this poem was written at some point in the nine intervening years. The contents of Book 9 and the title of *carm*. 9.10, on the other hand, call Rucco "bishop" (*episcopum*), thus dating this poem to the years subsequent to 576.

3.26
[*PL*, col. 149 (= 3.33); *MGH*, 75–76;
Reydellet, vol. 1, 125–26; DB, 234–35]

Good Rucco, minister, rock of Christ's altar,
I'm dashing off a *hello* from here.
The ocean swells around me, friend:
while Paris holds you, huddling the Seine,
Breton waves harass me, dear,   5
yet one love binds our separation.
Friend, no sea-borne fury banishes your face,
no northern wind carries off your name;
in my heart you're a lover who appears
as often as the ocean cuffs the wintry shore   10
like the sea shaken when the east wind blew:
so stands my soul without you, dear,
while a pleasant storm burns my docile heart,
bearing down on you in all its complication.
Requite my wish, Rucco: think of me,   15
share the gift that God gives to us both
to let Christ's grace make us more fully human,
to speak, to think only of who commands us.

9.10
[*PL*, col. 309; *MGH*, 216;
Reydellet, vol. 3, 32–33; DB, 492–95]

Father, no one higher in the land, Rucco, a sweet name to me,
binding the deep well of my heart with love:
a veteran friendship has gathered us in,
that swells endlessly, rich one, into my affection;
for no oblivion takes my lover from me—   5
I would sooner die than lose my love.
And so, father, blessed, accept a hurried *hello,*
hoping you remain long in your bishop's chair.
Your daughters, too, send hearty thanks from here,

for a gift, white, solid, of Parian marble—   10
the day's meals are sent around on it (a dish)—
in its beauty they see you, your piety;
and for a cluster of gems that decorates a cross
with an honor that adorns their sender.

11. To the Archdeacon of Meaux (fl. c. 570)

Until the ninth century there existed an Episcopal catalogue that might have shed light on the archdeacon of Meaux, the addressee of *carm.* 3.27. The only sixth-century figure with any certainty associated with Meaux is Medovechus (or Medoveus), who flourished in mid-century as bishop.[1] The figure to whom Fortunatus addresses this poem likely knew Medovechus, since he is described as caring for the "bishop's flock" in v. 7. Beyond this nothing more can be said. The poem may have been written while Fortunatus was making his way from Metz to Paris in 567, though a later date cannot be ruled out.

3.27

[*PL*, col. 150 (= 3.34); *MGH*, 76;
Reydellet, vol. 1, 126; DB, 234–35]

If it were given me to see your face,
for such a gift I would give a thousand words.
Your tender inclination sent wine my way,
a sweet gift proves you're a sweetheart.
You eagerly took up my satisfaction—though you never saw
                                                        me before;   5
what would you do if a friend ambled up?
You hold the care of the bishop's flock in a mind brimming
                                                        with faith;
great minister, may God be as generous to you.

12. To John (fl. c. 570)

The addressee of *carm.* 3.28, John, is called a deacon (*diaconum*) in the contents to Book 3 and in the poem's title. Reydellet is tempted to identify him with the son of the merchant Julian, whose epitaph, *carm.* 4.23, includes a couplet (vv. 15–16) that refers to John as someone who fulfilled the functions of the sacred. Gregory of Tours speaks of the leper John, who traveled from Gaul to the Holy Land, where he was cured in the waters of the Jordan before returning with relics of the Virgin Mary. But Reydellet cautions against connecting this John with our addressee, since it is unlikely that Fortunatus would fail to mention such a miracle in a poem composed in his honor.[1] On the other hand, there is nothing that militates against identifying John as the son of the merchant Julian, and the fact that Fortunatus wrote an epitaph for Julian strengthens the connection.

To so identify him offers no further context in which to read *carm.* 3.28, but references to Anthimius and Hilary, if only indirectly, do. Named in v. 5, Anthimius is the addressee of the next poem in the collection, and the warm intimacy there expressed is also a measure of Fortunatus' esteem for John. The connection to Anthimius is strengthened, too, by the repetition, in the initial lines of both poems, of the Latin word *pignus,* "token," a word used in either case to symbolize the poems themselves, sent as offerings of respect and affection (translated in both instances as "pledged"). The reference to Hilary (v. 7), on the other hand, takes readers back to *carm.* 3.16 and highlights the durability of the friendship that links John and Fortunatus. Shared diction confirms the bond, for the phrase "meager lines" (*versibus exiguis*) is used at *carm.* 3.16.5 and 3.28.2 to describe the sort of poetry Fortunatus has written to honor both men. Finally, shared wording also brings Paternus into the orbit of this friendship, for the final line of *carm.* 3.28 is identical to the concluding verse of 3.25. There, the poet encouraged Paternus to correct a manuscript Fortunatus had sent, but cast that injunction in terms of parental care, punning on Paternus' name, which means "fatherly" in Latin. Readers have good right, therefore, to see the same sort of care attached to deacon John.

3.28
[PL, col. 150 (= 3.35); *MGH,* 76;
Reydellet, vol. 1, 127; DB, 234–37]

A friendship etched in our minds is pledged
in meager lines, precious John—accept them.
My sweet: when I have gone to places we cannot know,
in your soul absence will be but an apparition.
Revered friend, through you I say *hello*   5
to father Anthimius, whose affection makes me whole,
and to Hilary, tenacious in his love,
(for I mention in my poems those I adore).
Eternity must be yours—you've earned it:
remember me when you read this again.   10

13. To Anthimius (fl. c. 570)

The contents of Book 3 and the title of *carm.* 3.29 call Anthimius a "deacon" (*diaconum*), most likely the same figure mentioned at *carm.* 3.28.5. Nothing else is known of him. The image of pledging links the first lines of this and the preceding poem, allowing the intimacy of each piece to carry over into the other.

3.29
[*PL,* cols. 150–51 (= 3.36); *MGH,* 76–77;
Reydellet, vol. 1, 127–28; DB, 236–37]

A lover is pledged in meager lines, Anthimius,
cast for you in a pure heart—have them.
When sleep agreeably coaxed your eyes,
body limp-lying on the bed:
wavering, then unwilling to vex your calm with sin,   5
my guilt left you undisturbed.
I crawled away, a thief in the night, no one will ever know of it;
but I didn't clasp your neck, brother, well-loved, I didn't
                                        say *goodbye;*
it wasn't given me to trust my soul's tender mandates,
not even an hour set aside for your words.   10
And now the Lord (my witness) prods my conscience,
because I stole away without hearing your voice,
irresolute to say more when I had you then:
let this meager poem now speak my longings to you.
Still, I ask before God: come to me like a gift,   15
to gleam dearly, always, to everyone, everywhere.
Let no one give me finery, treasure
but let no one deny me what sweetness demands.

14. To Sindulf (fl. c. 570)

Sindulf is described as a deacon (*diaconum*) in the contents of Book 3 and in the title of *carm.* 3.30, a poem written in serpentine couplets, a mode of elegiac composition in which the initial phrase of the hexameter is repeated in the conclusion of the pentameter. Fortunatus also composed *carm.* 8.2 and

App. 19 in this way. Is there a connection between the repetition of the poem's diction and the reliability of the friendship the words commend?

3.30
[*PL,* cols. 151–52 (= 3.37); *MGH,* 77–78;
Reydellet, vol. 1, 128–29; DB, 236–39]

Brother in God's love, etched in memory for the good you do,
fixed in my heart, brother in God's love.
Seize willingly the road that leads to heaven's palace,
so that you may rise higher, seize willingly the road.
Bear patiently the load, let no goodly burden weary you,   5
whence peace abides, bear patiently the load.
It is seemly to submit your neck because the yokes of Christ
                                                are sweet,
that we may merit his reward, it is seemly to submit your neck.
Who tills the fields swells the granary,
he will not be hungry, who tills the fields.   10
The sailor is a skipped stone, flying to his fattened treasury,
smiling at his wealth, the sailor is a skipped stone.
That man fears not death in the churning fury of the storm,
so that riches may be won, that man fears not death.
A soldier comes to arms seeking a palm for his wounds,   15
that he may become a victor, a soldier comes to arms.
Fight battles for me willingly, dear comrade,
there can be a triumph if you fight battles for me.
Whoever comes in love succumbs to no burden,
no burden to whoever comes in love.   20
Sending small poems to you, I return greetings I owe,
may you do better, I pray, sending small poems.

15. To Gregory (d. 594)

Fortunatus' closest male friend, Gregory, bishop of Tours, was born c. 539 into an illustrious Gallo-Roman family whose members included thirteen previous bishops of Tours. After Gallus, Gregory's uncle and guardian, died in 551, Gregory was raised by Avitus (No. 7), archdeacon and later bishop of Clermont-Ferrand (Gregory's mother went into seclusion soon after her husband's death but remained in contact with her illustrious son). Gregory assumed the Episcopal seat in Tours in 573 and died in office in 594. Gregory does not report his sister's name, but her daughter, Justina, became prioress of the Convent of the Holy Cross. His brother, Peter, was murdered in 574.

Gregory's reputation is assured on the basis of his *Histories of the Franks,* an accounting of Merovingian Gaul in ten books that begins with the biblical story of creation and wends its way through Roman, thence to Frankish, history. But he wrote a considerable amount beyond the *Histories:* the *Glory of the Martyrs (Liber in Gloria Martyrum Beatorum)*, in 106 chapters, on the miracles performed in Gaul under the Roman persecutions of previous centuries; the *Life of St. Julian (Liber de passione et virtutibus sancti Juliani martyris)*, in 50 chapters, on the miracles of a saint whose tomb in Gregory's day was a local site of pilgrimage; the *Life of St. Martin (De virtutibus beati Martini episcopi)*, on the miracles of Gregory's most illustrious predecessor and exemplar, in four books; the *Book of the Fathers (Liber vitae patrum)*, in 20 chapters, a work of hagiography; the *Glory of the Confessors (Liber in gloria confessorum)*, in 110 chapters, on the miracles of people of many stripes in Gaul; the *Miracles of St. Andrew (Liber de miraculis beati Andreae apostoli*, on the miraculous doings of this saint, in 38 chapters; the *Passion and Martyrdom of the Seven Sleepers of Ephesus (Passio sanctorum martyrum septem dormientium apud Ephesum)*, in 12 chapters, on the history of the seven men who, after their martyrdoms, await the day of resurrection in sleepful peace; and, not least, *On the Course of the Stars (De cursu stellarum ratio)*, in 47 chapters that link astronomical observations to monastic timekeeping.[1]

As the leader of an important bishopric, Gregory of necessity lived a life beyond the creative inquiries of spiritual and scholarly reflection, providing civic leadership in addition to the spiritual nurturance expected of a high church official.[2] Fortunatus' poetry sometimes captures Gregory performing these important roles, but mostly it centers on the warm intimacies of close friendship. To be sure, longer pieces not written in the glare of friendship go to the poet's support of his good friend in varied circumstances. *Carm.* 5.3, for example, the first poem written to Gregory, perhaps even before the two had met, celebrates the arrival of the new bishop to his Episcopal city. More ominously, in 580, when Leudast claimed that Gregory had spread a rumor that Bertrand, bishop of Bordeaux, had seduced Queen Fredegund, Fortunatus wrote a lengthy panegyric, *carm.* 9.1, to her husband, Chilperic, on whose mercy Gregory would rise or fall, balancing a deft praise of the king in the Roman mold with a subtle plea to him to do God's justice toward Gregory.[3]

The poems translated here, on the other hand, reveal the lineaments of a friendship that endured for over twenty years and offer intimacy, playfulness, devotion, and gratitude. They show good friends exchanging poetry, letters, and gifts both large and small. St. Martin, the most illustrious of Gregory's predecessors in Tours' Episcopal seat, is often the figure whose exemplarity enables Fortunatus best to offer praise to Gregory, but he is also a rich source of saintly lore that the poet exploits in order to make specific points about friendship's currency. *Carm.* 5.14, for example, focuses on a tree that harbors miraculous powers owing to the fact that St. Martin once prayed over it, but insofar as Gregory is a St. Martin–like figure, the tree's curative ability speaks also to Gregory's excellence. In the same way, *carm.* 8.20 recalls the time when Martin halved his soldier's cloak in the dead of winter to cover a half-naked beggar who Martin later dreamed was Christ, a signal event that Fortunatus recalls in order to equate Gregory's generosity with his predecessor's charity. Yet in doing so the poet brings himself into the equation as a latter-day beggar, who receives alms from St. Martin's venerable successor.

Some poems offer greetings or express happiness in discovering from Gregory's latest letter or poem that the bishop is well. We learn that travel between Tours and Poitiers, at least for Fortunatus, was often stymied by the latter city's bishop, Maroveus; and that Gregory gave to Fortunatus a farm. Throughout, Fortunatus relies on a stock of epithets to situate Gregory in specific contexts. These descriptive phrases, often repeated, usually with some variation, ratify the dynamic relationship of poet and bishop, with shifting centers of personal power contrasted to the always-superior status assumed by Gregory in the various roles he plays as bishop. As a habit of composition, Fortunatus deploys epithets as a means to say more with less, a constraint forced on him by the demands of the elegiac couplet. In the end, though, the stature affirmed in the epithets used of Gregory helps Fortunatus to articulate friendship in concrete terms by emphasizing the inequality of status and rank that comradeship overcomes. The epithets are in that sense perhaps the strongest token of alliance to be found in one of western poetry's most unique collections devoted to friendship.

5.4
[*PL,* col. 185–186; *MGH,* 107;
Reydellet, vol. 2, 18–19; DB, 294–295]

The contents of Book 5 records that *carm.* 5.4 was written "to bishop Gregory" (*Ad Gregorium episcopum*), but the poem's title adds that it is "likewise, a poem celebrating the *natalicium* of bishop Gregory, read at table, when the poet was asked to recite an antiphon" (*item versus in natalicium Gregorii episcopi, cum antiphonam dicere rogaretur, in mensa dictum*). *Natalicium* can mean literally "birthday" or refer to the anniversary of the taking of holy orders, when a Christian was thought to be "born" into the life of the faith. Meyer, claiming that the title is in error, thinks the poem celebrates Gregory's actual ordination as bishop, thus making it a companion to *carm.* 5.3, written to celebrate formally Gregory's arrival in Tours as bishop.[4]

The poem's contents comport to what might be said to honor an ordinand or to celebrate his anniversary, and thus offer no clue as to the specific meaning of *natalicium.* The fact that the title is unusually descriptive, however, works against Meyer's view. For its very specificity militates against the idea that its details are in error or, worse, were invented from whole cloth. Were it the case that it simply reported that the poem was recited at table, its invention could well be imagined. But it seems unlikely that someone guessing at the poem's function or seeking to cast it as a *natalicium* (however the term might be understood) would also bother to say, of the many things that might be said to support a ruse, that Fortunatus was asked to recite an antiphon. This detail seems too unique and distinguishes, rather than affiliates, the occasions celebrated in either poem.

So, too, their placement and themes. The more formal and rhetorically accomplished *carm.* 5.3 renders the brevity and concision of *carm.* 5.4 stark. If, as Meyer thought, *carm.* 5.4, like *carm.* 5.3, was meant to celebrate Gregory's installation as bishop, it is hard to see what rhetorical, social, or official needs it filled that were not already met by the earlier poem, which perhaps was recited publicly, not to mention formally solicited.[5] On the other hand, a piece that celebrates the anniversary of the signal event formally enshrined in *carm.* 5.3 would naturally be a more modest effort, since it stands in the same relationship to the longer piece as the anniversary to the actual event. In any case, it seems difficult to accept Meyer's view that the title, correct in its other details, is incorrect in its use of the term *natalicium.* But in accepting the authenticity of the term, it seems best to follow Reydellet in understanding *natalicium* to refer to the anniversary of Gregory's ordination rather than his actual birthday. [6]

The poem marks a milestone in the life of Gregory and of those, like Fortunatus, who count themselves among his friends, for which reason it makes good sense that the poem, as the title indicates, was recited "at table" (*in mensa*). Brennan presumes this to be a reference to a dinner celebrating the anniversary of Gregory's Episcopal ordination.[7] That the poet was asked to recite an antiphon, a brief verse from the Psalms or scripture sung or recited in various liturgical contexts, but chose instead to substitute his own composition about Gregory, makes good sense in the convivial setting of a meal.

Given that *carm.* 5.4 was written to memorialize an event, it makes good sense, too, that in it Fortunatus plays on the idea of memory. Martin's merits are writ large in the memory of Tours, and the poet hopes they will support

Gregory in his role as the great saint's successor. At the same time, Fortunatus hopes that Gregory's memory among his people will increase their honor, a process of modeling that Gregory's sermons can further. The poet enjoins Gregory's words to minister to Tours in such a way as to offer "sermons, like apostles" that can "be beacons to the people" (v. 5), thus evoking the memory of Christ's disciples. In doing this, the bounty of heaven is manifest in Gregory's own countenance, making him a model in this life of the plenitude of God through the humanity of Christ, whose life is remembered in Gregory's own best actions.

Nor, as a poem of friendship, is this poem exclusively one of high praise. As he does in the poems to Felix and Paternus, Fortunatus puns on the name of his good friend in the inflected form of the Latin word for "flock," *gregem* (v. 2), in which Gregory's name, *Gregorius,* can be heard. [8] Fortunatus thus introduces an element of playfulness that goes to the growing intimacy on the part of poet and patron that would not have existed on the day of Gregory's ordination—presumably the day on which Fortunatus and Gregory first met, strengthening readers in the view that the poem is an anniversary piece.

Finally, the esteem in which the poet holds Gregory, apart from any playfulness his verses might evince, is suggested through word placement in the poem's first couplet:

Martini meritis per tempora longa, **Gregori**,
Turonicum foveas pastor in urbe **gregem**.

Here, emphatically, Martin, the great saint of Gaul and Gregory's most famous predecessor, is linked through a long stretch of time to Gregory, his successor, an idea that "stretches" across the poem's first verse to connect Martin's name to Gregory's. So, too, Tours, the Episcopal city of Martin and of Gregory, is the first word of the second line, just as the flock, *gregem,* that connects Martin and Gregory to it is the final word of v. 2—and the word that puns on Gregory's name. Readers thus hear in the initial words of the first couplet Martin and Tours, while in the final words of either verse there is nothing but Gregory.

> Through the good that Martin did long ago, Gregory,
> city-shepherd, nurture Tours' sheepfold.
> Where the holy are gathered, be piety's life and measure:
> let honor grow and gain through the good that you do now.
> May your sermons, like apostles, be beacons to the people: 5
> let a heavenly gift glint in your glow.

5.8

[*PL*, col. 198 (= 5.9); *MGH*, 118;
Reydellet, vol. 2, 34–35; DB, 316–17; George, *Poems*, 21]

This poem negotiates the creative tension between public necessity and private feeling that informs much of Fortunatus' output. The poet acknowledges the prayers of the Gaulish countryside answered by Gregory's return (vv. 7–8) but the remaining lines are dominated by expressions in the first person: "I clasp" (*amplectende mihi*, v. 3); "I rejoice" (*gaudeo*, v. 5); "my heart" (*animo . . . meo*, v. 4); "to me" (*mihi*, v. 6); "with me" (*mecum*, v. 9). Even the closing epithet, "priest" (*sacerdos*) speaks to the privacy implicit in the relationship between priest and believer. It is the only single word epithet in a poem that boldly opens in Latin with three two-word epithets, "tower of honor, kindly glorious, rich beacon (*culmen honoratum, decus almum, lumen opimum*, v. 1), and includes two others, "sacred fortress," "a man revered" (*sacer arce*, v. 3;[9] *vir venerande*, v. 4).

The poem's title, "To Bishop Gregory after a journey" (*Ad Gregorium episcopum post itiner*) is controverted. A majority of manuscripts record for "journey" the ungrammatical Latin word *itinere*, but Leo, following several manuscripts (and good grammar), reads the Latin word *itiner*. In agreeing with Leo, Reydellet cites Lucretius' use of this word and notes a definition offered by Isidore that may explain both the sort of journey Gregory experienced and the relief expressed by the poet at his return. According to Isidore, an *itiner* is an arduous journey that involves much walking, while *iter* designates a journey easily made.[10] In this case, then, there is genuine relief at Gregory's safe return, quite apart from the normal happiness attending the arrival of a good friend.

> Tower of honor, kindly glorious, rich beacon,
> shepherd, enthroned like an apostle with your pleasant love:
> like a sacred fortress, Gregory, I clasp you endlessly,
> a man revered, never to be torn from my heart.
> I rejoice that Tours' priest has returned in honor,   5
> gladdened that father has come back to me.
> Raucous applause for answered prayers:
> you have relumed city and citizen with light.
> Priest, I commend the messenger with me now,
> hoping that the flock long follows you.   10

5.8a

[*PL*, col. 198 (= 5.10); *MGH*, 118–19;
Reydellet, vol. 2, 35; DB, 316–17; George, *Poems*, 21]

This brief poem contrasts Gregory's Episcopal duties with Fortunatus' pious
love, whose expression, while cast against the backdrop of Gregory's incom-
parable spirituality, is ardent, physical, and worldly. The structure of the
poem speaks to this contrast. Verses 1–4 focus on Gregory the bishop, loving
those in need of defense while hankering after the world of the saints that
redemption promises. In contrast, vv. 5–8 focus on the poet's love for such a
charismatic figure in terms that rightly stress humility in the face of spiritual
accomplishment. The two halves of the poem thus speak, at least in this
instance, to an equal friendship that has distinct qualities: the worldly and
spiritually subtle bishop loves in manifold ways, whereas the poet, living a less
public and less spiritual life, cultivates a love that is more single-minded.[11]

The poem is numbered as if it were of a piece with *carm.* 5.8, but this is
a matter of editorial convenience owing to the fact that it is not listed in the
contents to Book 5. Its title, in those manuscripts that report one, is simply
"to the same addressee as the previous poem" (*Ad eundem*).

> Nobly doing piety's duties, father, kind Gregory,
> mind full of redemption, seeking saintly precincts before
> our eyes:
> a defenseless soul quickened by your words
> will have in them the power of victory's sacred arms.
> Holy man, God's own, these words are wrapped in
> humility's urge   5
> to greet you with an endless, a pious, love.
> The less I write, the hotter I burn,
> what swells the heart, stymies the hand.

5.8b

[*PL*, col. 198 (= 5.11); *MGH*, 119;
Reydellet, vol. 2, 35–36; DB, 318–19; George, *Poems*, 22]

If the title, "To Gregory, for a book presented [to the poet]" (*Ad eundem pro
libro praestito*), is accurate, Fortunatus composed this complicated poem to
thank Gregory for a book. Luchi thought the poem "thoroughly obscure"
but hazards a guess that Gregory has composed a poem or a hymn intended
for public consumption for which the poet gives thanks.[12] Reydellet thinks
Gregory has put together an anthology of Christian poets and notes that if

Gregory himself had sent poems to Fortunatus, the poet would not have failed to praise the pieces directly.[13] Roberts thinks that Fortunatus has received two gifts: the book mentioned in the title, and the "sacred songs" mentioned in v. 1 (*carmina diva,* translated here as "psalms"); that the poem offers thanks for a gift received in the past (vv. 3–4); and that vv. 5–6 acknowledge the present book, for which Gregory will receive heavenly rewards.[14]

My understanding of the poem notices in the first verse the connection between selecting (*legens*) and preserving (*condens*) the songs that have been sent. Roberts sees the connection as one of reading and composing, rendering the line as "reading sacred songs and composing them by your inspiration."[15] But it is not clear how Gregory might compose what he is reading, especially under his own rather than divine inspiration, seeing that the composition in question is qualified as "sacred" (*diva,* v. 1). On the other hand, Reydellet connects reading with preserving, a more logical affiliation, so that Gregory reads, then stores away what he has read: "In reading the sacred poems, by preserving them according to your mood . . . ."[16]

Nisard's translation, "having collected these divine songs, having drawn them from your heart . . ." comes closest to what the poet would seem to be saying.[17] Reydellet considers Nisard's rendering contradictory,[18] but a pun in v. 2 supports Nisard's understanding, where the Latin word for "crown," *palma,* plays on the Latin word for "psalm, " *psalma*. That, coupled with the resonance of the phrase *carmina diva,* literally, "sacred songs," make it clear that Gregory is reading the Psalms. This makes sensible Nisard's phrase, "having drawn them from your heart," for Gregory, like all religious, would have set the book of Psalms to memory. It seems best to make the connection of "selecting" and "preserving" (*legens* and *condens*) one of gathering what has been stored in memory.

The book mentioned in the title is therefore a collection of Gregory's favorite psalms, the sharing of which with others fashions a crown of glory or of poetic victory for Gregory as the gatherer of such rich words (vv. 1–2). For this new collection and other psalms sent in the past the poet gives thanks (vv. 3–4) while offering his hope that all of Gregory's collecting will be amply rewarded by God (vv. 5–6). The poet claims not to have examined all of its riches just yet (vv. 7–8), but sends off his messenger, Prodomer, to give humble greetings and thanks (vv. 9–10). Finally, Fortunatus hopes that a future "palm" will grow for Gregory, betokening songs to be sung in honor of God that will smooth Gregory's path to salvation.

> Father, you pluck psalms from your heart's own keep;
> Pastor, sharing them fashions for you a crown of these and
> > other holy songs
> sung countless times to the sheepfold.

I thank you for them, I offer willing praise (for they deserve it).
Still, let gifts for you, heaven-sent, God-thundered, remain,   5
recompense for sacred riches that fed the man who needed them.
When I'm able to know what you've sent, I will sound your
                                          blessedness then
for offering so great a gift.
Priest, highness, father, sweet with love,
I humbly commend Prodomer, my messenger at the moment;   10
grant him his own deserts in accordance with your fair
                                          judgment;
by God's honor, let a future crown be plaited for you.

5.9
[*PL*, col. 199 (= 5.12); *MGH*, 119;
Reydellet, vol. 2, 36; DB, 318–19]

In his *Histories* Gregory reports that Maroveus, bishop of Poitiers (584–590)
was uniformly hostile to Radegund and Agnes in their respective roles as
founder and abbess of the Convent of the Holy Cross. After Radegund, with
the blessing of King Sigibert, had sent for and received a piece of the true cross
from Justin II and Queen Sophia, Maroveus refused her request to officiate
at a ceremony marking its arrival at, and deposit in, the convent. Nor was
this the lone snub the women suffered. As many times through the years as
Radegund asked Maroveus for assistance, she was turned down. He refused
her request for a monastic rule to govern the convent and was hostile, or aloof,
or both, to such an extent that Radegund eventually placed herself and her
women under the direct protection of the king.

As *carm.* 5.9 suggests, the relations between Fortunatus and this bishop
must have been, in the best of circumstances, strained, given Fortunatus'
intimate association with Holy Cross. Little wonder, then, when Fortunatus
attempted to visit Gregory, that Maroveus, who, as bishop, had a right to keep
Fortunatus from visiting other religious,[19] intercepted the poet and forced
him to return to Poitiers. At the same time, the inconvenience suffered by
Fortunatus becomes an occasion to celebrate his friendship with Gregory,
whose invitation, though it cannot be accepted for the moment, pales when
compared to the devotion that inspired its tendering and acceptance.

Holy Gregory, wrapped in Father's goodness, you invited
me to go to Tours, where the flock is pastured by your love,
where holy Martin, once bishop, teeming with goodness,
first held, then bequeathed, his sheep to you and

where the sheepfold now, in fields blooming with Christ,   5
is guided (rightly so) in shared custody.
But, just now, our honorable brother, with force
made me turn around, head back home, so that I couldn't rush

            to you:

I begged, pleaded, lobbed missives, endlessly,
my promise to return to him meant nothing.   10
A man pleasing with goodness, pastor in love with peace,
consider all this trivial (I pray) in the face of friendship's bonds.
Reverend, your own daughters say *hello,*
but, blessed father, I want to say *hello* in person—please.

5.10
[*PL,* col. 199 (= 5.13); *MGH,* 120;
Reydellet, vol. 2, 37; DB, 320–21]

Carm. 5.10 seems to speak to Fortunatus' role at the Convent of the Holy
Cross, where he perhaps facilitated contacts with the outside world, including,
if this poem is any indication, handling new recruits and, in this case, send-
ing them back if they or the sisters had a change of heart. Fortunatus uses an
epithet in v. 2, "sweet leader of Tours" (*dulce caput Turonis*), similar to that
used of Felix of Nantes at *carm.* 5.7.2, "sweet leader of the city" (*urbis dulce
caput*), thus linking Gregory and Felix in their roles as civic leaders.

Father, no one higher to home or hearth, piety's rich exemplar,
sweet leader of Tours, holy to the hilt,
endlessly tracking the heights, Gregory of the lenient heart,
you seek what seems best here: this is why your soul is noble.
High priest, the girl you commended to us on her way   5
now returns to you—take her in the fashion of a father.
May you be longer lived than the others, dear, as you return

            to me;

may your life be a harvest for me, for the rest.

5.11
[*PL,* cols. 199–200 (= 5.14); *MGH,* 120;
Reydellet, vol. 2, 37; DB, 320–21]

The poem imagines in close friendship a measure of protection. Verses 1–4
affirm the poet's devotion; the middle couplet (vv. 5–6) describes the situation
that occasioned the poem's writing, while its final lines (vv. 7–10) set devotion

to work in the parental figures of Martin and Gregory, styled as a "rich father";
and of Radegund and Agnes, both of whom are called "mothers"—all of
whom have, in their own way, assisted the poet to a safety he still cannot
quite fathom.

Holy Gregory, I need to embrace you, willingly, endlessly,
with my eyes I long to see you, to ask after you in slips of poems,
for to see you is sweet. But if we're often apart,
I hope, I pray, to send this poem to father:
leaving you (just now) I hurried home   5
through ice, skidded on roads of glass (I think that says it).
I crossed myself, Martin played protector
as I slid into the arms of mothers' safety.
Rich father, their double dignity venerates you
with *hellos*[20] but I pray thanks for my delivery.   10

5.12
[*PL,* col. 200 (= 5.15); *MGH,* 120;
Reydellet, vol. 2, 38; DB, 320–21]

Gregory is not named in *carm.* 5.12, whose reappearance in the collection
as *carm.* 9.8, written to Bishop Baudoald, reflects less on the sincerity of
Fortunatus' poetic motivations (it seems impossible that he would recycle
poems) than on the circumstances surrounding the gathering and publication
of the collection.

Highest of priests, richly provisioned in goodness,
towering in your honor, a beacon in my love,[21]
revered for duties sacredly done, piety's protégé,
you are held in my heart by friendship's pledge,[22]
abounding in learning, in the sacred laws of faith,   5
endless doer of good works that will shepherd you to God:
Father, I swear, I would give earth, stars, and sea—I pray it—
that you would wish to remember that I am yours when
                              sacredness is on your lips.

5.13
[*PL,* col. 200 (= 5.16); *MGH,* 121;
Reydellet, vol. 2, 38; DB, 320–21; George, *Poems,* 22]

Carm. 5.13 opens an intimate window on the affiliation of friendship and
gift-giving. The poet has received from Gregory cuttings from trees with

fruits still attached. As the fruits seem to be mature, we can assume it is late summer, so that the promise of further bounty symbolizes the enduring quality of Gregory's friendship that is continually full. At the same time, the fruit reminds Fortunatus of Gregory's connection to goodness, and goodness' ability to ease the way to paradise, where Gregory can pluck, so to speak, the richest bounty of all.

> Gregory, nobly doing piety's duties,[23] sacredly strong,[24]
> father on high,[25] you're gone, yet I see you in your gift:
> you've sent to me parents and their brood,
> slips with clinging fruits together with their branches.
> May God, insuperably strong, be filled with the bounty of
> your good;   5
> may you eagerly pluck the fruits that paradise holds.

5.14
[*PL,* cols. 200–201 (= 5.17); *MGH,* 121;
Reydellet, vol. 2, 39; DB, 322–23]

The initial focus of *carm.* 5.14 is the dead tree made famous by St. Martin, who, so the story goes, prayed before it, restored it to life, and thereby lent to it curative powers (vv. 1–6). As Fortunatus ponders this husk as a sign of Gregory's illustrious predecessor, a mother and father arrive, frenzied because their daughter, falsely accused of theft, has been sold into slavery as punishment (vv. 7–15). This allows the poet to claim impotency in the face of the parents' lament before stammering a couple of lines about Martin's presumed response to their plight. That response, in turn, sets up Fortunatus' plea to Gregory, in which the bishop's memory eventually braces the poet against his feelings of inadequacy, since Gregory is, after all, the new Martin, offering the hope that Martin held out to his flock long ago (vv. 16–20). For this reason, Fortunatus asks Gregory to intercede on behalf of the parents, examine the particulars of the case, and adjudicate it according to the evidence at hand.

Based on lineaments owed to Martin's career, Brennan and Roberts properly see in the poem's lines the creation of a model of Episcopal sanctity and duty that Gregory must uphold. Brennan rightly senses vestiges of *carm.* 5.13 in its successor poem. The branches and fruits that are parents and children in the earlier poem become in this poem the figure of one family. The daughter is the tree uprooted from her parents and, by analogy, just as Martin restored the tree, so Gregory must restore the girl. The heavy burden is to be like Martin in a new age.[26] Roberts notes the protreptic quality of the poem's conclusion, grounded in a topography that serves rhetorical ends:

Martin continues to aid the distressed through the tree, just as Gregory, his successor, must do in order to live up to the model Martin so amply supplies. There would seem to be literary modeling at work here, too, for Fortunatus follows in important details Horace, *Satires* 1.9.[27]

But as much as Fortunatus emphasizes Episcopal responsibility in the model supplied by Martin, it cannot be overlooked that *carm.* 5.14 is a narrative of miraculous activity and pious exemplarity used to express further Fortunatus' sense of friendship. For as much as the poet plays on the idea of the "uprooted" girl being returned to her parents by the paternal power of Gregory, so too does he assume a similar role. After all, in the same way that the girl is powerless in the face of unfair odds, so too is the poet an impotent figure, whose meager words cannot measure up to the strength required to smooth over the events the poem dramatizes (vv. 16–20). He is uprooted, out of his element, a victim of circumstance who must rely on Gregory's excellence as much as the girl must rely on Gregory's powers of judgment in order to come out of the situation unscathed.

The paternal imagery exploited in the poem, especially in the final couplets, is linked to shepherding for just this reason. Father Gregory can return this girl to her father and thereby add her to his own flock, in the same way that pastor Gregory can protect Fortunatus in his sheepfold. The poet, too, wants the same sort of protection Gregory the shepherd offers his flock, a plea that also reinforces the sense of subordination that the poet sometimes claims to feel when writing to Gregory. He dislikes, in any case, taking on the mantle of the shepherd precisely because it points up his powerlessness in the world. Rather, as Gregory's humble servant, Fortunatus simply wants to roam in his dear friend's flock because to do so is to feel the singularity of their friendship.

> Gregory, kind Father, as I beat a hasty path
> there were signs of your predecessor's piety:
> a tree dislodged, uprooted, lying flat (so they say),
> that heard Martin's prayer and exploded with leaves,
> now his faith props it up as it stands strewing cures,   5
> like a doctor healing bodies, its own body a husk.
> Here: the parents of a girl appeared,
> shouts filling salt-stained cheeks
> that rooted my feet, flooded my ears with words
> swimming in sobs: the girl is indentured.   10
> How did it come to this (I ask); then the father:
> the girl is to go under the yoke
> on the charge of thievery—but no evidence of theft;

he had wished to present witnesses
duly sworn by name—but he was too poor,
the judge never showed, the plaintiff pressed hard.   15
Holiness, what could a powerless poet do?
Then I said: "If holy Martin were here,
that shepherd wouldn't cotton to the loss of a sheep."
But still, eminence,[28] I gained strength in recollecting you,
in your goodness that recalls the hope Martin inspired.   20
Sweet father, examine the case, sort it out and, facts permitting,
make this girl your lamb; return her to her father.
Likewise, dear, I am a servant dutifully yoked to you;
rich shepherd, protect me in your holy asylum.

5.15

[*PL,* col. 201 (= 5.18); *MGH,* 122;
Reydellet, vol. 2, 40; DB, 322–23]

The title of *carm.* 5.15 indicates that this poem was written to Gregory "concerning the commendation of a foreigner" (*Item ad eundem de commendatione peregrini*) thought to be a messenger charged with delivering these lines to the bishop.[29] But, given the fact that he refers to himself in the third person in vv. 5–6, Fortunatus may well be this foreigner, who is also mentioned in v. 7. The adverb "likewise" (*item,* v. 7) coordinates separate circumstances, to be sure, but it seems out of character for Fortunatus to commend the happiness of a messenger as a means to praise Gregory, who, on this reading, has become shepherd and country to an unnamed, unknown figure. Instead, if my understanding of the poem is correct, its final two couplets refer to two aspects of Fortunatus' identity: vv. 5–6 attending to Fortunatus the poet, and vv. 7–8 describing Fortuantus the Italian emigrant; balancing these four lines are the poem's initial couplets that narrate Gregory's stature. The pangs of loneliness and alienation that Fortunatus goes on to expresses in *carm.* 7.21 (No. 29)[30] over the fact of his emigration are palliated here through the shepherding of Gregory's friendship, so great that it creates for Fortunatus a new home. The images cast in superlative terms in the couplets that describe Gregory further the emphasis on the incomparable ways in which Gregory rescued Fortunatus by becoming for him "shepherd" and "homeland" (*pastor, patria,* v. 8), while echoing Gregory's own praises of his guardian, Avitus (No. 7), who was, in Gregory's words, "at once a father and a fatherland."[31]

Good Gregory, whose merits gain a towering honor,
incomparable defender, esteemed bishop:

rank and genius lift you more worthily
in a piety productive and rich, enlarged by God.
Father, Fortunatus' poor poem wants your gentle love   5
to remember that he is your servant
and foreigner; eminence,[32] let him be glad to have found
a shepherd to come home to.

5.16
[*PL*, cols. 201–202 (= 5.19); *MGH*, 122;
Reydellet, vol. 2, 40; DB, 324–25]

The use of third person address connects this poem to *carm.* 5.15, while a
cluster of repeated epithets establishes the superlative powers necessary for
Gregory to do what Fortunatus describes as an Olympian task (*Olympus*, v.
5). The poet's use of ancient diction reminds readers of the space he inhabits:
worldly, secular, of a sufficient stature that befits the writing and reciting of
poetry, but not to be compared with the heights that Gregory surmounts.
The poet need not be expressing exclusively in v. 5 the idea of attaining
heaven, and Reydellet's translation, "Fortunatus asks that he be accorded the
assistance of Olympus," reflects its ambiguity.[33]

The flock cranes its neck to your honor,[34] priest of revered
                                                             strength,[35]
Gregory, your kindness glorifies the Fathers,[36] the reverent
                                                             love you,[37]
an ornament to priests, you have earned piety's trophy for
                                                             your goodness,
your rank soaring nobly to crown you by right:
your poet needs help of Olympian proportion,   5
intercede, make it happen, father, dear.

5.17
[*PL*, col. 202 (= 5.20); *MGH*, 122;
Reydellet, vol. 2, 40–41; DB, 324–25; George, *Poems*, 22–23]

Several of the poems to Gregory assume the guise of letters and/or were sent
with actual missives. This poem suggests the emotional quotient involved in
these exchanges. The safety that Gregory's letter reports becomes an occasion
for Fortunatus to demand a further, longer letter, whose receipt will, as the
poet says, "save" him (*recreet*, v. 6).

Your letter came running to me worthily,
tender father, sacredly close to God:
I devoured it with my eyes, rehearsed it in my heart,
cheered when I read that you were safe.
Gregory, papa, sign a longer letter,   5
let it save me as it says *hello*.

8.11

[*PL,* cols. 288–89 (= 8.16); *MGH,* 196;
Reydellet, vol. 2, 153–54; DB, 454–57]

In the *Life of St. Martin* Gregory of Tours speaks of "our priest Leo,"[38] who
seems to have been remembered also by Fortunatus in the third verse of this
poem, the occasion of which is the feast of St. Martin (November 11), to
which Gregory has invited Fortunatus. Explored already from a different
angle in *carm.* 5.14, the poet again plays on the connection between Martin
as a figure of miraculous cures and Gregory as a present-day healer. In this
case, the figure requiring ministrations is Fortunatus himself, prostrated with
fever. Gregory's words seem all that the poet needs in order to regain his
health, if slowly, and once the priest Leo reports them it is only a matter of
time before the fever breaks. Gregory is thus shown to be a healing presence,
even when absent.

Gregory, your words, nurturing, healing, from Tours,
came to me when I was sick abed, quarantined;
bright-faced Leo, the priest, fairly blurted them out:
I was to go to where holy Martin is fêted.
But I was pinched then with the pain of illness (I swear):   5
head hot with fever, all stiff below,
strenuously weak, vigorously lethargic,
my labored breath barely lifted my ribs,
like a vapor, desert-hot, it singed panting lips,
a burning blast blown from some secret place,   10
I was all heat, a sad pyre, a flaming furnace,
every fiber of my body wracked by fever, hidden, real,
until Christ poured help, streams of sweat,
even so, scorching flames stole the water's ice.
Yet I recovered my health—hello, kind father,[39]   15
be a remedy (I ask): a shepherd to your spindly lamb.

8.14
[*PL,* 290 (= 8.20); *MGH,* 198;
Reydellet, vol. 2, 156; DB, 458–59]

Fortunatus has learned that Gregory is well, and *carm.* 8.14 draws on epithets
previously used to offer brief thanks for this good news. In tone and intent
the poem is similar to *carm.* 5.17, especially in the emphasis it places on the
ability of words to elicit, and to harbor, strong feeling.

> Kind father, blessed, a beacon to the people,[40] Gregory,
> your towering[41] strength[42] rightly places you heads above priests;
> good news from you urges me to be grateful to God
> for your words now—holding them makes me glad.
> I am yours, Gregory, humbly, by prayer, by voice, *hello:*   5
> my heart's duty is to love you endlessly.

8.15
[*PL,* col. 291 (= 8.21); *MGH,* 198;
Reydellet, vol. 2, 157; DB, 458–59]

The placement of *carm.* 8.15 makes sense, given its reliance on imagery used
to good effect in the previous poem. Roberts notes the contrast of the moun-
tainous Auvergne, where Gregory was born, to the wide, flat countryside
of Tours and also the connection of geographical to personal exemplarity;
Gregory is taller than the mountains of his homeland and seems to fill the
broad plains surrounding Tours.[43] The bishop remains Fortunatus' defender
(*patrono,* v. 11), however, a word in Latin that blends the ideas of protection
and sponsorship.

> Father, no one higher to home or hearth,[44] a heavenly summit
>   open to all,[45]
> whose brave glory you are, Touraine cranes its neck to you:[46]
> luminous, arriving happily from the Auvergne,
> your words signal safety to the people, like a lighthouse,
> but higher, like the mountains that you've rushed across,   5
> and broad, like the plain where you sit, defending God's camps,
> lest enemies harm the sheepfold's faithful,
> singular, like a tower on the fields for the crowd.
> Gregory, dear, sweet head of the body politic:
> Martin's sacred seat makes you father.   10

I am humbly, fortunately, yours, Gregory, defender,
may your life spread before you longer still—be in the thick of
                                                    things for God.

8.16
[*PL*, col. 291 (= 8.22); *MGH*, 198;
Reydellet, vol. 2, 157–58; DB, 460–61]

Carm. 8.16 incorporates familiar diction but in the setting of poetic inspira-
tion that allows for more intimacy of expression. While the epithets situate
Gregory in his Episcopal milieu, only one of the poem's six lines is devoted
exclusively to his stature, the structurally important v. 3. Animating the
poem's energy otherwise are first-person expressions[47] that, while taking cog-
nizance of Gregory's standing, place him in the private world of Fortunatus'
friendship, where he can do the poet's bidding directly.

Holy, when inspiration whispers sweetly to me,
it prods from my pen a poem of longing.
Father, no one higher to home, hearth, world-revered,
you shine in God's attention, completely dear to me,
sacredly strong; Gregory,[48] humbly, I am yours: 5
pray to God on behalf of your servant, your own—that's what
                                                    I beg for.

8.17
[*PL*, col. 291 (= 8.23); *MGH*, 199;
Reydellet, vol. 2, 158; DB, 460–61]

Much as he does in *carm.* 5.16, Fortunatus uses ancient diction ("Thunderer,"
Tonans, v. 7) in this poem to position himself in a specific, worldly space that
betokens its own singularity—poets and poetry have their heights, too—but
that pales in comparison to the space cultivated by Gregory.[49]

Father, dear, if the messengers were to go on strike
I would wish to send poems on the southerly wind:
but my boy is here now, I send a poem
more affectionate than eloquent.
Rich in God, our glory, pious papa, sweet Gregory: 5
a couple of lines to say *hello.*
Don't forget: pray to the Thunderer on my behalf (please);
thus in honor, at his throne, may he make you his own.

8.18

[*PL,* cols. 291–92 (= 8.24); *MGH,* 199;
Reydellet, vol. 2, 158–59; DB, 460–61; George, *Poems,* 71]

Carm. 8.18 takes inspiration from the farm that Gregory gave to Fortunatus.
The conceit is that generosity diminishes language's ability to praise, so that
the flow of eloquence expected of a poet becomes a mere trickle. *Carm.* 8.19
and 8.20 add more detail to this general expression of gratitude.

> If my eloquence flowed like a cresting river
> or was driven by a whirling, watery storm,
> in rendering your high praises, Gregory,
> the flow would trickle to a drop.
> But so generous a father would make Virgil's Muse run dry: 5
> good Gregory, who has the power to sing your gifts?
> Holiness, serving your supremacy:
> I'm fortunate to have sent this drop.

8.19

[*PL,* col. 292 (= 8.25); *MGH,* 199;
Reydellet, vol. 2, 159; DB, 460–63; George, *Poems,* 72]

Carm. 8.19 memorializes a growing intimacy on the part of poet and bishop.[50]
Gregory has bestowed a magnificent gift, a small farm situated on the Vienne,
and has written a poem to celebrate it (no longer extant), honoring Fortunatus
further by means of a metrical gesture meant to delight the poet more for the
attempt than the result. Fortunatus acknowledges the gift and its beauty, but
says that he doesn't require it in order to be certain of Gregory's devotion. Like
the flock that Gregory shepherds, Fortunatus feels his friend's good presence
wherever the bishop might be. Each friend thus tries to match the other's
strong suit: the bishop gives a worldly gift while the poet takes comfort apart
from worldly goods in a space of spiritual repose.

> A letter, racing a generous path,
> was sweetened by your love into a poem
> that offered a present to me—a farm
> where the brash Vienne breaks the shore,
> where a sailor on his skiff, breaking the swell   5
> as the boatsman chants, sees fields under plow.
> Dear, brimming with piety's bounty, thank you
> for a poem whose decency is swollen by a gift
> I don't need. I am wherever you are, good shepherd:
> the flock is with you if the field is yours.   10

8.20

[*PL,* col. 292 (= 8.26); *MGH,* 200;
Reydellet, vol. 2, 160; DB, 462–63]

Inspired by the gift recollected in *carm.* 8.19, *carm.* 8.20 is connected to the previous poem through the adjective *munificus,* "generous," which appears there, as here, in the initial verse.[51] Fortunatus plays on a theme he has mined before, the excellence of Martin and Gregory's ease in modeling his illustrious predecessor. Here, however, befitting the event that has inspired the poem, Gregory is held up for comparison to what is arguably Martin's most famous feat, recounted in Sulpicius Severus' *Life of St. Martin,* in which the saint halved his cloak in the depths of winter and gave it to a beggar, after which Martin dreamed that the beggar had been Christ.

This act of charity becomes, in Fortunatus' hands, a means to organize the comparison with Gregory. Martin covers, but Gregory nourishes (v. 2); Martin leads, Gregory follows (v. 4); Martin halved his cloak, Gregory partitions his patrimony (v. 5); Martin is powerful in covering, Gregory in nurturing (v. 6); Martin relieved the beggar Christ, Gregory eases the burdens of the beggar poet, Fortunatus (vv. 7–8). In subsequent verses, Fortunatus expresses his willingness to return the land that Gregory has bestowed while offering thanks in a brief poem that can hardly do justice to such a gift. Be that as it may, the poet asks Gregory to intercede on his behalf with God, increasing his debt to him, but situating him in a fresh way as a friend in need.[52]

> Gregory, I see generous Martin in all you do:
> he cloaked a beggar, you nourish me with food,
> his peaceful teachings are the wise lesson you follow,
> where he sits the general, you hold a soldier's might,
> he divided his cloak, you parceled your farm,   5
> his power to protect like your graceful warmth:
> once he raised up a beggar, dear, as you've lifted me now,
> each becomes rich through the pauper he deserved,
> your beggar makes you rich—as did Martin's.
> The fields you gave will always be yours,
> restored to you for the asking (rightly so).   10
> Until then, a thousand thanks, sweetest leader,
> in a poem from a sheep, claiming his shepherd
> and bishop, to whom I give less than I owe.
> Please: soften God for this fortunate man.[53]

8.21
[*PL,* cols. 292–94 (= 8.27); *MGH,* 200;
Reydellet, vol. 2, 161; DB, 462–63; George, *Poems,* 72]

The first word of *carm.* 8.21, "excellent" (*egregio,* v. 1), puns on *Gregorius,* Gregory's name in Latin, playfully introducing a piece that celebrates Gregory's poetry writing and generosity (vv. 1–8) before specifically offering thanks for sandals recently sent, a gift described in the imagery that recalls those famously worn by Mercury (*talaria,* v. 11). In exchange for these, Fortunatus prays that Gregory will obtain from God the white cloak (*stola candida,* v. 13) mentioned at Rev. 6.11, 7.9, and 7.13.[54] That divine gift, which reminds readers of the cloak that Martin halved, links this poem to the previous piece, a connection affirmed also in the conclusion offered here, where the affiliation of Fortunatus to the beggar of *carm.* 8.20 is ratified. Fortunatus is "small" (*pusillum,* v. 9) and among the least of Gregory's flock (*minimis,* v. 14), and for his attention to the poet the greatest rewards await Gregory.

> Gregory, your poem, fitted in an excellent place,
> turned on a Sophoclean lathe, then gilded,
> richly watered my desert mouth,
> made me sound your eloquence when I spoke.
> Sweetly decent, dear, kind and fluent,   5
> a father to home, hearth, Gregory, holy and wise:
> your gifts are equal to your good works, your heart to
>   your habits,
> obliged to be loved in all you do.
> Small, lucky, I bow long and low to your eminence,
> I am yours, on bended knee, in prayer (rightly so)   10
> for the sandals you gave,
> whose soles are as snowy as the feet they now cover,
> or the white robe I pray God gives in return.
> Who does for the least gains the most.

16. To Aredius (d. 591)

The son of Iocundus and Pelagia, Aredius hailed from Limoges and was an official at the court of King Theudebert I (d. 548) before renouncing the secular world to become a priest at the urging of Nicetius, bishop of Trier (d. c. 565). Having previously taken over the management of the estates of his father and brother, who predeceased him, Aredius was able to draw on these holdings to further his spiritual concerns, establishing a monastery in Limoges that he served as abbot.[1] Gregory of Tours reports details attending to Aredius' famous saintliness: he was able to make water flow from the parched ground; to alleviate through his touch the pain of a man suffering from toothache; and, even after he died, to exorcise a woman possessed by the devil.[2]

Carm. 5.19 focuses on the unique spirituality of monastic life that would have made Aredius less visible to, though not less remembered by, Fortunatus. The monastic fervor shared by Agnes and Radegund and witnessed by Fortunatus in his daily exchanges with both women is of a kind with Aredius' integrity, for which reason the poet offers the women's greetings at the poem's conclusion. There, Aredius' "daughters" share "a holy love" with their "father," a token of monastic devotion that cultivates a special kind of honor. Yet if Fortunatus is excluded from the wholeness of this monastic "family," he can still demand that Aredius send some word by return messenger, demonstrating, in this instance at least, that friendship could be animated as much by the exchange of words as through actual contact.

5.19
[*PL*, cols. 202–204 (= 5.22); *MGH*, 123;
Reydellet, vol. 2, 41–42; DB, 324–27]

Kind father, my only option is to say *hello*
in a poem—for you're so rarely seen
that your honor, grown so large in my mind,
rushes these words sent in my place,
to ask, blessed father, that you remember me   5
as you savor Christ's sweetness, when you pray.
Aredius, shepherd, the gifts of God will come to me (I believe)
if you remember, kind one, that I am yours.
Dear, say *hello* on my behalf to your blessed mother,
send back with the messenger your mighty voice.   10
Rich father, Agnes and Radegund send their *hellos,*
with a holy love, daughters to none but you.

6.7
[*PL*, cols. 226–27 (= 6.9); *MGH*, 147;
Reydellet, vol. 2, 77; DB, 368–69; George, *Poems*, 52]

The title of *carm.* 6.7 in the contents to Book 6 is "On the villa at Cantoblandum" (*De cantoblando villa*); in the manuscripts it is, "To the villa at

Cantoblandum, a poem recited on the topic of fruit" (*Ad Cantumblandum villam de pomis dictum*). Aredius, the poem's addressee, links this piece with *carm.* 5.19. Less certain is the location of the villa mentioned in the contents and title. Aredius lived in Limoges, in the Auvergne, making that city or region likely locations, but there is no known place called *Cantum Blandum* in sixth-century Gaul, the closest recorded name being Cantobennum, or Chantoin, a town northeast of Clermont.[3] Brower thought that *Cantumblandum* referred to the pleasant sound of the birds, a view rejected by Nisard, who thinks instead that the name means something like "a quiet little place," seeing in *cantus* the misspelled *canthus,* from the Greek *kanthós,* "corner."[4] Since nothing can be known about it with certainty, I adopt Reydellet's literal translation, *Chantebland,* here. If its title is to be believed, this poem was recited, much as *carm.* 3.13a–d and *carm.* 5.4 were, at or after a dinner. While Aredius is mentioned in v. 2, the poem focuses on the perfect fruits Fortunatus discovers at *Cantumblandum,* devoured so quickly by him that he does not have a chance to savor their smells, a fact that sets up the poem's whimsical conclusion.

> I beat a happy path[5] into *Chantebland*
> and rejoiced to discover father Aredius.
> Since my hunger was prodding an insatiable belly,
> gilded fruits caught my eye
> on every side with so many shades   5
> you would think that I merited an artist's feast;
> barely in my hand, scarcely in my throat, chowed down,
> booty, quickly won, sent into the cavern of my belly,
> beguiled by their taste before my nose got wind:
> my hunger was conqueror; my nose lost face.   10

17. To Ultrogotha (fl. 567)

In 542 Childebert I brought back from Spain what was purported to be the tunic of St. Vincent, along with other ecclesiastical treasures, including a cross and chalices. To house them, he had built in Paris (but outside the city walls) a church in honor of St. Vincent, completed in 558 and dedicated by Bishop Germanus.[1] Prior to his death in the same year, Childebert also established adjacent to the church a garden, whose bounties are the topic of *carm.* 6.6, translated here.[2] Addressed to Ultrogotha, the widowed queen of Childebert, the poem is in one sense a consolation written against the backdrop of the king's death, in recollection of the good that he did in building the church of St. Vincent and in planting a garden next to it.[3] But Ultrogotha, as the poem's addressee, received these verses presumably a decade after the king's death, when she was much less in need of consolation over a loss now remote in time. Moreover, Fortunatus concludes his poem by hoping that Ultrogotha will find for herself and her daughters the sort of spiritual peace that Childebert has found and that God promises. He thus makes the poem function in the present of its composition, though it gains much of its thematic energy from the past embodied by Childebert's example. Not least, the tension between present hopes and past ideals is symbolized in God's paradise that Childebert now enjoys and that the earthly idyll planted by him betokens.

The poem cultivates in its opening lines the traditional *locus amoenus* (vv. 1–8), affirming the importance of the temporal world even as the symbols used to evoke it resonate also as markers for the promise of eternity.[4] Moreover, to the extent that it casts its gaze onto the bounties of nature, the poem is also one of friendship, whose words offer spiritual comfort, to be sure, but within the context of a life lived amid worldly allurements. After all, the perfections of Childebert's garden and the king's abilities in nurturing them render it dearer to Ultrogotha for having been fostered by him (v. 10). And if the perfections of the king's handiwork have inspired Fortunatus to see in them an emblem of heaven's idyll, still the feature that connects the poem's competing images is Ultrogotha's love—for the garden planted by her husband and for the worlds, both here and to come, that her husband inhabits in this poem.

6.6
[*PL*, col. 226 (= 6.8); *MGH*, 146–47;
Reydellet, vol. 2, 76; DB, 366–69; George, *Poems*, 51–52]

> Here crimson spring births the land to green,
> strewing roses that Paradise wafts;
> here a soft shoot defending summer's shadows
> yields leafy enclaves bursting with grapes;
> a full palette of flowers paints a garden   5
> whose trees dress in white before donning red,
> while fruits burden branches that summer feigns
> to endanger with breezes pleasant and soft.
> With love King Childebert sowed this garden,
> and dearer are those things that his hand gave;   10
> the sprigs coaxed by his gardening taste sweet,
> the honey he watered them with won't tell.
> The fresh grace of new fruits doubly honors this king,
> an aroma more seductive to the nose; a taste sweet to the lips.
> He alone protected us with an incomparable power,   15

even as he touched fruits that give fragrant pleasure.
May this tree bear blessed fruit forever
to remind us of a pious king
who once made his way from here to the church
that better keeps him now because he was good;   20
these holy precincts that he sometimes trod
are forever held now by this beloved man.
Be happy to have such things until the end of time, Ultrogotha:
rejoice with your daughters; a mother last though not least.

18. To Dynamius (d. c. 595)

Fortunatus met Dynamius in 566 at the wedding of Sigibert and Brunhilde. At the time, the poet had just completed one leg of his journey through Gaul, and Dynamius had made the long trek from Provence to Metz, undoubtedly with a cohort of Provençal nobility. That Dynamius' presence would be expected at Sigibert's marriage goes to his noble birth and the status he held in Provence among the ruling elite. This helps to explain the position he eventually assumed there, *rector provinciae*,[1] which effectively combined the political role of the Frankish count (*comes*) with the military powers of general (*dux*).[2] Fortunatus tells us that Dynamius was of noble birth, trained in the law, involved in meting out justice (*carm.* 6.10.33, 37) and a practicing poet[3] (*carm.* 6.10.57–62) who also tried his hand at hagiography, writing the *Life of Maximus,* abbot of Lérins and bishop of Riez.[4] His presumed date of death, c. 595, allows a birth of c. 545 to be conjectured.[5]

If Gregory of Tours' *Histories* are any indication, Dynamius led a full political life that sometimes placed him at odds with kings, bishops, and nobles. In one instance, Gregory reports that Dynamius appointed a man to the Episcopal seat in Uzès without consulting Childebert II; while in another, he refused to allow the military leader Gundulf access to Marseilles, with whose bishop, Theodore, Dynamius was also often at odds.[6] Dynamius also had dealings with Pope Gregory I, from whom he received a small crucifix and relics, and who placed him in charge of the papal patrimony in Gaul.[7] He was married first to Aurelia, then to Eucheria, a poet, from whose output a single poem is extant.[8] Gregory mentions a son, killed while on an embassy to the Byzantine emperor.[9]

Fortunatus wrote two poems to Dynamius, the longer and earlier of which, *carm.* 6.10, records many of the details of his life. The poem's seventy-two verses are heavy with classical imagery and allusion, a weightiness meant to honor Dynamius even if there is rebuke for a tardy gift of poems received through a third party. The shorter *carm.* 6.9, translated here, is more personal. The initial line of the poem links Dynamius in readers' minds to Bertrand (No. 5), Anfion (No. 8), John (No. 12), and Gregory of Tours (No. 15), all of whom are called "revered" (*venerande*).[10] Moreover, the Latin of the second line (*quamvis absentem quem mea cura videt*) is identical to the second verse of *carm.* 3.16, written to Hilary (No. 4), thus bringing this friend into the poem's thematic orbit.

It makes sense that diction would affiliate this cluster of friends, for Fortunatus shares with them an intimacy that *carm.* 6.9 helps to authenticate. The bold declaration in v. 1 that he is waiting for Dynamius allows Fortunatus to develop the theme that his friend is absent in all but love (vv. 2–6). Verse 7 then raises the question of Dynamius' commitment to a friendship observed more in the breach (v. 13), while subsequent verses use images of dreaming and wakefulness to declare the poet's devotion. The idea that Dynamius is, so to speak, the light of Fortunatus' life, whose absence makes all things gloomy, allows Fortunatus to hope at the poem's conclusion that he will have some word from his good friend, though he would welcome a visit most of all.

6.9
[*PL*, col. 229 (= 6.11); *MGH*, 149–50;
Reydellet, vol. 2, 80; DB, 372–73; George, *Poems*, 55–56]

I'm waiting, my love, revered Dynamius,
you're absent, though beheld in my poem.
I ask the wafting breeze where you might be,
gone from my eyes, unfled from my soul.
Metz is pleasant enough for me, Marseilles and environs
          satisfy you, 5
vanished, except in the junctures of my heart,
where some part of you (apart from you) forgotten until now
remained: do you not recall in your heart that part of you
          left behind?
If sleep has sneaked in, may your dreams tell on me,
where sundered souls are sometimes joined; 10
if you're awake, I confess, there's no forgiving
a friend sprawled in unjustified silence.
Twice now the zodiac's ambit of months has
wearied the horses' breathless race across the sun
that you snatched from me when you left; 15
lacking you I'm blind to the unfolding day.

Send a poem whose words flow like your voice,
so that to read it is to speak with you.
But, friend, still, I dearly want you here,
come at last—make me see again.   20

19. To Gogo (d. 581)

When Fortunatus met him in Metz in 566 at the wedding of Sigibert and
Brunhilde, Gogo[1] was already a close advisor to this king and may well have
been mayor of the palace, a post that would have placed him in the highest
reaches of Merovingian power. Sigibert relied on him to escort Brunhilde to
Gaul from her native Spain,[2] and Gogo remained a powerful figure even after
Sigibert's death, in 575, when he was named tutor (*nutricius*) to Sigibert's son,
Childebert II, and became an advisor in the regency established in the young
king's name under Brunhilde.[3]

Gogo and Fortunatus were linked in part by shared literary interests, for
Gogo was also a man of letters who more than once tried his hand at poetry.
Though none of his verse survives, Gogo's learning can be gleaned in the
four letters that survive from his hand,[4] in which his acquaintance with the
classical tradition is clear. Although Fredegar claims that Sigibert executed
Gogo under the malevolent influence of Brunhilde, this story is not reported
in Gregory of Tours, who notes without elaboration that Gogo died in 581.[5]

Fortunatus addresses four poems to Gogo, gathered at the start of the
collection's seventh book. The first of these, *carm.* 7.1, celebrates Gogo's role
in the political landscape, likening him to Orpheus, attracting through his
sweetness the weary and the weak, while praising Sigibert's wisdom in enno-
bling him. In a different vein, by commending his connection to the ancient
past, *carm.* 7.4 seeks rhetorically to know what Gogo might be doing,[6] while
the poet recommends himself to his friend as the one best able to concretize
Gogo's political aspirations in a language that suits them.

The first of the poems translated here, *carm.* 7.2, praises Gogo's abilities as
a littérateur and host, likening his talents to those of Cicero and Apicius. The
poet asks forgiveness for having eaten too much at Gogo's most recent banquet
and begs off any further attempt to write what amounts to a thank-you piece
perhaps delivered *in situ,* if not sent later. The poem is organized by the six
attributes that set Gogo's patronage and friendship apart: "nectar, wine, food,
clothing, learning, opportunity" (*Nectar vina cibus vestis doctrina facultas,* v.
1). Reydellet translates *vestis* as "hangings," and thinks the word refers to wall,
floor, or bed coverings used at the feast of which Fortunatus speaks.[7] Nisard

translates *vestis* as "clothes," [8] an understanding proven by the asyndeton of the line that demonstrates that *vestis,* along with the other words of v. 1 stand in apposition with Gogo, named in v. 2. Since *vestis,* like the other words of v. 1, refers to a gift the patron has given to Fortunatus, Nisard's reading is preferable. *Facultas,* the last word of v. 1, is used of Gregory of Tours at *carm.* 5.12.1, where it denotes the bishop's rich capacity for goodness. The sense is different here, since the word represents something Gogo gives to the poet, and more easily refers, therefore, to the "opportunity" to compose and to share poetry, of which this poem is a good example.

Unless Fortunatus wrote a poem that he meant to be entirely obscure, *carm.* 7.3 takes shape around a dispute involving separation. The poem's initial line may help in this understanding, especially if it sounds in its emphatic final word, "complaining," (*querellas*) the issue of severance so famously narrated by Horace at *Odes* 2.17, where this same word appears also in that poem's first line (*cur me querelis exanimas tuis*). Gogo apparently has complained about being apart from his good friend, but he is the one who has left Metz for Reims. Yet friendship, so Fortunatus assures him, has already overcome this spat, as the poem itself, especially in its final couplet, proves.

7.2
[*PL,* col. 234; *MGH,* 154–55; Reydellet, vol. 2, 87–88; DB, 380–81]

Nectar, wine; food, clothing; learning, opportunity:
Gogo, you satisfy me with such largesse,
you're like Cicero declaiming, or Apicius, from home:
talking my ear off as we eat.
But forgive me now, beef-bloated, half-asleep: 5
for if I mix flesh where beef now rests
my gut objects—chicken and goose will fly the coop,
the brawl between feathers and horns won't be fair.
Just now my eyes swim in their lids,
I'm only this side of sleep—as my happy poem proves.   10

7.3
[*PL,* col. 234; *MGH,* 155; Reydellet, vol. 2, 88; DB, 382–83]

Your letter reached me just now with such complaining:
but I claim immunity from blame;
your trip to Reims did more harm—

you sinned, yet I am accused of crime.
I'm still sweet on you, though, even after this scrap: 5
in the heart friendship's bounty lives—and endures.

20. To Lupus (d. post 587)

When Fortunatus met him, Lupus was already a powerful courtier of King
Sigibert, whom he served in military and diplomatic capacities, helping to
defeat the Saxons and Danes and participating in an embassy to Marseilles.[1]
Lupus wielded much of his power while duke of Champagne, a rank granted
him by the king, but more easily bestowed, perhaps, owing to his descent
from the Gallo-Roman aristocracy.[2] Gregory of Tours records the details of
an eventful and sometimes turbulent career. Like Gogo and Dynamius, Lupus
was well-educated, so much so that his encounter with the impressively learned
slave Andarchius led him to insinuate the slave into Sigibert's services.[3] After
Sigibert's death, when he was threatened by his rivals, Ursio and Berthefried,
Lupus came under the protection of Brunhilde, who at the time was serving
as regent for her minor son, Childebert II. Lupus eventually was forced to seek
the protection of Childebert's uncle, Guntram, while awaiting the defeat of his
enemies at the hands of his son-in-law. Instigated by Igidius, bishop of Reims,
Lupus eventually had a falling out with Childebert, too, who stripped him for
a short while of his dukedom. Gregory mentions a son, Romulf, who was made
bishop of Reims after Igidius was forced into exile.[4] No precise birth or death
dates are known, though Lupus was at Childebert's court as late as 587.

   The first of three poems written to Lupus, *carm.* 7.7 celebrates his appoint-
ment to the dukedom of Champagne. The poem was likely composed around
the time that poet and courtier first met, in 566, at the marriage of Sigibert
and Brunhilde. The poem not only is a formal panegyric on Lupus but also
contains praises for Sigibert, who has had the excellent sense to choose such a
noble to serve him.[5] *Carm.* 7.8 is more personal but exploits classical imagery
as a means to honor Lupus and frame more specifically the friendship shared
with the poet. The poem begins vividly with a description of a heat-stricken
traveler in need of assistance, whose woes the poet then uses to betoken his
own sorry state when he arrived in Gaul and was befriended by Lupus. The
anxiety Fortunatus recollects in his own circumstances turns out also to be
concern for Lupus' recent troubles, but the fact that Lupus is safe puts the
poem in the service of its recipient.

   The theme of rescue is revisited in *carm.* 7.9, translated here. Although
the two are separated, they form a pair that is joined by the strong bond that

friendship provides (vv. 1–4), but the current status of the affiliation mat-
ters less than the impetus that gave rise to it when Fortunatus first traveled
from Italy to Gaul (vv. 5–8). Alone in a strange land, having journeyed even
by today's standards a long distance and at considerable physical risk and
discomfort, Fortunatus suffered from a strong case of homesickness, made
all the worse for the dearth of letters received from family and friends (vv.
9–12). Then Lupus appeared and acted the parts of those loved ones absent to
Fortunatus, allowing him, as he says, to "live again" (vv. 10 and 14).

Shared diction also helps to specify the ways in which Lupus figures in
Fortunatus' estimation, for the first three words of *carm.* 7.9, "your nose to
piety's grindstone" (*officiis intente piis*) are taken verbatim from *carm.* 3.21.1,
written to Avitus, bishop of Clermont-Ferrand (No. 7), and form an epithet
used with some variation of Gregory of Tours (No. 15) at *carm.* 5.8a.1, 5.12.3,
and 5.13.1. Finally, the phrasing of v. 14 (*nectarei fontis me recreavit aquis*) is
virtually identical to *carm.* 7.21.8 (only the number of the verb is changed), a
poem addressed to Sigimund and Alagisilus (No. 29).

Lupus thus takes on the qualities associated with these figures, not least,
the support supplied by the grandfatherly Avitus and the protection and nur-
turance that Gregory consistently offered. These strong feelings are confirmed
in the final verse of the poem, where ambiguity serves the purpose of honor-
ing Lupus further:[6] the phrasing of the line—"who teaches what is done for
the least is done for him" (*quae minimis fiunt qui docet esse suum*)—features
the pronoun "he" (*qui*) and the adjective "his own" (*suum;* translated here as
"him"), which can refer to God or to Lupus, both of whom are mentioned in
the previous line.

7.9

[*PL,* cols. 245–46; *MGH,* 163–64;
Reydellet, vol. 2, 100–101; DB, 396–97]

Your nose to piety's grindstone, mindful of a lover,
poised willingly to tender your affection:
laid low by a friend gone too long, at such a price:
for love, secreted away, demands its pledges.
Do my deserts merit what is given me,   5
that of a sudden my hope was your kind care?
A wanderer from Italy nine years ago (I think)
to this place, whose shores are lapped by the sea;
so many seasons run their course; still no word
from a parent's sundered hand made me live again;   10
yet your tender love took their place and more:

did what brother, sister, nephew, neighbors, used to do;
the page you sent, pleasant, signed in kindness,
like nectar, eloquent, brought me back to life.
And more than nestled in your sweet letter,   15
what you've sent by messenger has now arrived.
Who can sing your bounty (I ask) mindful of such largesse,
for words can't reveal sweet affection?
But let the high king give all on high to you, who teaches
what is done for the least is done for him.   20

21. To Magnulf (fl. 575)

The placement of this poem subsequent to those addressed to Lupus makes
sense, since Magnulf, its recipient, is Lupus' brother. Nothing else is known
of him. Luchi, following Brower, rehearses the reasons why he cannot be the
more famous bishop of Toulouse mentioned by Gregory of Tours.[1] Fortunatus
tells us in *carm.* 7.10, translated here, that Magnulf is involved in governing
the Rhineland (*Rhenus,* v. 3; *regis,* v. 10) and Reydellet presumes he admin-
istered justice in the name of King Sigibert.[2] A pun on Magnulf's name in
v. 4—"**Magnulf**, decent, you please here with a **magnif**icent honor" (*hic,*
***Magnulfe**, decens, **magnus** honore places*)—lends a sense of intimacy to the
piece, while shared diction affiliates Magnulf with other friends. Sigimund
(No. 28) is mentioned in v. 5, for example, a figure Fortunatus addresses in
carm. 7.20 and whose presence here also brings to mind Lupus, since in *carm.*
7.9 Lupus is linked to Sigimund and Alagisilus (No. 29) in phrasing repeated
in *carm.* 7.21, a poem addressed to both men. Further, the adjective "power-
ful" (*pollens,* v. 9, here translated as "rock") is also used of Agricola (No. 6) at
carm. 3.19.2 ("mighty sower of fields," *cultor agri pollens*) and Rucco (No. 10)
at *carm.* 3.26.1, while Gregory of Tours (No. 15) is a "kind friend" (*alme*) at
5.8a.1, 5.14.1, 5.16.2, and 5.19.8, a vocative applied to Magnulf in v. 17.

7.10
[*PL,* cols. 246–47; *MGH,* 164;
Reydellet, vol. 2, 101–102; DB, 396–99]

How quickly word flies on crackling-sail wings,
fills the countryside, stirs its own storm.
Though the Rhine is yours and the Loire is mine (there it is,
                                        near to hand),

Magnulf, decent, you please here with a magnificent honor:
that's why the trumpet of Sigimund's herald has hastened   5
to send your goodness up and down the land.
Yet a letter, a few words jotted down, is scarcely adequate to
                                                    the task,
unable to sing what's needful, unwilling to keep silent.[3]
Rightly called a rock among equals, pitching a stemwinder
that evokes ancient habits in a fresh urge to rule   10
like a farmer obliged to plow a fair field with seeds
that mete out justice—people reap what they covet.
No one lacks his own, is laid low by others,
you ensure that there's no time for sin;
you solicit God for the people's salvation,   15
your solitary work becomes their repose, as your heart,
kind friend, runs steadily to the chorus that calls you
father and judge, just and good.
Forgive these few lines—the messenger paces—
I've said all I can about Lupus' brother.   20
God make your goodness a tonic to him:
I cherish him, I cherish you, with a heart-held love.

22. To Jovinus (fl. 570)

Having traveled from Provence to Metz for the wedding of Sigibert and
Brunhilde, Jovinus was, when Fortunatus met him, a powerful noble who
seems quickly to have struck up a friendship with the poet. Of Jovinus' long
career[1] Gregory of Tours recalls only the controversies, not least that Jovinus
was stripped of his office by Sigibert in 573 and replaced by Albinus, who
immediately became his enemy. Thereupon, in the presence of the king,
Jovinus accused Albinus of mistreating the archdeacon Vigilius.[2] He was
named to, but never assumed, the Episcopal seat in Uzès and in 581 was
arrested by Guntram, along with the bishop of Marseilles, Theodore, as both
were traveling to Childebert II to complain of Theodore's mistreatment at the
hands of Dynamius.[3] No secure dates for Jovinus' birth or death are known.
At *carm.* 7.12.121 Fortunatus mentions in passing Jovinus' father, Aspasius,
and Leo, his brother.

Of the two poems written to Jovinus, the much longer is *carm.* 7.12, which
begins as a traditional consolation that bemoans the passage of time and the
transitory nature of the world, themes developed through the use of ancient

diction and imagery combined with tags drawn from scripture. The poem is composed of two equal halves, each introduced by the phrase "time is fallen" (*tempora lapsa,* vv. 1, 63) but the second half is a private plea for attention and affection.[4]

George remarks that the initial lines of *carm.* 7.11, translated here, and of *carm.* 6.9, written to Dynamius (No. 18), put to the side the introductory niceties that normally mark Fortunatus' epistolary poems and instead tout the intimacy of the correspondents through bold declarations of the issues at hand. In the earlier poem, Fortunatus says to Dynamius that he is waiting for him (*expecto te;* 6.9.1), while here the poet notes that he has directed many letters to Jovinus, to no avail (*prosaico quotiens direxi scripta relatu;* v. 1).[5] He therefore seeks some word from him while making much of the desolations that result when friends are parted and silent.

7.11

[*PL,* col. 247; *MGH,* 165;
Reydellet, vol. 2, 102–103; DB, 398–99]

Jovinus, I've steered countless letters to you,
without answers from your loving cup,
to slake a soul you once watered more richly
with an eloquence now vanished from the Muses' springs.
If I had only loved you less, already   5
your neck would be pressed by my hand.
Now the more I covet, the less I have: seeing that I love
a great thing and desire it more, I'm left to grieve unrequited
                                                                                        prayers.
From your soul's safe keep you have decanted my heart
that longs to see your glinting eyes.   10
Friend, dear, in a poem at least I can say *hello:*
but send a letter with the power to return my gaze.

23. To Felix (fl. 570)

The contents to Book 7 simply says "To Felix" (*Ad Felicem*), but the title in most manuscripts reads "To Felix, his father-in-law" (*Ad Felicem socerum eius*), in some cases making explicit that "his" refers to Jovinus, the figure to whom the previous two poems are addressed. Luchi prints this title but believes it to be corrupt, preferring the reading in Σ, the lone manuscript that reports the title "To Felix, a companion" (*Ad Felicem socium*).[1] Leo and Reydellet also print this title[2] and agree with Luchi that the Felix in question is the bishop of Treviso, Fortunatus' boyhood friend.[3]

If *carm.* 7.13 is any indication, Felix was also an accomplished poet. Reydellet thinks its four verses are fragmentary and perhaps served in some capacity to introduce a more elaborate poem. Given the long friendship and current separation of Felix and Fortunatus, he reasons that a poem of four lines would otherwise be inappropriate.[4] As a poem of friendship, however, its length makes good sense, for the conceit is that Fortunatus cannot measure up to the poetic heights of his friend, so that he is scarcely strong enough to knock on the metaphorical door that represents the poetic abode built for Felix by the Muses. Only their long acquaintance enables the attempt, but the poet is braced by the love that friendship confirms. He can therefore beat on the door and trust his kind friend to respond. The poet thus refuses to write the long poem that one would normally expect in such circumstances and instead says only what friendship permits him to say. The brevity of the poem proves the truth of Fortunatus' claims: he is no match for Felix, but he is certain of his love.

7.13
[*PL,* cols. 250–51; *MGH,* 169;
Reydellet, vol. 2, 109; DB, 404–405]

You sit in a tower steeped in Pierian pride
that humbles a hand scarcely able to knock at its door.
But once, long ago, we were *compaesano,* kind friend:
I beat the door confident in your love.

24. To Berulf (fl. 575)

Berulf was a count (*comes*) when *carm.* 7.15 was written, as the contents to Book 7 and the poem's title indicate ("About Count Berulf," *De Berulfo comite*), and he became a general (*dux*) in 580.[1] As this poem is part of a collection published in 576, it makes sense that he would have held such a rank before becoming *dux.* The poem can thus be dated to the years between Fortunatus' arrival in Gaul in 566 and the publication, a decade later, of Books 1–7. The fact that Berulf was both count and general also points up the prominent place he held in Merovingian governance, since both terms designate formal positions awarded by the king, the one juridical, the other military.

Gregory recollects in some detail Berulf's stormy career. His responsibilities as *dux* under Kings Chilperic and Childebert II included the protection of Tours, Poitiers, Angers, and Nantes, and in each of these cities he was involved in due course in military activity. In Tours in 580 he imposed military rule when it was feared King Guntram was about to attack and, along with Count Eunomius, began surveillance on Bishop Gregory, who had recently been accused by Leudast of treason. Berulf also was involved in defending Tours from a threatened invasion from Bourges, the territory of which he also invaded in 583. In 585 he was replaced as *dux* by Ennodius and eventually arrested for having stolen property from Sigibert. For this crime Childebert ordered him decapitated but eventually relented under pressure from the bishops.[2]

All of this occurred long after *carm.* 7.15 was written, where, instead of a controverted political and military leader, we discover a host who fails to meet his guest's expectations. Fortunatus likely had enjoyed the count's hospitality on a previous occasion, for he describes Berulf as possessed of "charms" (*delicias*, v. 1). This time, however, Berulf's table is barren: no breakfast or lunch, only prayer (vv. 3–6), leading to what the poet calls a double famine (v. 2). But if Fortunatus remains hungry, he avers nonetheless that recording this experience in verse has sated him even more than the hoped-for meals could have.

The ambiguity of the poem's final couplet ramifies this sentiment, for in it Fortunatus seems to enjoin God to answer the prayers that Berulf offered in place of lunch ("whose prayers I hope God grants," *det tibi vota Deus,* v. 7). But when the poet goes on to say, "he made me full in writing these words" (*per quem . . . / haec quoque dum scribo, plus satiatus agor,* vv. 7–8), the figure to whom "he" refers can just as easily be Berulf as God. It may be the case that God has granted Fortunatus' wish in response to the fast that Berulf has imposed, in which case the ending is less sarcastic. Fortunatus' prayer to be made full has been answered. But the poem can also be read as a comeuppance, wherein the act of publicizing Berulf's lack of hospitality has sated the poet. A social slight thus leads in due course to a different sort of feast that satisfies just as well as the meals that were not forthcoming.

7.15
[*PL,* cols. 252–53; *MGH,* 170;
Reydellet, vol. 2, 111; DB, 408–409]

Berulf, gladly eyeing your charms,
damn if I wasn't doubly famished.
I thought breakfast would offer all I could eat,

but at noon the kind table was mute;
your meals taught me to how to fast: 5
your lunch was more a litany,
whose prayers I hope God grants to you. I smile:
he made me full in writing these words.

25. To Gunduarius (fl. c. 575)

Apart from what Fortunatus tells us of his friend in *carm.* 7.17, nothing is
known of Gunduarius.[1] It is clear that he was manager of the patrimony of a
Frankish queen (vv. 13–14), perhaps Brunhilde, and v. 18 indicates that he
was married. The poet protests his inability to express friendship's longings
(vv. 1–6), but the poem turns on the idea that Gunduarius possesses an elo-
quence that, if it does not do complete justice to their friendship, still goes a
long way toward satisfying Fortunatus, who is thirsty for some word from him
(vv. 7–10). Gunduarius' skills in managing the properties of the queen who
is also smitten by his charms (vv. 11–16) lead the poet, finally, to wish for his
friend's long life and longer repose, with his wife, in eternity (vv. 17–18).

7.17
[*PL,* cols. 254–55; *MGH,* 172;
Reydellet, vol. 2, 114–15; DB, 412–13]

If a lover could trot out his affection in words,
my notebook would be heavy with poems for you;
but eloquence mumbles close-confined in the heart,
whose din gives some verses that will have to do.
If you could glimpse desire through a poet's songs,   5
I would have sent a mountain, not this mound, of words;
yet your heart is wholly open to me, decanted in a sweetness
that makes your glad soul flash with a candor that guile
                                        disdains.
Words, like nectar, spill from your lips, like water
from an eternal spring that my soul gladly guzzles, and
                                        my heart.   10
Provident, guileless, watchful, respected, restrained,
your mind always spiced by soul as you manage
the noble estates of the excellent queen
who trusted you, swathed in a faith she sensed;

no one was dearer to that kind queen   15
than those who were like you in their goodness.
Gunduarius, live on to please as time grows long;
linger with your wife in an endless light.

26. To Flavus (fl. c. 580)

Fortunatus wrote two poems to Flavus: *carm.* 7.18, addressed to him alone and
translated here, and *carm.* 7.19, written to Evodius and Flavus and translated
in No. 27. The identity of Flavus is not known with certainty. Gregory of
Tours records the name Flav*i*us in identifying King Guntram's *referendarius,*
a figure responsible for correspondence in the royal household, who became
in 580 Bishop of Chalon.[1] Despite the difference in spelling, Meyer thinks
that this *referendarius* may well be the figure to whom Fortunatus addresses
both poems.[2] Roberts takes Meyer's tentative identification with a grain of
salt, since the failure to mention Flavius' royal master, Guntram, is, apart
from being in bad taste, out of poetic character, seeing that Fortunatus refers
to the royal patrons of the two *referendarii,* Boso (No. 30) and Faramod
(No. 34), to whom he also writes.[3] This observation lends weight to the idea
that Flavius, the *referendarius,* and Flavus, the friend of Fortunatus, are two
different people.

Whoever Flavus is, Koebner thinks he hailed from southern Gaul, for
he senses *Romanitas* in the possibility that Flavus could write to Fortunatus
in Latin (v. 15).[4] But, as Reydellet notes, this makes too much of the line in
question.[5] Latin is simply one option in a catalogue of languages that the poet
offers as impetus to get some word from Flavus' pen.

7.18
[*PL,* cols. 255–56; *MGH,* 172–73;
Reydellet, vol. 2, 115–16; DB, 412–15]

My letter makes its way again to Flavus dear;
I'm duty-bound to write something.
Whether a song in prose or verse, love more agreeably
whispers, coaxing me to mind my debts.
A traveler, wishing to make his way, never leaves without a
                                                    few lines   5
for you; no one slinks away from me, passing stealthily by
a friendship stoked in a demand that words be sent

often to you—and absent a messenger I use the breeze
that makes clouds slink through my reverie
with nothing to disturb it from your hand.   10
Has the turnaround on imports made paper scarce?
Can't love extort what time forbids
to make you write? Strip off a slice of beech
that becomes your sweetness when I read its bark;
it doesn't have to be in Latin; please,   15
use Hebrew to send some word,
or write in Persian since you know it well,
if you wish; or sing to me in Greek;
write barbaric runes on tablets made of ash:
it's as good as paper;   20
or send a page written on papyrus, easily hewn:
to read it again will be a lover's reward.

27. To Evodius and Flavus (both fl. c. 580)

The lack of identifying information for Flavus makes Evodius equally obscure,
though *carm.* 7.19 describes him as Flavus' identical twin. Surely if this Evodius
were the illustrious figure mentioned by Gregory of Tours, Fortunatus would
note his distinguished ancestry, both in this poem and in the previous one,
carm. 7.18, since Flavus would share the same pedigree. Instead, the lack of
honorific language suggests that Evodius and Flavus, while presumably well-
educated, were met by Fortunatus in contexts apart from royal or ecclesiastical
service of a sort that would require specific acknowledgment.

7.19
[*PL,* col. 256; *MGH,* 173;
Reydellet, vol. 2, 116–17; DB, 414–15]

How convenient for the father who raised them up,
whose single heart loves them both:
Evodius, Flavus—the twins—utterly
protected by my heart's single love.
It seems to see one is to see the other,   5
a brother's image gives a brother's likeness;
to know the first face is to know the second,
it seems, as if reflected in a mirror.

And so paired words greet a pair
among whom I will be a second third: 10
three hearts are one, held in sweet embrace
fastened by this poem—that's what I want.

28. To Sigimund (fl. c. 575)

The title of *carm.* 7.20, "Fortunatus says hello to dearest Sigimund, who is owed praises in every way" (*carissimo et omni gratia praedicando Sigimundo Fortunatus salutem*), suggests the closeness of poet and friend but nothing more. Sigimund is otherwise unknown. At *carm.* 7.10.5, in a poem written to Magnulf (No. 21), Fortunatus styles Sigimund the "herald of Sigibert" (*praeconis Sigimundi*). This would suggest a military role seemingly confirmed in the present poem, since vv. 9–10 mention fighting in Italy and the possibility of the Franks being at war.

The military situation imagined in these lines most likely pertains to the conflicts of the Franks and the Lombards, whom Guntram and his general, Mummolus, repelled in 573–574. Sigimund, though associated with the Austrasian court of Sigibert, could well have participated in this important defense of the Frankish homeland, especially if he is, as is supposed, a Saxon mercenary.[1] The Austrasian kingdom and the Byzantine empire allied to meet a fresh Lombard threat in 584, but, unless this poem is out of place in the collection, this cannot be the event the poet has in mind, since Books 1–7 of Fortunatus' collection were published in 576.[2]

Whatever the circumstances in which Fortunatus met Sigimund, *carm.* 7.20 reveals a powerful friendship currently impoverished through separation. While the sentiments of the poem accord well with those found in earlier pieces lamenting time spent apart from his friends, the concluding line offers a unique estimation of Fortunatus' devotion. For in his deployment of the words "halved" (*dimidiata;* here translated as "undiminished") and "part" (*pars*), Fortunatus recalls *Odes* 1.3.8, where Horace calls Virgil "the half of my soul" (*animae dimidium meae*); and *Odes* 2.17.5, where Maecenas is styled "a part of my soul" (*meae . . . partem animae*). In v. 12, therefore, Sigimund is both "part" (*pars*) and "halved" (*dimidiata*), thus making him a friend in the mold of both Virgil and Maecenas, arguably the two most important of Horace's many friends. While there is no evidence that Sigimund was, like Virgil, a poet, or even, like Maeceans, a patron, the diction culled from these two Horatian moments strengthens his image as a forceful presence in Fortunatus' life, even, and perhaps especially, in his absence.

Also written to Sigimund, App. 4 contains diction that recalls other important friendships, not least, "importuning" (*requiro*) at v. 4, which links Sigimund to Dynamius (No. 18) (*carm.* 6.9.3); Flavus (No. 26) (*carm.* 7.18.7); and Lupus (No. 20) (*carm.* 7.9.4).[3] The connection to Dynamius is strengthened, too, on the repetition, in v. 5, of "wind" (*flabra*), since that word is used in the same context at *carm.* 6.9.3.

7.20
[*PL,* col. 257; *MGH,* 174;
Reydellet, vol. 2, 117–18; DB, 414–15]

Pierced by your love, attending you with a vast desire,
I'm a busybody, dear, to know you're well.
If some hurried traveler pushes through from the north
I delay him with inquiries:
private citizen, public man, it matters not,   5
I importune all here before any proceed.
Dear, are you well? The latest trips?—
a checklist ordered by an all-curious love.
If harsh soldiers bear arms against Italy,
if the Franks are warring, I want to know: tell me.   10
Say what you're up to, please; but still, as I live,
may you outlive me: *the* undiminished part of my soul.

App. 4
[*MGH,* 279;
Reydellet, vol. 3, 146; DB, 638–39]

Saving souls is tiring to Christians eager
to see blameless salvation about.
But before all else I hang on your brilliance—
importuning any who come or go, tireless to get some news
of you;
my anxious eyes search the gusty wind   5
for a breath of your goodness—but when, from whom?
Let my sweet letter chiefly say this to you:
mine is the sorrow or fear that is yours,
you know that we run as kindred souls,
give me faith, send word that you are safe.   10

29. To Sigimund and Alagisilus (both fl. c. 575)

Given his description in *carm.* 7.21, translated here, Alagisilus appears to be a military leader, much like Sigimund, affiliated with the court of Sigibert. He is presumed also to be a Saxon.[1] Nothing else can be said of him. The references in vv. 9 and 10 to "parents" and "brothers" (*parentes, fratrum*), rather than indicating biological kinship, suggest that Sigimund and Alagisilus were figurative siblings to Fortunatus,[2] and styling them as such helps the poet to honor two men who were, as v. 9 suggests, familial surrogates upon his arrival in Gaul. Much the same role was taken up by Lupus (No. 20) in *carm.* 7.9, who also welcomed Fortunatus to Gaul and became in his own person a substitute family for the poet. Not coincidentally, v. 8, "by your words like nectar, eloquence that made me live again" (*nectarei fontis me recreastis aquis*) nearly replicates phrasing found at *carm.* 7.9.14: "like nectar, eloquent, brought me back to life" (*nectarei fontis me recreavit aquis*), where Lupus' letter, much like the presence of Sigimund and Alagisilus now, helps to revivify a poet thirsting for attention.

7.21
[*PL*, col. 257; *MGH*, 174;
Reydellet, vol. 2, 118; DB, 416–17]

A sweet letter opens on the names of my friends:
Alagisilus, who is upstanding, and brilliant Sigimund,
whose happy bounty tumbled on blustery winds
when the breeze announced men dear to me.
I swear (on your heads) my desires are furthered   5
like a field blooming gladly in the rain,
slaked in a summer wild with heat
by your words like nectar, eloquence that made me live again
after Italy, when you sent parents like brothers, whose arrival
(thank you, Rhine) meant I would wander no more.   10
Concord, new, joyful, rises up in the wake of war,
since these men have come, whom my love desires:
they have doubled the glory of this festive day for me.
May your glory swell in the gift of the king.

30. To Boso (fl. c. 567)

The contents to Book 7 and the title of *carm.* 7.22 identify Boso as a *referendarius,* a figure responsible for correspondence in the royal household, most likely of King Sigibert. Fortunatus presumably met Boso when he arrived in Metz in 566,[1] at the same time that he was introduced to a cohort of other men destined to become friends, not least Dynamius (No. 18), Gogo (No. 19), and Jovinus (No. 22). Nothing else is known of him.

7.22
[*PL,* col. 258; *MGH,* 175;
Reydellet, vol. 2, 119; DB, 416–17]

May God protect the king's gilded towers,
may heavenly arms rule his endeavors,
may divine power preserve lord and legions,
may the country's surety abide in his charge;
let God, supreme, pious, high, extend his hand   5
to our peaceful king as he once did to Peter,
let the king's ageless grace light on you,
that you may reap joys fixed in his garden.
Please, tell your messenger to make good time,
to lift my heart already burdened by delay;   10
he speeds to you my desire, certain, fixed,
that comes more sweetly if it comes in good time.
One thing else: words in the guise of an eager prayer
ask that you remember me to my lord.
Let the excellence in all you do abide, thrill you always,
but remember me, too, sweet friend—*goodbye.*

31. To Galactorius (d. post 592)

Galactorius was count of Bordeaux in the time of King Guntram, but nothing is known of him beyond what Fortunatus reports in *carm.* 7.25 and 10.19, translated here.[1] The poems are out of order in the collection: *carm.* 7.25 was written no earlier than 585, since Gundegiselus, identified as bishop (*antistes*) in v. 7, was ordained in that year.[2] *Carm.* 10.19, on the other hand, celebrates the promotion of Galactorius to the rank of count, a preferment already earned in *carm.* 7.25, where he is called by that title (*comes*) at v. 22.

As Books 1–7 were published in 576, *carm.* 7.25 must have been added later to the seventh book.

Fortunatus reports in *carm.* 7.25 that he once hoped to sail on the Garonne to Bordeaux but is now met by a fear of the river's turbulence, a sentiment cast in diction that recalls Virgil's *Aeneid*.[3] Held back from an in-person visit, the poet can nonetheless send this poem, with its epic bows and more intimate hopes. At the same time, the poem's length has caused him to run out of ink, a whimsical observation that ramifies warm friendship in the poem's final verse. *Carm.* 10.19 offers a series of puns that help Fortunatus articulate the grounds of friendship more intimately. Galactorius' worthiness, for example, is equaled by the worthy roles he has played (*dignus/digna*, v. 4); the judgment of the king is such that he makes Galactorius a judge (*iudicio/iudex*, v. 5); the power of the king powers Galactorius' rise (*potens/possis*, v. 7); Martin was blessed before he gave his blessings (*sacer/sacra*, v. 20); Galactorius rules under the king, for which reason he will be able more securely to enter the heavenly kingdom (*rege/regna*, v. 25); Fortunatus hopes that a high faith and a faithful love grow bright for his friend (*fides/fida*, v. 28). The received text of the poem is marred by a missing pentameter at v. 26, indicated here with asterisks.

7.25
[*PL,* col. 260–62 (= 7.31); *MGH,* 177;
Reydellet, vol. 2, 122–23; DB, 420–21]

I had hoped (quite often) to become a sailor,
my oar chopping head-on waves in a skiff,
on gusty gales piggybacking the Garonne,
making for Bordeaux untrammeled.
The north wind would consent to fill my sails,   5
skip me over the watery breeze, set me in the lap
of pious Gundegisilus, the bishop, who offers sacred things,
altarlike, eyes glinting, a towering presence to the people;
and bring me to you, Galactorius, friend, famously filled
with goodness, dear, never far from my care,   10
for whom Guntram, the excellent king reserves
further honors (rightly so), generous to a fault so far.
I wished this once—then fear as high as the Himalayas arose,
water like a mountain, raging, soapy, a cloud speeding head
                                                    over head
discourteously dashed your invitation to the rocks,   15
love's call prohibited by my fear.
What remains is to send this letter to you,

scurrying to return your love in kind.
Sweet friend, I say to the utmost now—*hello,*
hoping God gives you many days.   20
Stand close to Him with your minions, family, friends,
be a count, knowing that a dukedom must come.
Rich one, in your prayers remember me to the lofty bishop,
and reach to heaven—your due for being so good.
What remains to be said is that I've said too much: 25
I send poems now; but, please, give me some ink.[4]

10.19
[*PL,* cols. 345–46 (= 10.23); *MGH,* 251–52;
Reydellet, vol. 3, 99–100; DB, 544–45]

Finally, friend, what's owed is yours,
a *de facto* count, now *de jure.*
Long were you a lover and protector of Bordeaux,
a worthy, juggling two worthy roles;
the king judged you capable, made you judge,   5
(your reputation preceded his diktat);
his power owes it, to empower your rise,
he stands tall for you, bestowing the arms of a duke
that allow you wisely to protect borders, gain cities
for the one richly ennobling you,   10
make the Spanish tremble, make the Basques grow
white with fear and quit their mountain wars.
God, holy, unique, author of things, sees to it—
as a grandee says—high and low are braced by the Lord:
Justinian, a lowly recruit, rose in the ranks   15
to be emperor—not the first to do it.[5]
In church Christ allows such stories to flow:
the glory of a bishop in rooting out evil,
like Martin in his exceptional goodness,
blessed before he gave his blessings;   20
like God, all-powerful to create the world,
ponder the greatness made by his might.
I pray: be happier now ruling in your citadel
but hope, reasonably, wisely, for greater things,
flourishing under the king, seeking eternity's kingdom;   25

* * * * * * * * * * * * * *

brandish justice and piety, make them comrades-in-arms,
let one at your side, and one in front, guard you.
May your high faith and faithful love grow bright;
but, Count, be a full love to your fortunate friend.   30

32. To Chilperic I (d. 584) and Fredegund (d. 596/7)

King of Neustria from 561 until 584, Chilperic I was the grandson of Clovis and one of four surviving sons of Lothar I, whose third wife, Aregund, was Chilperic's mother.[1] He was briefly married to Gelesuintha, a Visigothic princess and sister of Brunhilde, Sigibert's queen, but she was murdered in 568, not long after her arrival from Spain, perhaps by, or on the order of, the king or of Fredegund, who was at the same time also married to Chilperic. Fortunatus composed *carm.* 6.5, in 370 lines, on Gelesuintha's sad history.[2] Chilperic's first wife was Audovera, with whom he had four children, all of whom predeceased him.

Gregory of Tours calls Chilperic the "Nero and Herod of our time,"[3] and reports in detail depredations leveled against family and country. His tendency to overreach is perhaps apparent as early as 561, when, upon the death of Lothar I, he seized Lothar's treasury at Berny-Rivière and entered Paris to take the throne once held by Childebert I. His three half-brothers, Charibert I, Guntram, and Sigibert I, expelled him from Paris and gave to him Lothar's kingdom instead, with its capital at Soissons, while dividing up the rest of Frankish Gaul among themselves. Chilperic warred on Sigibert and took for himself Charibert's kingdom when that half-brother died in 567, territory that was later retaken by the combined forces of Guntram and Sigibert. A series of subsequent incursions into Sigibert's kingdom, occasionally with Guntram's aid, ended poorly and likely would have led to Chilperic's execution had Sigibert not been assassinated in 575, perhaps on orders from Fredegund. Until his own assassination in 584, Chilperic attempted to consolidate his position, especially after Sigibert's death, but met continued resistance from Guntram and Sigibert's successor, Childebert II.[4]

It can scarcely be said that Fredegund acquitted herself with any less brutality in her role as Chilperic's queen. She may have been responsible for the assassination of Sigibert, and Gregory reports that she was involved in the murders of several of her stepchildren, not to mention more than a few Frankish nobles. Gregory also notes that she pondered, but was not successful in carrying out, plots to kill Sigibert's successor, Childebert II, as well as Sigibert's widow, Brunhilde. Her son by Chilperic came to the throne eventually as Lothar II (d. 629). She outlived her husband by a dozen years, dying in 596.

The first five poems of Book 9 are addressed to Chilperic and/or Fredegund, or memorialize their two young sons, Chlodobert and Dagobert, who died in an outbreak of dysentery in 580. *Carm.* 9.1, a panegyric to Chilperic in 148 lines composed just before the outbreak, was occasioned by a synod of bishops convened at the king's request at Berny-Rivière.[5] Gregory of Tours had been accused by Leudast, count of Tours, of spreading the rumor that Queen Fredegund had committed adultery with Bertrand, bishop of Bordeaux (No. 5). The synod was meant to clear the air, and Fortunatus' poem presumably had something to offer in this regard. While comporting to the order of topics traditional to classical panegyric, Fortunatus takes this poetic opportunity to offer a formula for rapprochement among the king and bishops, acknowledging the authority of the king to investigate the charges leveled against Gregory, but noting, too, that bishops are loyal to kings who are just and fair.[6] Gregory was in any case cleared of wrongdoing.

Carm. 9.2 is addressed to Chilperic and Fredegund in consolation over the death of their sons. Its 140 lines do not comport to the normal tripartite division of classical prose consolations—*laudatio, lamentatio, consolatio*—since the poem lacks a *laudatio* and has only a brief *lamentatio*. The thrust of the poem is thus to offer literal consolation in a time of grief, rather than to praise the two dead princes or to lament the cruel fate that took them from their parents.[7] *Carm.* 9.4 and 9.5 are epitaphs written to the memory of the two princes. *Carm.* 9.4, to Chlodobert, the elder son, may have been inscribed on or near his tomb, in the Church of St. Crispin and St. Crispinian.[8] *Carm.* 9.5 to Dagobert, is an acrostic spelling the prince's name, a visual cue that may indicate the poem was inscribed on the prince's tomb in the church of St. Denis.[9]

Carm. 9.3, translated here, is datable to spring 581, the first Easter after the princes' deaths.[10] Koebner thought the poem was composed during a journey made by Gregory and Fortuantus to Chilperic's villa at Nogent-sur-Marne, a few months after the council of Berny-Rivière.[11] But, as Reydellet suggests, Gregory does not mention Fortunatus as a companion on this visit, which was, in any case, not a casual call but a royal summons in which Fortunatus would have had little reason to be included.[12]

George suggests that this poem, when read as a companion piece to *carm.* 9.2, represents on the part of Fortunatus a careful strategy of drawing the royal couple out of their grief.[13] Where *carm.* 9.2, written presumably much closer to the time of the princes' deaths, uses poetry to assuage a present hurt, *carm.* 9.3 acknowledges grief but places it in a wider context, affiliating the lives that the king and queen must live against the backdrop of eternal life represented in the coming of spring and the Christian celebration about to unfold in it (vv. 1–10). The poet thus tugs Chilperic and Fredegund back into the world, and the poem, far from merely reflecting on grief's purgations, encourages the royal couple to be open to the energy of the season (vv. 11–18). Not the least of the ways in which the poet accomplishes this is through the ancient pedigree of his language, reminding readers also of Chilperic's literary pretensions.[14]

9.3
[*PL*, col. 303; *MGH*, 209–10;
Reydellet, vol. 3, 21–22; DB, 480–81; George, *Poems*, 87]

After tempests and lowering clouds
that hold the land in an icy vise,
after white-out days, wintry woes,
whose howling winds vex stubbly fields:
spring shambles forth to the world again,   5
whispering taunts to the warming day,
reviving fields that again waft perfume,
every grove strutting green treetop leaves,
branches hunchbacked with savory fruits,
soil tickled by its green-growing hair, just back.   10
Majesties, after your mountain of griefs,
I pray: be better of spirit—rejoice,
look: Easter is come, Christ pacifies a world
that roars fresh prayers all around.
Let joys befriend you more in your kingly towers,   15
bid the servants prepare a blessed feast,
let God account you well again in the world:
tower over the nation for a long while still.

33. To Droctoveus (d. c. 580)

Droctoveus was born in Autun and studied with Germanus, bishop of Paris, as Fortunatus notes (v. 3) in *carm.* 9.11, translated here. Droctoveus devoted his considerable energies to living as a monk and eventually as abbot, a position he assumed first in Autun, at the monastery of St. Symphian, and then at the monastery of St. Vincent and the Holy Cross (now St.-Germain-des-Pres), built for Germanus by Childebert I.[1] *Carm.* 9.11 praises Droctoveus' connection to the eminent Germanus (vv. 1–4) but also notices the ways in which he imitates his great teacher (vv. 5–6), not least in continuing God's work in this life while always desiring to leave it for the next. The word "adored" (*venerande*) in the first verse of the poem links Droctoveus to a cohort of friends who are identically styled, including Anfion, Anthimius, Bertrand of Bordeaux, Dynamius, and Gregory.[2]

9.11
[*PL*, col. 310; *MGH*, 217;
Reydellet, vol. 3, 33; DB, 494–95]

Adored man, holy in your goodness, cultivated by honor,
Droctoveus, I love you like a father,
who, of all the disciples of blessed Germanus,
is exemplary in superintending souls;
his holy footsteps you now retrace, despising   5
the world, wishing to make the journey to God.
Go gladly on your heavenly way, while lingering in the world
yet longer; and, please, pray to God for lowly me.

34. To Faramod (fl. c. 575)

The title of *carm.* 9.12 and the contents to Book 9 call Faramod a *referendarius,* a figure responsible for correspondence in the royal household, and Koebner places him in such a role at Chilperic's court.[1] Meyer believed him to be the brother of Ragnemod, bishop of Paris, who failed, so Gregory of Tours relates, in his effort to succeed Ragnemod upon that bishop's death in 591.[2] If these figures are one and the same, Faramod seems not yet to be a cleric at the time *carm.* 9.12 was composed, for this is something Fortunatus would not fail to mention. That Faramod may well be the brother of the bishop of Paris is strengthened by the fact that *carm.* 9.10, written to Ragnemod, stands but one poem removed from this piece.

Carm. 9.12 reveals an intimacy controlled now by separation that seems not to have lessened the poet's attachment. As he often does in such poems, Fortunatus describes the emotional terms upon which friendship is founded (vv. 1–2), bemoans the separation that the poem in some measure lessens (vv. 3–4), and asks that his greetings be sent to others in anticipation of a response that will requite his love (vv. 5–8). Reydellet notes that the phrase, "to courtiers, to kings" in v. 5 (*domnis . . . regibus*) refers to Chilperic and

Fredegund (No. 32), but I prefer to see it as formulaic, given that it reappears at *carm.* 9.13.8 (No. 35).

Falling as it does in a cluster of poems written to friends living in, or associated with, Paris, that is, Ragnemod, bishop of Paris (No. 10, *carm.* 9.10), Droctoveus, abbot of St. Vincent and the Holy Cross (No. 33, *carm.* 9.11), and Chrodinus, a duke associated with Chilperic (No. 36, *carm.* 9.16), *carm.* 9.12 links Faramod more securely to Ragnemod and Chilperic. Reydellet conjectures that the thanks the poet offers in v. 6 is for a gift that Chilperic and Fredegund may have given to the convent of Holy Cross. Fortunatus thus imposes on Faramod's good offices to relay the convent's appreciation to the royal couple.[3] In this the king and queen would be repeating an act of largesse also performed by Ragnemod, and reported by Fortunatus in *carm.* 9.10. I understand the lines in less specific terms, following more closely Nisard's sense that they express a general thanks to the powerful people the poet and Faramod know in common.[4] To view it otherwise requires one to explain the failure of the poet to mention the gifts involved and the recipients in question, something he explicitly does in *carm.* 9.10.

9.12
[*PL,* col. 310; *MGH,* 217;
Reydellet, vol. 3, 34; DB, 494–95]

My sweet friend, the name of a lover I can't forget,
prompt in the goodness that duty demands, Faramod:
if I've been absent, let this poem say *hello,*
let it wash you in a loyalty purchased less in person;
commend me (I pray) gladly to courtiers, to kings,   5
say the world is obliged for the might of their devotion;
let your letter track me down with a vehement affection;
kindly one: when this returns to you give as good as you get.

35. To Lupus and Waldo (fl. c. 575)

The recipients of this brief poem are difficult to locate historically. The touchstone provided by Gregory of Tours, who mentions a deacon named Waldo,[1] perhaps helps to control the title of the poem and what is reported in the contents of Book 9: the title calls both men "deacons" (*diaconos*), but only Waldo is so designated in the contents. If, as Nisard believed,[2] Gregory's Waldo is the figure addressed by Fortunatus in *carm.* 9.13, translated here, then he was baptized under the name Bertrand, in Bordeaux, by Bishop Bertrand (No. 5), who also designated this younger Bertrand his heir and Episcopal successor. But Gregory also mentions an archdeacon of Paris named Bertrand, who in 586 became bishop of Le Mans.[3] Ewig believes that they are one and the same person—the nephew, as it turns out, of Bishop Bertrand of Bordeaux, a fact that perhaps explains the bishop's actions toward his baptismal name-sake. Reydellet conjectures from this tentative identification that Waldo was a deacon in Paris at the time Fortunatus wrote *carm.* 9.13.[4]

This would comport to the principle that organizes the cluster of poems at this point in Book 9, many of which have Parisian recipients. Droctoveus (No. 33), mentioned in v. 9, who has incontrovertible connections with Paris, strengthens the idea that Waldo is in or near this city at the time the poet wrote to him, which leads Reydellet to presume that the bishop mentioned in v. 7 is Ragnemod, not, as Nisard believed, Bertrand of Bordeaux.[5] Gregory of Tours offers some evidence regarding the identity of Lupus, too, for in the *Glory of the Martyrs* he mentions a deacon so named who hailed from Bordeaux.[6] That would perhaps explain the connection to Waldo, in which case Lupus would have traveled with his friend, for whatever reasons, to Paris.

How the two came to know Fortunatus is unclear. Whatever the circumstances, the men are held in different regard by the poet, for while Waldo is, expectedly (if he is who he seems to be) a figure of holiness (v. 3), Lupus is charming (v. 2). This might explain the discrepancy between the listing in the contents, which calls only Waldo a deacon, and the title, which styles both men as deacons. Several other figures mentioned in the poem, which otherwise laments friendship's absence, help to situate more securely Fortunatus' connection to Lupus and Waldo, not least Droctoveus and Ragnemod, both of whom are recipients of their own verses. Caesarius and Constantine, mentioned in vv. 11–12, are unknown, while Mummolus, mentioned in v. 11, is a functionary at the court of Chilperic. Reydellet identifies him with the figure called by Gregory of Tours a "prefect," who, so Gregory relates, died from a stroke brought on by torture suffered at the hands of Chilperic and Fredegund.[7] The fact that Mummolus, according to Gregory, was from Bordeaux, is unlikely to be coincidence.

9.13

[*PL,* cols. 310–11; *MGH,* 217–18;
Reydellet, vol. 3, 34–35; DB, 496–97]

A ceaseless piety, a parent's heart, demand that
you be cherished: Lupus, they're the source of your charm,
Waldo, they make you holy; ministers equal in goodness

and grace, always fixed, a side-by-side love in my heart.
From afar I try to pay the greeting I owe,   5
if I can't see you I can seek you with this trifle.
Commend me to the lofty bishop (I pray),
take my best wishes to courtiers and kings,
tell sweet Droctoveus, tell citizens and clergy,
what I would do if I were there.   10
My best to excellent Mummolus and Caesarius,
don't let me slip from my Constantine's mind.

36. To Chrodinus (d. 582)

Gregory of Tours reports that Chrodinus was at least seventy years old when
he died in 582; this secures a birth year of no later than 512.[1] Fredegar notes
that Chrodinus refused Sigibert's offer of the mayoralty of the palace, because
he feared he could not be impartial. Gogo (No. 19) was named in his place.[2]
Gregory of Tours calls Chrodinus a duke (*dux*), as does Fortunatus in *carm.*
9.16, translated here (*inclite dux,* v. 1).[3] Both Fredegar and Fortunatus make
much of his illustrious pedigree, and Gregory speaks in detail of his interest
in the poor and in the assistance he often gave to other clerics and churches.[4]
Whether or not, as Di Brazzano senses, the poem was composed in a convivial
context,[5] it is less an affirmation of deep friendship than a poetic reflection on
Chrodinus' beneficience, whose effects are widely cast and deeply felt.

9.16
[*PL,* cols. 312–14; *MGH,* 219–20;
Reydellet, vol. 3, 37–38; DB, 498–99]

Glorious Duke, your goodness is spoken worldwide,
your glowing reputation bubbles over, Chrodinus:
I can't miss tossing your praises to heaven,
I can't appear to be the only one inured to your greatness.
Italy, Germany, applaud alike,   5
endlessly your praise is on everyone's lips.
An ancient lineage made you more nobly born,
your promise a tonic to country, to king.
Some call you a guardian or foster father
and wrangle over your piety,   10
yet your bounty is available to every comer:

enriching others, you enrich yourself.
If there's someone to prop up, you seek him out,
you want to be among the crowd, to make it your own.
Goodness for all, never sharp, impartial,   15
refusing spoils, comrade of justice,
soft-spoken, peaceful, pleasing, discreet,
you are given every reward, that you may bear every glory.
Committed to the Franks, adored by the Romans:
endlessly happy to linger on the lips of the world.   20

37. To Armentaria (fl. c. 575)

The mother of Gregory of Tours, Armentaria was the granddaughter of
Gregory, bishop of Langres, and the wife of Florentius, whom she married
c. 534. She came from and married into illustrious families. Her life is reported
in a few details at various points in her son's *Histories:* she was in the Auvergne
in 543; she later lived in Burgundy; she was cured of a longstanding ailment
during a visit to Tours immediately following Gregory's consecration as bishop
in 573.[1] Fortunatus ennobles Armentaria in *carm.* 10.15 by affiliating her with
the mother dramatized at 2 Macc. 7, who, along with her seven sons, was mar-
tyred at the hands of Antiochus IV Epiphanes. The poem seems more directly
to compliment Gregory, who is the source of pride and reward for Armentaria
(vv. 7–10), but the role played by the Maccabean mother informs Fortunatus'
words, too, in the ways she was a model to her martyred sons in forming their
faith and in insisting that they live and die by it. In v. 1, I render the adjective
Machabaea literally "Maccabean woman," as a name, "Maccabea."

10.15
[*PL,* cols. 342–43 (= 10.19); *MGH,* 248–49;
Reydellet, vol. 3, 94; DB, 538–41]

Maccabea for her goodness was doubly blessed, for herself
and for the world, but motherhood made her blood run bluest:
she sent seven victors from her nest to heaven,
her womb gorged with marytrs' grace.
Armentaria, you smile at Gregory's power (you should),   5
you are no less a mother than Maccabea:
she had the greater number of sons, but you have the greatest
son in one, who does on his own what seven once did,

who brings you fame, surrounds you with rewards;
Gregory is victor, crown, and glory to you.   10
With reverence I sign myself lowly Fortunatus;
for my part, please: I plead the heavenly might of your prayers.

38. To Sigoald (fl. c. 575)

In *carm.* 10.16, translated here, Fortunatus remembers that King Sigibert sent
Sigoald to accompany him as the poet made his way from Italy to Metz in
566;[1] and Gregory of Tours reports that Sigoald was sent by Sigibert's succes-
sor, Childebert II, as an emissary to King Guntram.[2] Fortunatus adds that,
at the time *carm.* 10.16 was composed, Sigoald was a count (v. 12) and his
hope that his friend might become a duke perhaps reflects Sigoald's aspira-
tions, if not political reality. George dates the poem to 592, the year in which
Guntram died, when Childebert came into the inheritance agreed to by the
Treaty of Andelot. This is likely the sense in which Childebert is imagined
as "rising" (*crescens,* v. 11) in the poem,[3] but ambiguity complicates the final
couplet, where the reference to "lord" can apply to Childebert or to Sigoald.

Two other poems are written to, or are about, Sigoald: *carm.* 10.17, a praise
piece on Sigoald's concern for feeding the poor in his capacity as count; and
carm. 10.18, translated here, written to an unnamed *defensor* on a meal pre-
pared to Sigibert's liking. The title of the poem and the contents to Book 10
call this meal a "lunch" (*De prandio defensoris*). A *defensor* normally oversaw
the protection of church property,[4] but this poem suggests that in this instance
he was responsible also for the laying out of a meal according to the tastes of
Sigoald, a connection that prompts Fortunatus to write and perhaps to recite
lines that honor him. Di Brazzano, following Meyer, considers it likely that
the poem was composed during an actual meal.[5] The ambiguity of several
of its verses may speak, however, to something other than extemporaneous
composition: in v. 3, "lord" (*domini*) can refer to Sigoald or to Christ; while
in vv. 7–8, "king" (*regis*) can apply to Childebert or to Christ; and "honor"
(*honor*) to Childebert, Christ, or Sigoald.

10.16
[*PL,* col. 343 (= 10.20); *MGH,* 249;
Reydellet, vol. 3, 95; DB, 540–41]

On the edge of Italy, when I first ventured into his realms,
King Sigibert saw to it that you were my prop,

to point the safer way, tag along,
provide a fresh horse, offer a meal.
Your duty long done, you've come back to your friend,   5
my keeper finally returns to me now.
Sweet friend, after a canyon of time, how is it that you're here—
magnificent in your grace, greater still in my love,
prompted by your vassals' affection, kind Sigoald,
a godly name to me, friend?   10
Let Childebert, the rising king, make you rise as he goes:
a count today, a duke tomorrow;
in such a lord may the faithful see their own desires;
may a life lived in triumph become their path to honor.

10.18
[*PL,* cols. 344–45 (= 10.22); *MGH,* 251;
Reydellet, vol. 3, 98; DB, 542–45]

Easter blooms here, etched in memory,
the *defensor* feeds us the count's pleasure;
the lord's delicacies supplied by season and prayer:
heaps of fish, fruit, fowl.
Sigoald, you wear Childebert's power well,   5
may position and rank raise you higher still;
let the realm be happy in the king's happy love,
let the faith of the good count swell in honor.

39. To Agiulfus (fl. c. 575)

Though it is presumed he was of some importance at Childebert II's court,[1]
nothing is known of Agiulfus, who appears only in App. 7, translated here.
The poem hints at more than a passing acquaintance, not least in the play-
fulness of its first verse: ***Nomen*** *dulce* **mihi,** **mihi** *semper amabile* ***nomen.***
Here, "name" (*nomen*), betokening Agiulfus, brackets the line in which it falls,
enclosing the pronoun "me" (*mihi*), standing for Fortunatus, within its fold
and depicting in the placement of its words the embrace for which Agiulfus
is praised in v. 3.

App. 7

[*MGH,* 280–81;
Reydellet, vol. 3, 148; DB, 642–43]

A name sweet to me; to me an endlessly pleasant name
(no one doubts it); but to me more brilliant for your soul:
embracing every lover in your heart, making each one your own
as you love and are loved in return, dear, eminent
(no one demurs),
distinguished, Agiulfus, kind companion.   5
Your service sits well with the powers that be,
bound by amity to the world, a man decently good,
a picture of happiness, faith confident in your heart.
Let your rich grace abide awhile longer still for those
holding sway,
let their salvation be your glory, dear;   10
through you remember me to their high power (please),
may you flourish, happily, while the days remain.
Great friend, say something on behalf of Audulf—(he belongs
only to me);
and so, abiding in this world, may your life be noble,
let all happy things flow to the royal will,   15
and may God grant you the day of days.

40. To Radegund (d. 587) and/or to Agnes (d. no later than 589)

Radegund was the daughter of Berthar, King of Thuringia, where she was born, c. 510. Her mother died a few years after her birth, and her father was murdered by his brother, Hermann, leaving the princess an orphan at a young age. Hermann's scheming cruelty eventually caught up with him when the Frankish kings Theuderic I and Lothar I invaded Thuringia in 530. In the aftermath of Hermann's defeat, Radegund was awarded to Lothar as booty and spirited off to Gaul, where in due course she became his wife. Throughout her time in Gaul and even more so once she became Lothar's queen, Radegund practiced a powerful ascetic version of Christianity that involved mortification of the flesh, penitence, alms-giving, and service to others, the details of which are recollected by Fortunatus in the biography he wrote about his close friend.[1] The turning point in Radegund's complicated life came when Lothar murdered her brother, who had traveled west with her after their uncle's defeat, at which point she left her husband, fled to Noyon, and submitted herself to the protection of Medard, the bishop of that city, who in due course consecrated her a deaconess.[2] In short order she made a pilgrimage to the shrine of St. Martin at Tours and then decided to found her own religious community in Poitiers, thus establishing the Convent of the Holy Cross while gaining the protection of the city's bishop, Pientius.

The political skills praised by her other biographer, Baudonivia,[3] were clearly put to good use at this point, for Radegund managed to weave together the support of many Gaulish bishops, including, most importantly, Germanus of Paris, whose advocacy enabled her to gain a modicum of financial security for her convent while ensuring her liberation from Lothar. When she died, on August 13, 587, Radegund was mourned throughout Gaul and beyond, not least by Fortunatus, whose many poems written to her reveal, as the translations here suggest, an intimacy grounded in a profound respect for morality, asceticism, and suffering.

Refusing to administer the convent that she founded, Radegund instead named as abbess her protégé, Agnes, about whom little is known, apart from what is gleaned from the poems Fortunatus wrote to her, most of which are translated here. Both Gregory of Tours and Fortunatus tell us that Agnes was adopted by Radegund, who raised and educated her. Gregory further relates that Bishop Germanus consecrated her, a fact that makes sense given the assistance he provided to Radegund.[4] A birth year of c. 525 can be conjectured based on details found in the poems. From Gregory's observation that Leubovera was abbess of Holy Cross in 589, it is surmised that Agnes died no later than this year.[5] Radegund and Agnes had good relations with Pientius, the bishop of Poitiers at the time Holy Cross was founded, but his successor, Maroveus, was dismissive of the women and unresponsive to their requests for spiritual, not to mention actual, guidance. In the instance of attempting to institute a rule to govern Holy Cross, Maroveus was particularly unwavering in his neglect, which led Radegund to take up on her own authority the rule established for women earlier in the century by Caesarius of Arles, one of the most stringent then available to women religious. Fortunatus uses the tendency of his friends to mortify their flesh as a touchstone for more than a few poems.

Fortunatus met Radegund and Agnes in 567. He had made good on his vow to visit Tours to honor St. Martin, and behind him were the heady days in Metz, where he had met Sigibert and Brunhilde and made lasting friendships with Dynamius (No. 18), Gogo (No. 19), and others. It is unclear what brought the worldly poet to a convent devoted to worldly retreat, but in part Radegund's reputation must have preceded her, in which case she would be one more important Frankish figure the itinerant Italian poet wished to meet. Yet the fact that Fortunatus remained in Poitiers for the rest of his life, which ended, in the early seventh century, with him sitting in the city's Episcopal seat, suggests the extent to which he became devoted to both women. Along with Gregory of Tours, Radegund and Agnes were the most intimate of the poet's friends, and the poems through which we glean their devotion form one of the richest collections in the western literary tradition.[6]

Not all the poems concerning Radegund and Agnes are of the sort translated here. *Carm.* 8.3 and 8.4, for instance, take up the topic of virginity through the examples of the two women, while a cluster of poems, App. 1, 2, and 3, were written in support of or about Radegund's eventually successful effort to acquire from the Greek east a relic of the true cross. Against the backdrop of writing on her behalf to Constantinople, Fortunatus takes the opportunity in App. 1 to relate in Radegund's voice the fall of her homeland, Thuringia, at the same time as she speaks to her cousin Amalfrid, who had fled from there to the Byzantine court during the upheavals that led to Radegund's own exile and who presumably could influence the emperor to part with a piece of the true cross. But, as App. 3 makes clear, Amalfrid had died some time before, and Fortunatus takes the opportunity in this piece, also written in Radegund's voice, to lament losses both past and present. More happily, App. 2, a *gratiarum actio* to Justin II and Sophia, shows that this emperor and his wife were forthcoming with the relic, whose reception in Poitiers was celebrated by Fortunatus in *carm.* 2.2, *Pange, lingua,* and 2.6, *Vexilla regis,* two hymns that are today the best known of Fortunatus' compositions.

By and large the remaining poems, most of which follow, attend to daily life at Holy Cross, where Agnes took responsibility for the administration of an important and prominent religious community, and, if her biographies are to be believed, Radegund attended to cultivating her asceticism while performing tasks within the community both menial and of consequence. At the same time, Fortunatus reveals himself in these pieces to be, to use George's apt phrase, a "mini-chancery," composing poems that do the women's bidding in a form that adds to their power, resonance, and persuasiveness,[7] when he is not simply writing for the occasion, celebrating the gusto of the moment, or longing to confirm in the women's absence friendships that will endure until death.

8.5

[*PL*, col. 286 (= 8.10); *MGH*, 193;
Reydellet, vol. 2, 148–49; DB, 450–51]

Written to Radegund during her annual Lenten retreat, the poem is an acrostic, a form used by Fortunatus also in *carm.* 2.4, 2.5, 3.5, and 9.5. In *carm.* 3.5, written to Felix of Nantes (No. 2), the poet joins his and his friend's names on counterpoised axes while punning on the idea of happiness, since in Latin *felix* and *fortunatus* are also adjectives meaning "happy." In *carm.* 8.5 Fortunatus is not so bold as to insinuate his name into an acrostic that features Radegund's, for that might suggest spiritual equality. Instead, her name is inscribed on both axes, thereby affiliating her with the Christian cross that her name forms in order to affirm her incomparable spirituality—a connection not inappropriate, given the liturgical season in which the poem was written. The cross formed by her name also speaks to the two worlds Radegund inhabits, a horizontal world of physical and material action, and a vertical world divorced from it.

The first word of the final verse of *carm.* 8.5 is contested. Leo prints *solo*, "alone,"[8] while Reydellet (following Luchi) has *salve*, "hail."[9] There is manuscript authority for both readings, but the ambiguity that readers expect from Fortunatus, especially in the closing couplets of his poems, makes *solo* the better reading. The poet seemingly claims that Radegund's soul has its "own lord" (*Dominus . . . suus*), which might be God but could be the poet himself, in which case *solo amore*, "singular love," heightens the exemplarity of the poet's veneration. Given that the poem trumpets the opposition between worldliness and eternity, ambiguity becomes a means to point both to the worldly love the poet feels and to the eternity of God's love that Radegund desires.

> **R**oyally born, powerful in the world, **RADEGUNDES,**
> **A**waiting heaven, despising the world,
> **D**ue to earn Christ,
> **E**ternity glimmering in your cave,
> **G**rasping the universe, crushing Satan   5
> **U**nderfoot as you walk the happy stars,
> **N**estled in a cave become heaven,
> **D**ripping tears on ground that blooms joy,
> **E**mptying, cutting, fatten the soul
> **S**ingularly loved by its own lord.   10

8.6
[*PL,* col. 286 (= 8.11); *MGH,* 193;
Reydellet, vol. 2, 149; DB, 450–51; George, *Poems,* 70]

The title of *carm.* 8.6 and the contents to Book 8 indicate that Radegund is
the recipient of this poem, but Agnes is also addressed, as v. 4 makes clear.
The poet apologizes for not sending lilies or roses in a season that offers only
violets. Their colors ramify early spring, the season of Easter: white, betoken-
ing purity; the lily, representing Easter; the violet, indicating royalty but also
Christ in his humility; the rose, symbolizing both passion and martyrdom.
The importance of color, too, is underlined at v. 9, where the phrase " royally
tinged" (*murice tinctae*) forms an allusion to Horace, *Odes* 2.16.36 (*murices
tinctae*), a line that takes readers back to a moment in which the Roman poet
encourages the exchange of worldly for spiritual things. In Horace's case the
substitution involves embracing the beauty of language as an antidote to fleet-
ing wealth. Here the idea is that the simple beauties of nature that take in,
ultimately, the incomparable smell of violets affirm what is properly a source
of pleasure while simultaneously pointing to what is truly to be enjoyed in
eternity's bliss.[10]

> If it were the season when lilies glittered white for me
> or roses dazzled brilliantly red,
> I would have freely plucked them from field or garden,
> and sent small gifts to two great souls;
> but I lack even these, all I have are violets   5
> tendered with a love that calls them roses.
> Amidst sweet-smelling grasses that I've sent
> are noble buds of royal hue
> that breathe out purple, royally tinged,
> and drown their leaves in whiffs of beauty;   10
> the violet bears both fragrance and grace; may you each
>   have both:
> let the scent of the gift with its flower be endlessly glorious.

8.7
[*PL,* col. 287 (= 8.12); *MGH,* 194;
Reydellet, vol. 2, 150; DB, 450–53; George, *Poems,* 70–71]

The title of *carm.* 8.7 indicates that the recipient is Radegund, but v. 19 proves
that Fortunatus wrote with Agnes also in mind. The poem mines ancient
diction, not least that of Claudian,[11] in its opening couplets, while subsequent

verses imagine battle lines being drawn (v. 11)[12] as the ancient colors of the circus teams, the "Blues and the Greens,"[13] depict the vivid flowers adorning the altar at the Convent of the Holy Cross. The circus competitions, which evoke in context images of the Byzantine east, may be prompted, according to George, by Radegund's contacts with the court there in her search for relics.[14] In that case, it would make good sense for the poet to think about the true cross as he ponders the gloriously adorned altar at the convent. The beauty of the flowers placed on it betoken an image of competition that points to the true cross, while connecting this world to Paradise—the place, in fact, to which the poet takes his readers in v. 20. There, the ambiguity of the word "odor" (*odor*) complicates the poem's conclusion. It can refer to the fragrances of the flowers with which Agnes and Radegund have bedecked their altar, but it may also denote the incomparable fragrance of the women themselves, a fresh instance of their exemplarity.

> The world is chained in winter's ice,
> light dies away from the flowerless field,
> but Spring, when the Lord laid Tartarus low,
> tousles the grass' heads, rising, unused to attention.
> Men decorate pulpits, doorposts with flowers,   5
> a woman's lap fills with wafting roses;
> for Christ—not for you—these aromas are strung,
> for the holy churches you give these buds.
> You have dressed festive altars in colored wreaths,
> painted them fresh with flowery threads.   10
> A golden, crocusy line goes forth, and here a purple row
> of violets, flushed scarlet meets milky white.
> The Blues and the Greens take their stand, colors wage a
>   flowery war;
> imagine—in this place of peace, plants drawing up
>   battle lines:
> the lily, pleasantly white, the rose with ruddy allure,   15
> the lily teasing fragrantly, the rose prettier in pink,
> flowers arrayed for a various war whose colors are brighter
> than any jewel, nor incense more fragrant than they;
> Agnes, Radegund, this is what you built.
> May your fragrances breathlessly mingle with eternity's
>   flowers.   20

8.8

[*PL,* col. 287 (= 8.13); *MGH,* 194–95;
Reydellet, vol. 2, 151; DB, 452–53]

Carm. 8.8 celebrates Radegund's return from her Lenten retreat by suggesting
that the flowers of spring are an indication of the beauty that heaven promises.
There is a connection, Fortunatus insists, between nature and God, for which
reason Radegund can more credibly attend to the poet's presence in the world
she otherwise scorns, using the hints provided by nature to brace herself as
she prepares for eternity's bliss. The poet expresses the wishes of the season's
flowers that clearly mirror his own desire to see Radegund again (vv. 15–16),
but their especial fragrance, which he has heretofore stressed, is diminished
in the face of Radegund's return. She now is the focal point, and all that the
flowers offer must be directed to her honor, for which reason they more prop-
erly belong in her hair.[15] Are we to imagine the poet placing them there?

Mighty queen (who reviles purple and gold):
a lover venerates you with buds;
not golden objects or purple cloth, but their colors
dress a grassy bouquet: purple in violets, crocuses in gold.
Rich in the love of God, you have shunned the rewards   5
of this life, despising them to sustain his wealth.
From me, accept this bouquet for you, a gift
(your blessed life better calls you to flowers)
as you mortify your flesh, to be revived in a light you will
                                        come to know.
Yet from here you spy what sort of field will sustain you in
                                that time to come: 10
in frail branches strung with odors (my gift to you just now)
ponder how great the aroma is that will revive you in the
                                        lap of God;
when you reach it (you're owed its rewards) I pray
that the gentle hand of your goodness tugs me up after you.
The beauty of the flowers of Paradise awaits you (no doubt),   15
but the flowers I've sent wish to see you again
in the world—and though their singular smell may seem
                                pleasant enough,
you've returned—they more properly belong in your hair.

8.9

[*PL*, col. 288 (= 8.14); *MGH*, 195;
Reydellet, vol. 2, 152; DB, 452–55]

Carm. 8.9 celebrates Radegund's return from Lenten retreat. It matters little what occurs in nature, with its longer days and increasing light that also symbolize the promise of spring and Christ's redemption. The ability of the poet to see depends instead on Radegund's presence, and her longed-for arrival is dramatically narrated before the reader's eyes in the final line of the poem. There, in v. 16, following a prayer for Radegund's safety, the poet declares that "a double light returns to me" (*et nobis pariter lux geminata redit*): the poet's vision is returned to him in the vision of his returned friend. Roberts notes the inconcinnity of the present indicative verb of v. 16, *redit* ("returns") following the present subjunctive verb in the previous line, *referant* ("return").[16] I recognize the inconcinnity as a means to dramatize the power of the moment: the poet's perspective is restored by Radegund's return, and the shifting moods reflect this restoration, not to mention the power of Radegund to restore her good friend in fact, not just potentially. The "double light" can thus be understood to indicate the double joys of Easter and of Radegund's arrival, as Reydellet suggests;[17] or it may be, as my translation suggests, the restoration of the poet's vision in the presence of Radegund's visage.

> Mind pregnant with God, Radegund, bedrock of the sisters,
> you burn your flesh to stoke your soul:
> a Lenten vow to take to the cloister hurries you to your cave
> today where my heart will wander, claiming you.
> In a flash I'm unable to see,   5
> I'm weighed down, in a thick fog, lacking you,
> you've shut the world out—your cave will keep you—
> you make me a prisoner in a jailhouse world.
> You're a fugitive, a recluse, for just a few days
> that will seem more like a year than a month to me,   10
> subduing time, hidden to your lover,
> when I see you again I will scarcely believe it.
> Until then we will be as one in prayer:
> my soul follows you to a forbidden place.
> May the joys of Easter account you safe (I pray).   15
> A double light returns to me: my sight, your face.

8.10
[*PL,* col. 288 (= 8.15); *MGH,* 195–96;
Reydellet, vol. 2, 153; DB, 454–55]

It is clear that *carm.* 8.10 was written to Radegund, due to both its placement
in the cluster of poems in Book 8 that attend to her Lenten practices and
to the association of her return with a power that upends nature, though,
except for the title, she is unnamed in the poem. Fortunatus returns to images
exploited in *carm.* 8.8 and 8.9, but whereas Radegund's return was longed for
in *carm.* 8.8 or immediate to the narrative of *carm.* 8.9, it is now established
fact, ramified through a series of natural descriptions that jumble nature's
expected functions. Planting, growing, and reaping occur at once; buds and
fruits appear simultaneously; grapes can be pressed even though it is only
April. As was the case in *carm.* 8.9, the ability of Radegund to "double"
reality is suggested anew.[18] In the earlier poem she was a "double light" that
embodied the poet's restored vision gained through her physical proximity.
Here, she increases the festive quality of Easter, making it doubly enjoyable
by dint of her presence. She is equivalent, in other words, to the joys implied
in Christ's resurrection, an eternal renewal that she has effected, at least for
Fortunatus, in simply coming into her good friend's presence again. For this
reason George rightly senses in v. 4 an "almost blasphemous joy."[19]

> Your face, irradiant, has returned to me—from where?
> What delays held you so long?
> You had carried off my contentment that you now recall,
> you double Easter's sanctity.
> Although shoots just now poke through the furrows,   5
> I gather their harvest in your sight again
> and collect fruits, laying aside quiet handfuls,
> April acts as if it were August;
> although buds and shoots scamper forth just now,
> already autumn with its grapes has come,   10
> the apple, the high peach, fan fragrances now,
> but with their blossoms bear fruit to me.
> Although no harvest dresses the barren field,
> everything bursts, thrives, at your return.[20]

11.2

[*PL,* cols. 351–52; *MGH,* 258;
Reydellet, vol. 3, 113; DB, 546–47]

While the placement of *carm.* 11.2 in Book 11 among a group of poems addressed to Radegund confirms her as recipient, only its title ("And also something to Lady Radegund"; *Item aliud ad domnam Radegundem*) identifies her as such. Like the cohort of poems written to her in Book 8, *carm.* 11.2 contrasts images of light and its absence in order to bemoan Radegund's Lenten retreat. In this instance, however, Fortunatus speaks on behalf of the sisters of Holy Cross, not merely for himself, in enjoining Radegund to return as quickly as possible. Everyone is blinded in Radegund's absence and all are anxious to see—by seeing her—again.

Not the least of the poem's literary attributes is the elegiac diction mined by Fortunatus to articulate the strong feelings occasioned by Radegund's absence. In particular, the phrase "my light" (*mea lux,* v. 1) recollects Ovid's identical wording in more than a few of his elegiac pieces. Consolino argues that in the five hundred years separating Ovid from Fortunatus, such diction has lost its erotic sense and now functions in Fortunatus' deployment in a spiritual way.[21] Roberts notes that the same words (*lux mea*) are found on a Roman inscription that records a son addressing a mother, thus demonstrating that the phrase was appropriate to a number of loving relationships, not least between children and parents.[22] Be that as it may, the question remains: by what procedure does the original erotic context of such diction evanesce, to be replaced by spiritual resonances that are not, in any case, to be denied?

> My light—banished from eager eyes, without me,
> but where—holed up, unyielding to my gaze?
> All things seem indistinct: sky, rivers, the land
> are as nothing to me when you're gone from my sight.
> Although dissolving clouds clear the sky   5
> your hiding brings on a blackening day
> that makes me pray time doesn't falter,
> that the days wish to quicken their pace.
> Let me, let the sisters, insist on this:
> show your face to those caressed by your love—relieve us.   10

11.3
[*PL*, col. 352; *MGH*, 259;
Reydellet, vol. 3, 114; DB, 546–49]

The title of *carm.* 11.3 and the contents of Book 11 indicate that this poem was written for Agnes' *natalicium,* a word that can mean, literally, "birthday" or refer to the anniversary of her installation as abbess of Holy Cross, the definition that applies here. The poem is symmetrical, with vv. 1–8 attending to the special parenting—God as father, Radegund as mother—that nurtured Agnes; while vv. 9–16 announce the festive day and feature a list of injunctions to both women that ends with the wish that they possess the love that will join them in Paradise. In v. 10 the poet writes "a lamb in the world gave you this Agnes" (*Agnen hanc vobis Agnus in orbe dedit*); to preserve the pun of *Agnen/Agnus,* "Agnes"/"lamb," I translate *Agnus* as "angel," which sounds enough like *Agnes* to perhaps suggest Fortuantus' playfulness here.

The "lamb" of v. 10 can refer to Radegund or to Christ. The accompanying prepositional phrase "in the world" (*Agnus in orbe*) thus highlights Radegund's incomparability, or designates Christ, the lamb of God who takes away the sins of fallen humanity. Reydellet translates, "the Lamb gave you this Agnes in the world;"[23] Di Brazzano has, "the Lamb has given that Agnes to the world for you."[24] Both versions have Christ as lamb and otherwise suppress the ambiguity. The "you" (*vobis*) of v. 10 functions in much the same way. If the lamb is Radegund, then "you" designates the sisters of the Holy Cross who are set to celebrate Radegund's beneficience. If the lamb is Christ, then "you" takes in both the sisters and Radegund. The ambiguity is purposeful, since it links Radegund with Christ as the lamb of God, while affiliating Agnes, too, with Christ, through the pun provided by her name.

> Rich mother, graceful, in a blessed prayer reveal your joy
> and rejoice: sweet Agnes is abbess for another year.
> Not your womb but grace made her your child,
> in love Christ gave her, not your flesh,
> our Founder gathered her to you that she might be
>   eternally yours,   5
> our Father in and out of time gives a daughter who will
>   never die,
> a happy heiress for whom time stands still
> remains with you in and out of time.
> Let this glorious day honor holy Radegund now,
> an Angel in our midst gave Agnes to us.   10

May you both celebrate joys tumbling down the years,
may you be the answer to the people's highest prayers,
(teaching songs of eternity to virgin choirs)
parcel out the work of eternal life,
be well, live long in this place, partners toiling in the flesh,   15
until love joins you once more in eternity's light.

11.4
[*PL*, col. 352; *MGH*, 259;
Reydellet, vol. 3, 115; DB, 548–49]

This poem is linked to *carm.* 11.3 through that poem's closing injunction
that Radegund and Agnes "be well" (*longinqua salus teneat vos*, v. 15), a theme
picked up in *carm.* 11.4, an appeal to Radegund to take some wine to relieve
her exhaustion. That she would have suffered from world-weariness (*lassata
nimis*, v. 4) makes good sense, if reports of Radegund's activites at Holy Cross
are to be believed. In his biography of her, for example, Fortunatus has left
this report of Radegund's work in the convent kitchen:

> How can anyone describe her excited fervor as she ran into the
> kitchen, doing her week of chores? None of the nuns but she
> would carry as much wood as was needed in a bundle from the
> back gate. She drew water from the well and poured it into basins.
> She scrubbed vegetables and legumes and revived the hearth by
> blowing so that she might cook the food. While it was busy boil-
> ing, she took the vessels from the hearth, washing and laying out
> the dishes. When the meal was finished, she rinsed the small
> vessels and scrubbed the kitchen till it shone, free of every speck
> of dirt. Then she carried out all the sweepings and the nastiest
> rubbish.[25]

Although Fortunatus also reports that she was ill on at least one occasion, it
seems unlikely, as George suggests, that *carm.* 11.4 was written during sick-
ness: Radegund is overworked, not sick.[26]

A pun on her name in v. 3 links Agnes to Fortunatus: "in verse: Fortunatus
the **agent** and **Agnes** pray" (*Fortunatus agens, Agnes quoque versibus orant*).
This line has been cited as evidence that Fortunatus held an official position at
Holy Cross, that of *agens*, which, to preserve the pun, I translate as "agent."[27]
There is nothing that militates against understanding *agens* to designate such
a title, since the word was regularly used in sixth-century Gaul to designate a
"manager" or "overseer,"[28] but George's view is the *opinio communis*: "verses,
not vegetables, were Fortunatus' livelihood."[29] The question remains: what

exactly did Fortunatus do at Holy Cross apart from writing poetry, which clearly could not have consumed all his waking hours for over two decades? Perhaps it is no coincidence that the verse in which the pun occurs follows a line in which the poet speaks of being a "servant" to Radegund (*famulos . . . tuos*, v. 2). *Agens* might therefore be understood to qualify how precisely the poet performs his role as servant. Given her role as abbess, Agnes' servitude is self-evident.

The power of the injunction to drink is heightened by the scriptural tag Fortunatus indirectly recalls in the poem's closing couplet. There, in vv. 11–12, Radegund is linked by analogy to Timothy, in need of the medicine wine provides, in his case, for stomachache (1 Tim. 5.23). At the same time, Agnes and Fortunatus, perhaps speaking for the women of Holy Cross, take on the role of Paul as they, like him, enjoin someone to drink whom they wish to be well, not least to sustain the friendship they share.[30]

> If piety, if inviolable love, are as good as answered prayers,
> so abundant in both, let those who serve you have their say
> in verse: Fortunatus the agent and Agnes pray
> that you drink kindly of some wine when world-weariness sets in.
> May Christ grant whatever you seek   5
> as we seek from you the best way to live;
> our petition comes wrapped in humility, rich mother,
> no offense is meant—but, please, give us leave
> to say: let the effect, not the taste, make you sip this wine,
> a draught such as this slakes a weary heart: 10
> Timothy drank some, on Paul's command,
> lest a clarion call to the gentiles stumble on stomachache.

11.5
[*PL*, cols. 352–53; *MGH*, 260;
Reydellet, vol. 3, 115–16; DB, 548–49]

The title of *carm.* 11.5 and the entry in the contents to Book 11 are identical: "A poem to the abbess on her birthday" (*Item aliud ad abbatissam de natali suo*), that is, the anniversary of Agnes' installation as abbess, the same event celebrated in *carm.* 11.3. It is unclear, however, how the content of the poem comports to this title, and, unlike *carm.* 11.3, its words offer no clues. Because it is Agnes' *natalicium*, Reydellet thinks that Agnes and Radegund have devoted the day to prayer and abstinence, for which reason the poet has been excluded from their intimacy.[31] I understand the poem to make explicit the idea that Radegund has also been denied Agnes' presence, both in vv. 5–6, where Agnes' absence makes Radegund long to hear her voice, and in v. 15, where Fortunatus admits that Radegund put him up to writing.

The poem focuses on two themes: in vv. 1–8 the poet laments Agnes' absence (from him and from Radegund equally), then, in vv. 9–16, he worries about the specifics of Agnes' retreat. He gives every indication that she has been in retreat for some time, not simply on this day, and the images of fasting and seclusion suggest a genuine concern on his part for his friend's welfare, an apprehension that Radegund seems to share, given the fact that, as the poet says in v. 15, she ordered him to write to Agnes. On a reading of v. 4 that substitutes the word "unsatisfactory" (*inexpletam*) for Leo's "unaccustomed" (*nec solitam*), and that understands the Latin word *opem* to mean "food," rather than "riches,"[32] Reydellet thinks the line indicates the poet's displeasure at having been brought only a cursory meal owing to Agnes' obsession with praying and fasting.

But it is difficult to know how Agnes can be in retreat and still supply a meal, however cursory. To do this, in any case, would presumably imply some sort of contact with Radegund, the lack of which seems to be the impetus behind the poem's composition. Further, if a meal has been produced, why does the poet describe himself as enduring a fast? Finally, reading "unsatisfying" (*inexpletam*) rather than "unaccustomed" (*nec solitam*) steps on the parallelism provided by the negative particle *nec,* in vv. 4–5, both of which introduce descriptions of what her good friends miss most in Agnes' absence. On this view, *opem* (v. 4) designates not a meal but what Agnes' presence brings, such as the sweet melodies of her voice that Radegund misses (v. 5).

An obvious if unexpected bow to Catullus' Attis at the poem's midpoint also helps more securely to understand Fortunatus' (and Radegund's) concern. For v. 9, the first line of the second half of the poem, contains the phrase, "radiant little eyes" (*radiantes . . . ocellos*) that recalls Catullus 63.39–40: "with radiant eyes" (*radiantibus oculis*).[33] Catullus' words personify the sun, which possesses, in his depiction, eyes that banish the shades of the night, clear the heavens, and take Attis out of the realm of sleep. At just this moment, when the sun, so to speak, shines its light on this setting, Attis recollects his prior night of frenzied devotion and recognizes for the first time that he has made himself a eunuch.

In Fortunatus' rendering of Agnes' latest retreat, therefore, it is difficult to suppress Catullus' Attis, who plies his devotion to a god in bouts of extremism that do him harm. This harm carries over into Fortunatus' poem, betokening the dangers involved in Agnes' devotion that begin, as the poet has made clear, with fasting. The poet, who presumably sent the poem to Agnes in real time, thus imbeds at his poem's midpoint a red flag, so to speak, that directs Agnes' attention in token of the dangers he feels she faces. In this sense, then,

Fortunatus performs the same act of revelation that the sun performs for Attis, revealing the landscape in which Agnes finds herself, for which reason her good friend is fearful. Just as Agnes and Fortunatus worried about Radegund's overwork in *carm.* 11.4, now Radegund and Fortunatus worry about Agnes' ascetic practices, demonstrating the ways in which personal and spiritual devotion could come into conflict.[34]

> Our sweet grace, Christ's holiest virgin,
> Agnes, goodness keeps you pure
> but were you pleased to spend today
> ignoring me—you hadn't given what I'm accustomed to—
> and ignoring our mistress, who grows fat on sweet words   5
> when you deign to send them?
> I've heard yet again that you're not eating:
> you might say that I'm famished along with you.
> I listen: has sluggish sleep numbed radiant eyes;
> or are you wide awake, rehearsing your soul through
>   endless nights?   10
> Aren't these long spaces of quiet enough
> for you—day or night, it's all the same?
> Everything lingers now in mists, moon, stars, blotted out,
> dissolving, fleeing only if your soul is glad.
> For our mistress, who bade me write to you, I pray a joyous
>   translation,   15
> may she flourish with you on her way to heaven.

11.6
[*PL,* col. 353; *MGH,* 260–61;
Reydellet, vol. 3, 116–17; DB, 550–51; George, *Poems,* 103]

Carm. 11.6 speaks of charges leveled against Fortunatus and Agnes, its recipient, and makes the case for a love grounded in spiritual, not corporal, devotion. The poem keeps to a theme already mined in earlier pieces written to Radegund, in which she is a spiritual mother to the poet and to Agnes. Here, in the face of scandal, the poet focuses on the ways in which that maternity proves the devotion of her children, who are, logically, spiritual siblings rather than lovers. The poem presents not a few interpretive difficulties. First, as he often does in his poetry, Fortunatus relies on ambiguity to provide complication, not least in v. 1, where Agnes is called "mother" (*mater*) and "sister" (*soror*), the only time in the collection that the poet so designates her. But these descriptions blur the line the poet seemingly is anxious to observe between the corporal and spiritual worlds. For the word *mater,* when it appears again in v. 9, is used of specific and erotically charged parts of Radegund's body, albeit in a narrative whose goal is to affirm spiritual purity.

Moreover, in v. 13, where the poet expressly bemoans the charges leveled against him, he uses two ambiguous words, *tenui* and *susurro,* that complicate what is otherwise a straightforward declaration of worry. For though the phrase *tenui . . . susurro* here is comprised of the adjective *tenuis* and the noun *susurrus* that together mean "weak/soft/tenuous whisper," both words are also erotically charged, first person singular verbs, *tenui* meaning "I held/embraced," and *susurro,* "I whisper."[35] The poet thus seems to suggest the grounds for innuendo in the very words that articulate gossipmongering.

Apart from these ambiguities, readers have been troubled, too, by the eroticism implied in Fortunatus' description of Radegund's body. Roberts, for example, argues that the language of soulful affiliation deployed by Fortunatus in vv. 9–12 harbors spiritual, not carnal, meanings,[36] and George, too, while noting the gossip it elicited, holds up the "passionate friendship" of Jerome and Paula as normative for understanding Fortunatus' friendship with Agnes. Given the tradition symbolized by Jerome and Paula, she concludes that "there is no reason not to accept Fortunatus' apologia at its face value."[37]

In a poem that seeks to deny corporal attachment, however, it seems odd for Fortunatus to choose diction that could be construed in any but the most straightforward way. To do anything less invites the sort of scrutiny the poem has received over time and tends to lessen, rather than confirm, belief in the poet's protestations. Moreover, the phrase *tenui . . . susurro* is further complicated by the fact that it seems to recall Juvenal, *Sat.* 4.110, where that poet speaks of dangerous rumors bandied about by an informer at Domitian's court.[38] This lends to the line a sinister quality that may portend the infighting that broke out among the nuns at Holy Cross after Radegund and Agnes had died. Leo, in fact, thought that the poem was written after Radegund's death, given the fact that Fortunatus calls her "blessed" (*beata*) in v. 11.[39]

If this is the case, then the difficulties the convent faced after Agnes died were already percolating in the brief interval that separates the deaths of Radegund and Agnes. As Roberts notes, it is clear from Gregory of Tours' account of the revolt that abbesses were likely to be the subject of gossip and innuendo, as was unfortunately the case with Agnes' successor, Leubovera.[40] Reydellet seems to concur with Leo, noting that, in any case, gossipers would not likely have had free rein during the lifetime of Radegund.[41] Nisard's objection that the "you" (*vos*) of the poem's final line proves that Radegund was alive seems to be a misunderstanding of the Latin.[42] Rather than designating the community of sisters, as Reydellet believes,[43] it is simply the royal "you," designating Agnes alone. For it makes no sense for Fortunatus to speak to the community, nor even to Radegund, in the poem's final line. The poet cultivates a private space in his closing verses, and the plural is a token of the respect demanded by friendship.

In my translation I have moved to v. 12 the final word of v. 10, *eram* ("I have been" in the translation), in order to facilitate sense.

> Honor makes you mother to me, love makes you sweet sister,
> with piety and faith, in my heart and soul, I cherish you
> with a divine love, not with any bodily guilt:
> I love what the spirit covets; my flesh is still.
> Christ swears it, Mary, Peter, Paul   5
> and the company of saints
> all know that I have loved you in this way,
> as if you were Titiana, sister of my bone and flesh,
> as if mother Radegund had birthed us both
> from the chastity of her womb, as if the dear breasts   10
> of that blessed woman had nourished us with their milky flow—
> that's how I've always been to you.
> I grieve these rumors, whispering weakly but
> with venom enough to trample my sense;
> but I'm standing my ground, this is how I feel—   15
> if you wish to tend me with your sweet love.

11.7
[*PL,* cols. 353–54; *MGH,* 261;
Reydellet, vol. 3, 117–18; DB, 550–51]

The repetition of "mother" (*mater*) and "sister" (*soror*) in the initial lines of this and the prior poem perhaps influenced their placement in Book 11, but unlike *carm.* 11.6, this poem is written to both Radegund and Agnes. While expressing in general terms the longing that arises when friends are apart (vv. 1–6) and the urge in the face of absence never to allow separation to impede friendship's progress, the poet also speaks in his own person as somehow having let Radegund down, perhaps through his own absence or through disability caused by illness. In any case, he asks Agnes to make good the deficiency before going on to hope that the three friends never have to be apart in this life or the next.

Roberts understands this poem to be a lament over Agnes' and Radegund's latest retreat that keeps these good friends from Fortunatus; or, more sinisterly, an indication that the two women are purposely keeping the poet away.[44] My reading of the poem has Fortunatus emphasizing the place (*locus,* v. 3) that separates him from his friends, especially since, if he has fallen out of favor with the women, it would seem impolitic to ask Agnes to attend to Radegund in his absence. Given the poem's ending, in which the reliability of the women's presence in his life is affirmed, Fortunatus seems simply to lament another of his friends' frequent retreats, tinged now with the guilt of being an inadequate son to Radegund, a fault that absence seems to have set into high relief.

> Dear mother, sweet sister, what words suffice,
> alone, in my heart, lacking your love?
> A mind worry-plagued cries out to you, close-confined in
> > your cave,
> just as it begs to see you again, pleading prayers laced with good.
> Dear sister, I ask your daughterly devotion—   5
> since I've been less of a son to her—to incline to our mother's
> > beck and call.
> My stake? Let her live with you for uncounted days,
> let her only salvation be with Christ as he Fathers and haunts
> > the world.
> Not now, not in the days to come, let us never be apart,
> but let salvation alone protect us and the day of days carry
> > us away.   10
> In this world, still, I hope time remains a friend
> that keeps sister and mother my reliable repose.

11.8
[*PL,* col. 354; *MGH,* 261;
Reydellet, vol. 3, 118; DB, 550–53; George, *Poems,* 104]

Carm. 11.8 exploits the role that Agnes played in superintending souls and stomachs, for she, like Radegund, often took part in preparing, serving, and clearing meals. The poet, who makes no bones about his healthy appetite in succeeding poems in Book 11 and in the Appendix, plays on his tendency to overindulge at mealtime in order to honor Agnes. For while she goes about preparing and serving a meal to the nuns, she offers to Fortunatus something much more filling and worthy, a spiritual sustenance supplied by her presence. Verse 8 summarizes the poet's view: because his friendship is so deep, Agnes' attentions are all the sweeter. This allows the poet to pray for Agnes' long life (and Radegund's) while noting Agnes' position as the one who reins in the nuns in her role as abbess (vv. 9–12).

Fate, most agreeably, has granted my wish,
my prayers deserved a savory gift
that fed the sisters, but did more good for me:
they're sated by food while I'm nourished by love,
glittering with decency as you fashion two meals: 5
restoring my heart as they eat what you serve,
food feeding their bodies, love nourishing my soul—
because I need you all the more, you come a sweeter meal
                                                          to me.
In pious prayers may great God hear your petitioning
and wash over your lips an unending feast.   10
Grow green in the length of time with our mother at your side,
let the sisters' chorus stand firm for God, but bridled by
                                                    your hand.

11.9
[*PL,* cols. 354–55; *MGH,* 262;
Reydellet, vol. 3, 119; DB, 552–53]

This and the following poem celebrate the bounties in food and friendship
that Fortunatus receives at Holy Cross. In *carm.* 11.9 Agnes feeds the poet
a mountainous meal whose variety and volume weary the server and sate
the poet. His overeating gets the best of him at poem's end, for which rea-
son Agnes is a "conqueror" (*victrix,* v. 16). Although there is no doubt as to
Fortunatus' self-depiction in these lines—he is an avid observer, and con-
sumer, of food—the concluding image of Agnes as conqueror is ambiguous.
She is a conqueror, to be sure, because her stupendous meals have conquered
the poet physically, making him drowsy and forcing him to end his poem. But
she is also someone who stands victorious over her own appetites, something
Fortunatus admires in her but never replicates in his own life in the light of
Agnes' good example.[45] The poem thus celebrates the fact that Fortunatus
can have his cake and eat it too (literally): Agnes' abstinence makes her the
better friend, for it serves as an example to the hungry poet who nonetheless
can indulge his appetite. Not the least of the contrasts this ambiguity supports
is the picture of Agnes drawn by Fortunatus in *carm.* 11.5, where he worries
about her fasting.

Your sisterly concern never lets me forget
how the meals you bring keep me alive.[46]
The bounty of today's supper was prime,
at your table vegetables drizzled in honey

ran twice up and down the board,   5
the smell alone could have fattened me,
the server could barely manage the loads,
his feet were blistered at meal's end.
Then a haughty mound of meat appeared,
a mountain—with adjoining hills,   10
fish and ragout girding them,
a little garden for supper within.
Gluttonous, greedy, I scarfed it all down:
mountain and garden in a sluggish gut.
I can't remember much after this, since your gifts conquer me.   15
Off to heaven, conqueror Agnes, above the clouds, fly away.

11.10
[*PL,* col. 355; *MGH,* 262–63;
Reydellet, vol. 3, 120; DB, 552–55]

When compared to *carm.* 11.9, this poem seems more concerned, as Roberts notes, to "impress with the richness of the food and its presentation."[47] Not the least of the ways in which Fortunatus accomplishes this, as Reydellet suggests, is by emphasizing the materials of which the table setting is made—silver (*argentea gavata,* v. 3), marble (*marmoreus discus,* v. 5), wicker (*pictis canistris,* v. 9), glass (*scutella,* v. 7)—which seemingly are as important as the foods they hold.[48] The concluding verse, in which the poet calls himself "third" (*tertius,* v. 13), reminds readers of the final verse of *carm.* 6.6, where Ultrogotha was so styled. The affiliation is apposite, since she is the third member of a trio that includes her two daughters, whereas Fortunatus is the third member of a group that includes his spiritual mother and sister. The intimacy of this trio of friends is akin to that shared by parents, children, and siblings.

From all sides, a flood of food rushes out.
I can't go wrong—what first to try?
A silver plate bears a mound of meat,
a thick gravy where vegetables were swimming,
a marble dish deposits a garden's brood,   5
a honeyed taste flowed over my lips,
a saucerglass swelled with a burden of chicken—
removing feathers doesn't lighten it.
Apples in abundance rush from colorful wicker,
their fragrance, pleasant-flowing, sated me.   10
An indigo jar gives snowy draughts of milk,

haughtily come—it knew it was set to please.
Lady and mother, and her child: let the third man,
your servant, speak of these gifts, chained by a godly love.

11.11

[*PL,* col. 355; *MGH,* 263;
Reydellet, vol. 3, 121; DB, 554–55; George, *Poems,* 105–106]

Carm. 11.11 portrays a feast lavish in its presentation: amidst a panoply of
flowers—roses, violets, lilies (vv. 3–5)—numerous enough to fill a field (v.
4), is a table whose cloth is rosebuds (vv. 7–8), surmounted by a wall of green
ivy and a floor covered in roses that appear to bleed when trampled (vv.
11–12). The room seems to be a slice of nature that transmogrifies into the
allurements of Paradise, personified and addressed directly at v. 16. The scene
perhaps takes place in the monastic refectory, where flowers strewn on table
and floor become, in the poet's mind, a tableau of paradisiacal beauty. Yet the
severe asceticism practiced by Radegund and Agnes runs at cross-purposes
to the setting imagined here and raises questions about the austerity of life at
Holy Cross. It is possible, of course, that the poem reflects convivial practices
thereafter abandoned for more austere habits; or perhaps exceptions could
be made in the case of meals honoring special guests. George notes that the
poem might describe a "parlor" that was often used in convents, in which the
rules governing monastic life were relaxed, if only for a few hours.[49] Whatever
the specific setting, the poem affiliates Radegund with the beauty of flowers,
recalling *carm.* 8.7 and 8.8, and is in its own way an offering whose devotion
equals that of the banquet so carefully fashioned by Agnes.[50]

Lucky guest, consider these glad delights
that fragrances furnish and taste proves:
burning red, a horde of flowers softly smiles;
a table of roses nearly as full as the fields,
in the lap of lavender, milky lilies fade to white,   5
a place freshly flagrant with rivalry's smells.
Dinner is an insult to dewy buds made to play tablecloth—
why accost these lovely roses so?
Yet the table was more pleasing without its cloth,
covered by sweet smells with their colorful gifts.   10
A wall hung in green clusters of ivy stood out,
roses trampled on the limestone floor bleed red,
an incomparable fertility makes you think soft fields
with glad buds grow green under the eaves.

If fugitive time, with its vanishing pleasures, satisfies,   15
may your meals prove alluring to us, Paradise.
My sister plaited this together with hands like Daedalus
that made it thrive: Mother deserved to have such beauty.

11.12
[PL, cols. 355–56; *MGH,* 263–64;
Reydellet, vol. 3, 122; DB, 554–57]

The gifts of which Fortunatus speaks in *carm.* 11.12 are presumably verses, perhaps the poem itself. They have been sent to Agnes but they remain her property because she inspires them (vv. 1–2) through the meals she serves and by her conversation, both of which are honeysweet (vv. 3–4). But the gift of food has proven too large and the poet is full, for which reason he can return some of the "food," that is, his own verses inspired by the bounty his friend has sent (vv. 5–6). The gift he offers is hardly enough, however, for food and good company are much superior to a poem. For this reason, the poet must beg forgiveness; his love presumes to send a lesser for a greater gift, but the inspiration it has furnished, while making it Agnes' own, also provides a fine setting in which Fortunatus can exploit the connection he always emphasizes between Agnes' worldly and spiritual habits.[51]

I sent gifts, but not mine—don't doubt this confession—
that come to you more properly your own,
for you send everyone meals dripping in honey,
like the sweet combs flowing from your devoted lips;
so the surfeit of your gift that remains for me—   5
believe it—I'm returning now since my gut is full.
But let your heart, kind, venerable, pardon me,
let the presumptions of love be forgiven.
On my behalf let that revered chorus adore Christ,
easing my guilty conscience.   10

11.13
[PL, col. 356; *MGH,* 264;
Reydellet, vol. 3, 122; DB, 556–57; George, *Poems,* 106]

In *carm.* 11.13, Fortunatus offers two gifts to Radegund and Agnes, a basket he fashions from simple twigs and chestnuts gathered from the ground that fill it. The simplicity of the gifts and of the poem set the poet in the proper spiritual relationship to his friends. What complication exists in the poem comes in the form of an allusion, in v. 4, to Virgil *Ecl.* 1.81, whose phrase "soft chestnuts" (*castaneae molles*) seems to control Fortunatus' identical wording.

> This twiggy basket was made by my hands,
> believe me, dears—mother, kind sister—
> and in it, country gifts borne by the fields,
> I send soft chestnuts, tree-tossed to the ground.

11.14
[*PL*, col. 356; *MGH*, 264; Reydellet, vol. 3, 123; DB, 556–57; George, *Poems*, 106]

The gift recalled in *carm.* 11.14 is milk, set out for Fortunatus by Agnes—but with the imprint of her fingers left behind in the cream gathered at top. There is no reason to think, as Nisard does, that Agnes actually sculpted something in the cream.[52] That goes against what the poet says in vv. 1–2 and relies on a too-literal understanding of v. 4. The imprint is a work of Daedalian skill because Agnes made it, not because it is high art: even the sweep of her fingers over the morning's cream becomes a thing of beauty in Fortunatus' eyes. The transience of the imprint, which dissolves in the breakup of the "skin" that holds the sculpture briefly in place, contrasts with the permanency of the image of Agnes in the poet's mind.[53] This mental imprint is thus expressed in a poem that celebrates a friendship that the poet hopes will be evoked in this way for many years to come (vv. 9–10).

> I spied fingers splayed through a milky gift,
> a cast of your hand where you snatched some cream.
> I must know: what made your soft nails sculpt it so?
> Was Daedalus your teacher in the plastic arts?
> Cherished love, the heist that you pulled off   5
> conjured an image of your absent face
> in my mind—a hope that cracked under flimsy skin,
> not even a dollop remained for me.
> God grant that you do this for a long time to come
> in this world, with mother long remaining at your side.   10

11.15
[*PL*, col. 356; *MGH*, 264; Reydellet, vol. 3, 123; DB, 556–57]

1 Cor. 3.2 provides a scriptural context for *carm.* 11.15, written to Radegund and Agnes to thank them for sending milk. Paul tells the Corinthians that

he fed them milk because they weren't ready for solid food, a sentiment
Fortunatus exploits in order to situate himself with proper humility in rela-
tion to his friends. Their milk, though real, nonetheless reminds him of his
spiritual state, which recollection brings some measure of spiritual health.

> What could mother and sister have given as sweet
> as the gift they sent to me just now—just so, mighty milk,
> on the authority of the apostle Paul, preaching to the
> > Corinthians,
> who ordered milk to be given to infirm souls?
> Your mind worries about my fortune;   5
> may God's goodly care always worry of yours.

11.16
[*PL,* cols. 356–57; *MGH,* 265;
Reydellet, vol. 3, 124; DB, 558–59]

The bold beginning of *carm.* 11.16, "I didn't know, believe me" (*nescivi, fateor,*
v. 1), suggests an urge to get to the matter at hand, which, beyond avowing
ignorance, includes in v. 2 a plea that the poet be returned to Agnes' good
graces: a deceitful doctor, so Fortunatus says, kept him from Agnes' meal (v.
4), the rub that has occasioned the poem's composition. While it is not clear
precisely how the doctor deceived Fortunatus, the poet's anger at being kept
from his friend's aid leads him in the poem's conclusion to condemn the doc-
tor's gluttony and incompetence (vv. 11–14).

More important are the details of friendship revealed in vv. 5–6, for in
these lines the poet uses a phrase, "my soul's delight" (*delicias animae . . . meae,*
v. 6) that cannot help but make readers recollect Catullus' Lesbia poems.
But to what end? By examining the resonances of the Latin word *delicias,*
"delight," in Fortunatus' poetry, Roberts denies the eroticism clearly pres-
ent in Catullus' use, claiming that the word refers in Fortunatus' hand to
"delights that appeal to the senses . . . [and] most often . . . and always in the
poems to Radegund and Agnes . . . to food delicacies."[54] My understanding
of these lines has them imagining a potential moment in the future when
Fortunatus is once again ill and, due to the slight of the present moment,
Agnes' good presence is not forthcoming. The poet wonders who might tender
him meals in such a circumstance if Agnes won't (*Quis mihi det reliquas epulas,*
v. 5), then bemoans the fact that her absence will mean that he will have no
one to call "my soul's delight," a term of endearment that evokes Catullus
and Lesibia (v. 6).[55]

If, as I understand it, the line is an instance of reported discourse in which Fortunatus quotes Catullus to Agnes, there can be no doubting the tone of *delicias:* since it is Catullus' word, it evokes in all its complexity the emotional and erotic habitats created by him in his Lesbia cycle. More apposite is the fact that Fortunatus quotes Catullus at all, and that he fears his recovery will be in doubt absent Agnes' sure presence. That presence becomes as much a part of Agnes' ministrations as the meals she offers, and part of the thanks the poet holds out comes, therefore, in this playful quotation.

The moment imagined here seems to run against the grain of expectations for monastic life: seemingly Agnes and Fortunatus were permitted to be alone together. But under what circumstances such meetings occurred, if at all, remains unclear.[56] However one wishes to read *carm.* 11.16, on the other hand, what better way to compliment the woman whose ministrations Fortunatus has unwittingly scorned than with these words; or to express the extent to which the hurt he might have caused runs at cross-purposes to the friendship that makes it matter so much?

> I didn't know sick-meals were prepared for me—truly:
> on that score I deserve a return to your graces.
> No one ever plucked me from your charms
> until a conniver's cheap trick put one over on me.
> Now who will minister meals to come,   5
> where I call you my soul's delight—and mean it?
> We're apart: I've taken to cultivating fasts
> for in losing you I've lost my appetite.
> Some word from you would be better for this hungry heart
> than a plate piled high—sweet words would fill again my soul. 10
> Strange to say, the doctor caused a grievous wound
> in tricking me—that's how a conniver proves his skill.
> Fish, fowl, it matters not, no meal ever satisfies him,
> yet he thought I could feed myself.
> But now, forgive me, please, well-stocked with goodness: 15
> it's the doctor's fault; don't make me shoulder the blame.

11.17

[*PL,* col. 357; *MGH,* 265;
Reydellet, vol. 3, 125; DB, 558–59]

Carm. 11.17 develops a theme pursued in *carm.* 11.13, where Fortunatus sent to Agnes and Radegund a handmade basket filled with chestnuts. Here the idea is similar, especially given the emphasis on the gift's size, which in this case is the poem itself rather than a basket.

I built this gift of love, hand-hewn,
I hope you or my Lady finds it sweet,
though, to all appearances, barely formed,
let a trifle swell in my affection.
Think of it: among lovers it's always the same: 5
to small gifts belongs a greater grace.

11.18
[*PL,* col. 357; *MGH,* 265–66;
Reydellet, vol. 3, 125; DB, 558–59]

The poet sends plums but anticipates some hesitancy on the part of his friends, especially Radegund, in accepting them. Has he sent them less savory gifts before? In trying his "pure meal," in any case, Fortunatus is sure the women will soon allow him to send even better, though unspecified, gifts.

Sent your way, a meal of black plums (as they're called);
please don't hate what the woods tossed to me,
for if you deign to taste these foresty fruits
I'll be able to satisfy you all the better with gifts, God-given,
not something hung from a shadowy branch (never fear),   5
not mushrooms that the earth gave up, but tree-tossed riches.
I'm not crude enough to send mother improper gifts:
to your lips, down your throat, don't resist a pure meal.

11.19
[*PL,* cols. 357–58; *MGH,* 266;
Reydellet, vol. 3, 126; DB, 560–61; George, *Poems,* 106–107]

Reprising the theme of illness found in *carm.* 8.11 and 11.16, the sick poet on doctor's orders cannot eat, but Agnes relieves him with a gift of milk that seems, given his hunger, incomparable. The conclusion is ambiguous. Fortunatus often uses the first person plural to stand for the singular, but in v. 8 either singular or plural makes sense. The poem can thus be understood to honor Agnes for a gift that pleases but also to include her in the joy of the table she sets simply by being the good friend that she is.

Amidst countless feasts you send a fast
and burn my soul gazing at mounded meals
that the eye covets but the doctor forbids,
a purring gut is muzzled by his hand on my mouth.
Still, when you drizzle creamy milk on my lips,   5

it's a present that any king would prefer.
I pray now, sister, with good mother, be happy,
for a kindly table of joy holds us.

11.20
[*PL*, col. 358; *MGH*, 266;
Reydellet, vol. 3, 126; DB, 560–61]

Agnes (possibly with Radegund) has sent eggs and prunes. If read as a companion piece to *carm.* 11.20, these gifts are perhaps a further ministration to the now-recovering poet. But Fortunatus has gorged on the eggs. Told to eat two, he scarfed down four, though he admits to his gluttony in order to make a spiritual point: in the same way that his belly obeyed Agnes by doubling the number of eggs she ordered him to eat, the poet hopes his soul can be doubly obedient to any spiritual orders she sends.

> All around, your delicacies wrapped in grass
> fatten me; eggs appear, and then prunes,
> gifts, pallid, dark, offered in tandem provide
> so varied a meal that I worry my gut won't keep the peace.
> Too late you ordered me to eat two eggs;   5
> I drank down four (I wouldn't lie to you).
> May my soul be privileged for all my days
> to obey you in the way I obeyed my gut just now.

11.21
[*PL*, col. 358; *MGH*, 266;
Reydellet, vol. 3, 127; DB, 560–61]

Fortunatus regularly uses amorous diction to prove friendship's staying power, and the words of *carm.* 11.21 are no exception. Here, away from Holy Cross, he avers that he would have returned had not inclement weather hindered him. The poem is written to Agnes, though the "you" of v. 2 (*nesciretis*) is plural, which may be an instance of poetic plural for singular or indicate that Radegund is also its recipient.

> If the rain-soaked wind hadn't held me back,
> unbeknownst to you, your lover would have returned.
> I'm unwilling to be detained one hour more,
> I can see again when my lover appears.

11.22
[*PL*, col. 358; *MGH*, 267;
Reydellet, vol. 3, 127; DB, 560–61]

This brief poem demonstrates that in some instances Agnes and Fortunatus were permitted if not to dine together, then at least to be in each other's presence when the poet took his meals. The ambiguity of v. 3 does not allow readers to know whether the poet is merely enjoining Agnes to speak when she dines with him, or whether Fortunatus simply eats in her presence, since the use of "we" in v. 3 (*nos*) may be the plural of respect. I translate it as a singular here.[57] The title of the poem and the contents to Book 11 style the meal as a "banquet," a "feast" (*convivium*), but this only underscores a copyist's understanding.

> For goodness' sake—and God's, for the sake
> of all that mother loves, your brother has one wish:
> say something when I sit down to eat;
> if you do that will be my desert.

11.22a
[*PL*, col. 358 (= 11.23); *MGH*, 267;
Reydellet, vol. 3, 127–28; DB, 560–63]

This poem is not listed in the contents to Book 11, for which reason Leo assigned it the number 11.22a. In nearly all the manuscripts, on the other hand, the title is "Likewise concerning the same thing as in the previous poem" (*Item de eadem re*). A subscription in four manuscripts notes that the poem contains ten rather than six lines, thus demonstrating that some copyists understood *carm.* 11.22a to go with 11.22.[58] A case could surely be made that *carm.* 11.22a describes the meal that Fortunatus enjoys after requesting that Agnes speak to him when they dine. It is more than an ordinary meal, to be sure, and on that score would fit the requirements of a banquet or feast, the *convivium* mentioned in the title to *carm.* 11.22. It would also point up the weightiness of Agnes' words, since it is a meal comprised of rich foods: milk, vegetables, eggs, and butter. But whether read in close connection to *carm.* 11.22 or separately, this poem links Radegund, but especially Agnes, to the pleasures of a fine meal.

> I spread myself over jumbled delights that gorged my belly
> as I scarfed it all down: milk, vegetables, eggs, butter.
> Now platters fitted out with new dishes appear,

a polyglot meal, more sweetly pleasant.
Butter was served to me with milk: 5
fat calls to mind what it once had been.

11.23

[*PL,* cols. 358–59 (= 11.24); *MGH,* 267;
Reydellet, vol. 3, 128; DB, 562–63; George, *Poems,* 107]

This and the poem that follows it are considered in some manuscripts to be of
a piece, since a subscription to *carm.* 11.23a notes that it is a poem of sixteen
lines, that is, comprised of its two lines plus the fourteen verses of *carm.* 11.23.
The longer poem offers a variation on the theme of overindulgence explored
elsewhere. Here the emphasis is on drinking too much, which, so Fortunatus
claims, has inhibited his ability to articulate clearly what he would like to say,
not to mention his capacity to write it down. Still, the love that friendship
fosters has coaxed a poem from his impaired hand.

It is easy enough to read *carm.* 11.23a as the concluding couplet to 11.23,
not least owing to the ways in which it offers the sort of shift in perspective
that often characterizes the endings of Fortunatus' poems. In this way, the
declaration that logically concludes the description of intoxication, in which
Fortunatus admits that he managed to write something despite his debility,
is followed by a couplet that brings Agnes into the poem's narrative. She
becomes a figure of recovery, at which point the potential for Fortunatus to
overindulge recedes, replaced by the pleasant conversation she offers.[59]

Pleasures to the right, flavors to the left,
while I was dozing and being fed
(mouth open, eyes closed,
chewing as dreams danced before my eyes),
dears, believe me, I was embarassed   5
to slur words already hard to find;
my fingers couldn't clasp a pen, paint a verse,
tipsy *Musa* had made my hands shake;
the wine was so well suited to me, to my friends,
that the table seemed to swim in a sea of red.   10
Still, for mother and sister I was able to manage
this brief poem, sweetly spoken.
Though sleep now reins me in from all sides,
love coaxed a halting hand to scribble these words.

11.23a
[*PL,* col. 359 (= 11.25); *MGH,* 268;
Reydellet, vol. 3, 129; DB, 562–63]

A charming mistress talked and fed me back to life,
a plate of delicious jokes tops things off.

11.24
[*PL,* col. 359 (= 11.26); *MGH,* 268;
Reydellet, vol. 3, 129; DB, 562–63]

In part, daily life at Holy Cross consisted in the keeping of the divine office, that is, praying at set hours throughout the day. The completion of the last of these hours, Compline, also marked the closing of the convent for the night, after which the nuns were inaccessible until Lauds, or morning prayers, around 6:00 A.M. In *carm.* 11.24, Fortunatus uses the deadline imposed by Compline as an excuse to send to Agnes and Radegund a mere four lines. Anything longer might delay the poem's arrival, and time is of the essence as night begins to fall. A pun in v. 1 on "completed" and "Compline," found, respectively, in the Latin words *conplestis* and *conpleta,* helps to further the point that less is often more where friends are concerned.

If you haven't completed Compline (as they call it here),[60]
I ask humbly that you own these words—take them gladly.
Don't turn your nose up because there aren't many. My
                                        heart would say
(if you were to ask) that in this narrow gift is a widening love.

App. 10
[*MGH,* 282;[61] Reydellet, vol. 3, 151; DB, 646–47; George, *Poems,* 119]

Having been banished from their presence, Fortunatus has heard that Agnes and Radegund may allow him to return (vv. 1–2). He asks for a note to confirm the rumor, since the handwriting will prove their love. Based on its proximity to App. 11, a poem that seems to commemorate Christmas, Nisard understood this poem to celebrate a reconciliation that occured on that festive day.[62]

A sweet-spoken story is on peoples' lips
if I'm welcome again at your kind table;
jot down, send on, your souls' good intentions[63]

in a letter, handwritten to prove your love:
with a loyal affection, equally sweet, mother, sister,   5
celebrate gladness with dancing sounds.

App. 12
[*MGH,* 283;
Reydellet, vol. 3, 151–52; DB, 648–49]

Given the reference in v. 13 to a daughter presumed to be Agnes, App. 12
seems to be addressed to Radegund.[64] The poem contrasts its author's poetic
debility with protestations of filial love. Fortunatus is embarassed by the
sluggishness of a Muse who withholds inspiration, forcing him to look to
his own heart for poetic motivation. He is goaded by a love (vv. 1–6) that
reminds him of his father's honor, his mother's affection, and the habits of
his grandmother (vv. 8–10). Verse 13 indicates that Agnes is with Fortunatus
and that Radegund is excluded from their company, though not from their
thoughts.

In a poem I want to run up and down the plectrum;
   not unusually (but more slowly) I start to clop a beat,
but the smart-talking Muse refuses her pipe,
   disoriented, ignorant of her own metier.
Though this rickety poem makes my heart waver,   5
   its solitary love made me write with abandon.
To me: dear, kind, decent, sweet, good forever,
   your affection braces me like a father's honor,
through you my heart reclaims my mother
   and the way her mother always acted—in you I see her again.   10
In a trembling poem I say *hello,* humble, lowly,
   a servant commending my soul to you
with the daughter birthed in the grace of your heart:
   God keep them in the world for a long time to come.

App. 15
[*MGH,* 284;
Reydellet, vol. 3, 153; DB, 650–51; George, *Poems,* 120]

Fortunatus hurriedly composes six verses before Holy Cross is locked for
the night. Sharing with *carm.* 11.24 the conceit of the convent's impending
close, App. 15 puts to the side the prior poem's emphasis on the paucity of
a poetic gift in order to focus on the safety of Agnes and Radegund, which,

in the poet's hands, transmogrifies into a moment of cosmic implication in which angels direct the women's souls. The poem plays on the meanings of the verb *ferre,* "to bear, to carry," and its compounds: night is "safety-bearing" (*salutifera,* v. 1); the poet demands that his prayers be "borne" to the ladies (*ferant,* v. 2); and he commands the women to "bear" to him two verses for the six he has sent (*ferte,* v. 6).

> Mother, sister, linger in the safety that night brings on,
> let the lucky prayers of a son and brother say it:
> let a flight of angels return to your hearts
> and rule your souls with their own consolations.
> Night creeps in to cut me short: 5
> for only six little verses please send back, say, two.

App. 16
[*MGH,* 284;
Reydellet, vol. 3, 153–54; DB, 650–51]

Given that the addressee of App. 16 is in a position to order Fortunatus to compose poetry (v. 9), Radegund seems the likely recipient,[65] though the title simply reads, "Likewise, something else" (*Item aliud*).[66] Dronke sees in the poem's opening a bow to passionate love (vv. 1–4) that dissolves in v. 5 into patristic *amicitia.*[67] Perhaps it could be said that the poet imports amatory discourse in order to better animate the bonds of friendship in the here and now, which serves as prelude to the friendship that will be shared in eternity (vv. 5–8).[68] We have seen the poet in prior poems, such as *carm.* 8.8, gently tug Radegund back to the realities of temporal life, and the concluding couplet clearly places poet and addressee in present time (the Latin *hinc,* v. 10, "from this place," is emphatic). Nor, as Reydellet notes, would it be appropriate for Fortunatus to claim that he will recite poems to Radegund (or Agnes) in heaven, should one choose, as Blomgren does, to see in the final verse of the poem a depiction of eternity.[69] This helps perhaps to strengthen the argument that has Radegund as the poem's recipient.

The space implied in the poem's concluding line does not seem to be in question, but its temporality is, for the final word of v. 10, *loquar,* "I say, I speak," can be present subjunctive or future indicative. If the first, then the idea is purposive, that is, "take [the poems that I've been ordered to write] with you from this place, so that I might say only worthy things to you." On this view, the poet is inspired by the fact that Radegund (or Agnes) commands him to write, while her acceptance of his compositions inspires him to write more. If the verb is future, on the other hand, the idea is that in taking his poems with her, Radegund (or Agnes) will be able to hear the voice of the poet, even though he is otherwise absent. I prefer the second of these readings and translate the final line accordingly, but the ambiguity heightens the ways in which the poet seeks to honor his friend—whichever of the women it is—by managing to say in one line both that she inspires him and that his poetry can in his absence bring him into her presence.

> I coveted what the shadows dispersed,
> but that darkness didn't steal you entirely from me:
> the soul sees lovers even vanished from view,
> my soul was there—where I could not be.
> Incomparable the place that lovers never leave,   5
> who light their eyes on those they covet,
> with Christ, prince of goodness, in their midst,
> his love a sacred ligature that binds the heart.
> Let more poems be ordered down the years:
> take them away from here—and there I will say worthy
>   things to you.   10

App. 17
[*MGH*, 285;
Reydellet, vol. 3, 154; DB, 652–53]

As the vocative "sisters" (*sorores*, v. 1) indicates, App. 17 is addressed to the nuns of Holy Cross, but it is unclear who the unnamed woman (*hanc*) in v. 3 might be. The poet is emphatic that he is excluded from this woman's presence and, implicitly, from the community of nuns, while the woman and the sisters are holed up like lovers (*amantes*, v. 3). It would seem likely that Radegund or Agnes is meant, for there are any number of poems earlier in the collection that worry about separation during times of spiritual retreat while framing in amatory diction the longings that absence cultivates. Roberts senses in Fortunatus' words more than the usual intensity owed to spiritual retreat, betokening perhaps a fresh resolve on the part of the sisters to keep male visitors at a distance. His translation of v. 4, "it is the common wish that we keep apart," thus picks up on the idea of punishment or even banishment.[70]

I would stress the implications of the verb *retinere*, "to keep," "to hold in check," and so on. The emphasis is not so much on the poet's exclusion, though that is mentioned, as on the communal decision to keep this woman, whoever she is, secluded—not to punish Fortunatus or to enforce some tightening of the convent's rules, but for her own good. That sense is explicit in the primary meanings of this verb, which include "to prevent from escaping," "to detain a person forcibly," "to hold prisoner," and so forth.[71]

In this case, perhaps the always-active Radegund, who keeps herself busy, as Fortunatus and Baudonivia tell us, cleaning, cooking, and serving the sisters, has fallen ill due to overwork or old age. In such a circumstance, even more than normally is the case, she might desire to keep to her typical routine, as if to doubly mortify her flesh with illness and with work. The sisters are lovers to her in their care and concern, while the poet is a different sort of lover, but no less insistent or caring—hence this poem. Not least, this reading is strengthened by the hope Fortunatus expresses in vv. 5–6 that Radegund might live longer still for the community and for him. The "we" of v. 5 (*nobis*) seems to be a true plural that takes in the sisters and him, while the phrase, "for each" (*per singula*, v. 5) pertains to the poet's hope that in the future Radegund can be a good presence in all lives, one person at a time.

> Sisters: in God's face clap your voices into prayers,
> for joys so tantalizing that abide with you.
> I'm cut off, on the outside looking in: you keep this woman
> > as lovers do,
> your common pleasure is not common to me.
> May she live for a long time, for each of us yet,   5
> may she blossom—involved in every good thing.

App. 18
[*MGH*, 285;
Reydellet, vol. 3, 154–55; DB, 652–53]

App. 18 reprises the situation imagined in *carm.* 11.3 (and, presumably, 11.5), which also celebrated Agnes' *natalicium*, the anniversary of her installation as abbess of Holy Cross. The joy of the earlier poem is absent here, however, since Fortunatus is not present for the latest celebration. His isolation is juxtaposed to a happiness that seems, at least to Fortunatus, to surround the world.[72] Though the poems of the Appendix are assumed to be randomly gathered,[73] the placement of this and the previous poem seems purposeful, since both play on the senses of the verb *retinere*, used by Fortunatus in App. 17 to qualify Radegund's separation from him. Here the verb assists the poet in describing his own predicament: he is the one kept away, though for reasons otherwise unstated (v. 10). It is tempting to associate this separation with the gossip mentioned in *carm.* 11.6,[74] but the fact that a poem has been sent, with the idea that it will be received and read, lessens the likelihood that Fortunatus has been banished or censured. While it is true, in v. 10, that the poet bemoans

the fact that he has been kept from the latest festivities, his phrasing is, as
Roberts notes, vague.[75]

> Alone in a world that fêtes you as abbess,
> my absence is a bitter pill today.
> If I were hiding in the hinterlands (let us say),
> posthaste I'd be on my way to you.
> The world sends gifts—I have nothing for sister   5
> but what I've gathered in this spot: fruits—mulberries—
> and a plot in your heart where absent love abides.
> I've sent a gift: please, willingly have it,
> let God, all-powerful, spare a mother and sister
> who haven't urged me to return to them.   10
> May pious celebrations down the years unfold
> to your maturity, making Radegund happy—and brother.

App. 20
[*MGH,* 286;
Reydellet, vol. 3, 156; DB, 654–55]

Inspired by Fortunatus' concern for Radegund's well-being, App. 20 seems
to be missing a couplet, since the shift from v. 4 to v. 5 is otherwise abrupt.[76]
This goes to the nature of the poems gathered in the Appendix, some of
which are in various states of completion. The sentiment of App. 20 does
not suffer for the presumed lacuna. Fortunatus frequently worries over his
friends' well-being and is overjoyed when he hears fresh news of their safety.
This is hardly unusual in an age of primitive medicine, especially given the
fact that Radegund pushed herself physically even, and perhaps never more
intensely than, when she was ill, as App. 17 suggests. The similarities linking
that poem to App. 20 point to principles of ordering that argue against a
haphazard collation.

> A servant worries over a kind lady's care:
> is this a happy day at Holy Cross?
> As you rejoice and clap your prayers, my joy is greater still
> for answered vows—as long as you thrive.
> If the messenger has already said goodbye, he's that much
>   closer to a good reply: 5
> no hiding for him under cloak of night—he better be
>   standing here first thing.

App. 21
[*MGH,* 286;
Reydellet, vol. 3, 156; DB, 654–55]

App. 21 plays on the idea of separation by imagining Radegund to be a sheep whose lamb, Fortunatus, has been taken from her. Without the sustenance of her milk, the lamb is lost, frightened, and can find no pleasure in the world (vv. 1–6).[77] Agnes is brought into the poem's situation, too, for, in Radegund's absence, she offers comfort to the aggrieved poet, at least affording him the chance to reclaim a part of his equilibrium. For Agnes and Radegund each hold one half of the poet's soul, and he can never be whole until he finds himself again in their good presence (vv. 9–12).

At the same time, the concluding references to Martin and Hilary refocus attention on Radegund, now in the company of these two exalted men. While there is perhaps a subtle bow to Gregory of Tours suggested in the mention of his glorious predecessor, St. Martin, more than geography informs the reference to Hilary, for this fourth-century bishop of Poitiers was also a champion of Christian orthodoxy. His devotion to the faith thus highlights Radegund's Catholic Christianity, an important point to stress in sixth-century Gaul, where more than a few powerful figures were adherents to heresies of several stripes, not least Brunhilde, whose conversion from Arianism to Catholicism Fortunatus celebrates in *carm.* 6.1a.

The presence, in v. 11, of the verb *retinere,* "to hold back," "to retain," "to keep," reminds readers of App. 17.3 ("you keep this woman as lovers do," *vos hanc retinetis amantes*) and App. 18.10 ("who haven't urged me to return to them," *quae non egerunt me retinere sibi*). In the first piece, Radegund seemed to be held back from the poet's presence, perhaps owing to overwork or illness (or both); whereas, in the second, Fortunatus bemoans the fact that his good friends have not seen fit, for whatever reason, to keep him among their fold. In App. 21 the issue is no less that of separation, but now it is the poet's soul that is sundered, with one half kept by Radegund, the other half by Agnes. This separation is such that the poet, so he says, feels whole only when he is in their joint presence.

> Yesterday was a blur of hours.
> I wasn't granted the privilege of mother's voice,
> like a loving lamb snatched from mother's milk
> sad, bewildered, wayward in fields of grass,
> now skirting the meadows, bleating to the wind,   5
> now returning to the fold: nothing pleases without mother:
> thus I suffer when deprived of your words,

four walls could scarcely hold me here.
But I say *thank you* to sister, peaceful, dear,
who soothed me with the power of goodness.   10
You hold the half of me, that lady keeps the other:
I am whole again only when I see you both.
Dear, my prayer for you now is this: let Martin and Hilary
                                        be your props;
let God, our single hope, tuck you and your children in.

App. 22
[*MGH,* 286–87;
Reydellet, vol. 3, 157; DB, 654–57]

App. 22 recollects a time when Fortunatus worked side by side with Radegund,
cooking a meal and cleaning the kitchen. He calls this moment "a revelation"
(*splendor,* v. 13) and presents it as proof that, were he present, he would do
whatever Radegund ordered, viz., sing in German (vv. 3–6), fetch water, tend
the garden, and so forth (vv. 7–12).[78] As thanks, and owing to his absence,
the poet sends his *Life of Marcellus,* a biography still extant that praises an
early bishop of Paris. Despite any stylistic foibles in his telling of Marcellus'
life, Fortunatus hopes that this figure's saintliness will prove rewarding (vv.
15–18) but concludes that nothing would be sweeter than some direct word
from Radegund (vv. 21–22).

If I can't be at your side, from afar I can make an offering
                                        to you
that proves my passion, mother, beloved.
If I were before you I would do your bidding
and, finessed by little things, my bumblings would perhaps
                            prove pleasing to you.
With my heart's abandon I would sing in German   5
on a shepherd's pipe sounding in mother's ear,
I would run myself ragged, serving the whims of the moment,
my neck, in service to its mistress, bowed,
my fingers would never excuse themselves, the hand that
                                    wrote this
wouldn't hesitate to run the deep well of water dry,   10
to weed vines, aerate the garden,
to plant, to nurture, sweet seeds (glad to do it).
It was a revelation to burn with you—in the kitchen,
to bathe in clean water—the scorched pot.

I've sent now Marcellus' bounty for you, recompense,
                              something to take my place,   15
heavens' habitat was granted his blessed life,
and if the way I've related his story rankles,
let his saintly yarns capture your soul.
For my sake live down through time, with daughter, with
                              a crop of sisters,
and in the company of a virgin choir let God's sheepfold grow.   20
Whiffs of flowers drizzled in bee-dropped honey
wouldn't be sweeter than your *hello*.

App. 23
[*MGH,* 287–88;
Reydellet, vol. 3, 158–59; DB, 656–59]

Addressed to Agnes, this poem fits into a cluster of similar pieces gathered in the Appendix that speaks to Fortunatus' separation from Holy Cross on account of gossipmongering. App. 24, to follow, is clearly written in this vein, as is *carm.* 11.6, in which the poet claims a spiritual love for Agnes amidst whispers that his devotion is in fact physical. Here, a rapprochement has apparently been achieved, since the poet speaks in v. 29 of returning to Holy Cross. Part and parcel of that return, however, is the composition of App. 23, whose words, so the poet notes, he has been ordered to write (v. 29). The topics the poem takes up—the impermanence of the world, the brevity of life, the power of Christ and of lives lived in holy imitation of him—make the poem appear to have a penitential function: if the rumors have merit, then pondering these themes can only brace Fortunatus spiritually in the future.

By affirming Agnes' exemplary spirituality and chastity, the figures of Thecla and Susanna further Fortunatus' meditation on these themes. As told in the apochryphal Acts of Paul and Thecla, Thecla was converted to Christianity by Paul himself, abandoned a young suitor while she was still a virgin, renounced the life that had been planned for her, followed Paul to Antioch, Myra, and Seleucia, and suffered ridicule, derision, and even torture for her beliefs. The affiliation thus does much to ennoble the abbess of Holy Cross, but it goes, too, to Fortunatus' interest in depicting the aspersions leveled against Agnes in the most derogatory light. They are akin to those cast against Thecla herself, a paragon of virtue and exemplar of spiritual power—utterly groundless.

Although there is a saint by this name, a virgin and martyr who died around 295 C.E., Fortunatus must mean by Susanna the figure whose story is told in the Old Testament Apocrypha as part of the book of Daniel. Susanna's beauty, so the story goes, obsessed two Jewish elders, who, seeing her one day bathing in her garden pool, told her they would accuse her of adultery unless she submitted to their passions. She refused and, on the authority of the two elders would have been sentenced to death but for the intercession of Daniel, sent by God, who heard Susanna's prayer. Daniel exposed the elders' fraud, who were themselves put to death instead. Thus an innocent girl was saved from an unjust death.

If *carm.* 11.6 and App. 24 are any indication, Susanna's story points to the ways in which Agnes, too, may have been unfairly accused of indiscretion, but it provides a means by which Fortunatus is able to assert Agnes' innocence and his own. For it is the rumormongers, like the elders of Susanna's story, who are to blame, not the innocent Susanna, for which reason, along with Thecla, she is fitting company for Agnes' entry into Paradise. Agnes and Susanna are further connected in the catacomb images that imagine Susanna to be a lamb, a depiction that points to a pun on Agnes' name in the Latin word for "lamb," *agnus.* The poem's final verse is perhaps surprising: after composing a poem that trumpets the power of otherworldliness, Agnes must still, Fortunatus says, think of him when she re-reads his words.

> A pool of nectar is no sweeter to me than your goodness, Agnes:
> I cherish you heart and soul, God knows.
> See: change is swift around us all,
> our lives a tuft of bird's down in the wind,
> seconds, hours, a sop to uncertainty,   5
> who divines a man's beginning or end?
> Today: deep snow has burdened the crests of trees
> and hard winter bows branches rigidly deformed,[79]
> but tomorrow, perhaps, if the sun flashes limpid
> in the east, snow and ice will flow away.   10
> For we are fallen, beguiled by things we can't know,
> how we should live, when we will die,
> and since the ambit of all things yields to ruin,
> who is wise knows eternity's embrace.
> Christ be your dignity, your hope—and lover,   15
> fasten on his powerful safety to the exclusion of all else,
> with your all unhesitatingly turn to his love,
> let your chaste body preserve its faith after he is bridegroom
>   to you.
> If sleep sneaks in, hold Christ to your heart:
> in darkness you bear the armature of light,   20
> cultivating him in your mind, you are flanked by a noble guard;

and if a bandit should suddenly rage, peace is a protection for
your heart;
fall into Christ's arms freely, completely,
whoever is his fears no foul.
Do this—and when the world's judge comes to your bed,   25
you will glint, unblemished, your body unspoiled;
then let Thecla and Susanna take you in,
sisters to your coming with a shining lamp, a joyous choir.
Words, mandated, I give over to you in brief as I now return:
think of me when you read them again.   30

App. 24
[*MGH,* 288;
Reydellet, vol. 3, 159; DB, 658–59]

This and the previous poem ought to be read in tandem, though App. 24 is presumably earlier than 23, since in it the poet reveals, not for the first time, that charges have been leveled against him. App. 24 also brings to mind the details of *carm.* 11.6, where the poet speaks of rumormongering while denying any physical longing for Agnes. But the measured tone and earnest determination of the earlier poem are replaced here by a significantly harsher stance. The stakes have clearly been raised: Fortunatus cannot write, his heart races, he lacks focus, the man of words loses his poetic bearings (vv. 1–4). And whereas in *carm.* 11.6 the poet was not separated from Agnes, banishment clearly is an issue now, since Fortunatus pleads to Radegund, the poem's addressee, to be allowed to return to her and to Agnes (vv. 13–16).

The shifting numbers of key verbs in the poem—"take" (*reddite,* v. 11) is plural but "believe" (*crede,* v. 12), "justify" (*excusa,* v. 13), and "whisper" (*feras,* v. 14) are singular—led Nisard to suggest shifting addressees: Agnes for vv. 1–6; Agnes and Radegund for vv. 7–10; Agnes and the other sisters at Holy Cross for vv. 11–12; and Agnes alone for vv. 13–16.[80] But the plural *reddite* can be understood to be spoken to the clouds (*nubila*) mentioned in v. 5 that would bear Fortunatus' words, if only he had an audience to hear them.[81] The shift from the plural to the singular witnessed in vv. 11–12 thus indicates that Radegund is the addressee, the "you" mentioned earlier in the poem, in v. 6 (*tibi*) and v. 8 (*vos*). This shift is perhaps also a measure of the poet's initial description of himself in vv. 1–4, a way to suggest that he is flustered, unable to think straight or to put his jumbled thoughts into words, addressing now himself, now Radegund, now the clouds, in an effort to make some sense of his predicament.

On the other hand, the final four verses of the poem are clearly addressed to Agnes, who will plead the poet's case to Radegund, the "mother" mentioned in v. 14 (*matris*). Roberts understands the poem's concluding verses to represent Fortunatus' embarrassment at having disappointed Radegund: she had requested Fortunatus' presence, but for unstated reasons he was unable to comply with her request (v. 14). In v. 15 he promises to make the attempt to come soon.[82] I hear in v. 14 Fortunatus' plea to be allowed to return to Holy Cross and in v. 15 an eagerness to be on his way. The striking final line of the poem, in which the poet asks to be scolded and beaten is, given the seriousness of the supposed charges and the forboding of the poem's opening lines, an admission on Fortunatus' part that he deserves to be reprimanded and punished. He may be free of guilt, as he says in v. 12, but that he has somehow acted in a way that invited misinterpretation seems to weigh on Fortunatus' mind, especially since this is not the first time gossip has flown.

> Unfocused, vexed, stooped under a burden of worry,
> my heart beats against a thousand feelings, I'm unable to
> > > send a poem;
> slashed by gossipy whispers, I can't find the fluency for songs,
> flummoxed, I don't know what to say.
> Damn, if you were willing to listen: of a sudden, on clouds   5
> I would send my sad confession to you; if I knew how
> I would take up Daedalus' faltering wings
> and already a lover would have returned to you, faster than
> > > these words can say.
> God, who quickens the hungry heart,
> has known what trouble vexes my soul, but keeps it always
> > > to himself.   10
> Take my promises to a kind lady (since I can't);
> still, believe that the fault wasn't mine:
> justify things, if perhaps you can (I swear the firmament as
> > > my witness)
> and whisper in mother's ear that I wish to return.
> Plead for a servant: I will pack my sack and come at once,   15
> and when I am back in your good presence, I wish to be
> > > scolded—I want to be beaten.

App. 25
[*MGH,* 288;
Reydellet, vol. 3, 160; DB, 658–59]

App. 25 may well speak to the circumstances recounted in App. 23 and 24 that attend to gossip and banishment. The poet is separated from his friends, who are always in his heart, but if words can ease separation by calling those who are absent to mind, then absence might be considered a fiction. Because the addressees of the poem, "mothers and ladies" (*matribus ac dominis*), are plural, Fortunatus may be addressing the sisters of Holy Cross collectively. Reydellet understands the phrase to mean "Radegund and Agnes,"[83] a plausible reading, given that Fortunatus regularly uses the plural of respect in addressing his closest friends. On the other hand, if the phrase is truly plural, the emphatic first word of the poem, *supplicibus* ("supplication"), might suggest a repentant poet working his way by stages back to the good graces of the women of Holy Cross.

> Let this poem, sent with words like wagging tongues,
> say *hello* to mother and to lady, with prayers dressed in
> > supplication.
> While the road wends away, refusing to let you see me again,
> at least let me prove my affection by sending a poem in
> > my stead:
> if its sweetness holds us always in a present resolve,   5
> in a loving heart— I never left.

App. 26
[*MGH,* 288;
Reydellet, vol. 3, 160; DB, 660–61; George, *Poems,* 120]

Like *carm.* 8.6 and 11.13, this poem exploits the contrast of small gifts offered in handmade vessels. The container in this case is a "wrapper," that is, the papyrus on which the poem is written, the Latin for which, *fano* (v. 5), puns on *fanum,* "church" or "temple."[84] The poem is thus a "temple" made of words that holds the poet's offering, a conceit that links the sacral world of Holy Cross to the secular realm of poetry writing and gift-giving. The presents of fruits and words may well be in token of Fortunatus' return to his friends' good graces. In any case, the unity the poet trumpets clearly places this poem outside the events recalled in App. 23 and 24.

I'm a son to mother, at the same time a brother to sister:
I bear smalls gifts in a resolute heart.
Joined to you, one-third of three, I offer three gifts to you two:
sugared fruits fitting for souls so sweet.
But forgive me for the sort of wrapper they've got: 5
let these gifts be carried in a basket of words.

App. 27
[*MGH*, 289;
Reydellet, vol. 3, 160–61; DB, 660–61]

In the first verse of App. 27, the verb *direxi* ("I have directed, steered, sent")
reminds readers of *carm.* 7.11 and 11.12, where the same verb, falling also in
these poems' initial lines, is used to send letters to Jovinus and gifts of food to
Radegund and Agnes. Rather than words or food, the gift this time is a cross,
sent to Agnes, who is enjoined at the poem's end to bear the poet's greetings
to Radegund. The word "brothers" (*fratres*) in v. 2 would seem to designate
Radegund and Agnes in their mutual roles as monastic "brethren," but sub-
sequent verses tug readers away from this understanding, since Fortunatus
conceives of the cross as a gift that brings him closer to Agnes (vv. 3–4). Thus
the word more likely designates Fortunatus and Agnes.[85] The poem plays on
the idea of mediation. The cross that Fortunatus sends negotiates the space
that separates him from Agnes in the same way that Christ mediates divine
and human space. The poem beckons Agnes to its own wisdom in the same
way Christ will beckon from the cross to Agnes when she spies it hanging on
her wall (v. 10). But when she sees it she will think of Fortunatus, too.

To you I have sent a symbol, an incomparable gift:
let this cross protect two brothers as one,
let it govern our hearts, now yours, now mine,
let love become the common good.
When it comes to you it will still be mine;   5
since you love it, nothing will do me more good.
In your soul evermore covet its beauty
where Christ will then have eternity's might;
he hung once in goodness on that hallowed cross,
he extends his hand when he hangs for you now.   10
Reverently I say *hello* to the mother we share,
let her linger as comrade a while longer still.

App. 28
[*MGH,* 289;
Reydellet, vol. 3, 161; DB, 660–63]

App. 28 strikes a theme similar to that of *carm.* 11.4, in which Fortunatus asks Radegund to drink some wine as an antidote to her wearying workload. Here there is no injunction to drink, only a celebration of Radegund's capacity for hard work: she sweats in the kitchen, burns her hands (vv. 5–6), and otherwise presents to the world a flurry of activity (vv. 3–8). The poet feels guilty—presumably he writes in order to assuage the emotions he expresses in v. 7, where he depicts himself, for whatever reason, as unable to interrupt Radegund's toil. But now, back at his writing, Fortunatus admits that he is too lazy to offer help (v. 10). Agnes, he decides, can lighten the load (vv. 11–12). The theme of hard work and the shared burdens of administering Holy Cross are mirrored, in the poem's conclusion, in the aid God must grant the two women for all that they do in their respective roles at the convent.

> Sweet, rich, full of decency, you manage your duties with
> such care
> that you make a great harvest from a single seed;
> you exhaust your limbs without complaint, while time wends
> its fugitive way:
> peace without remit will come with Christ.
> You drip sweat as you put up meals for the sisters,   5
> you burn your hands, douse them in water.
> I pray for the strength to interrupt you,
> but your mountain of work stomps on my will.
> And now you're back to cooking meals, lighting fires
> and naturally I'm too lazy to help mother.   10
> But let a daughter pitch in once more, since she's here,
> lightening the load by doing her share.
> Let the redeemer of the world give his help to you both:
> let him foster this aid a long while still.

App. 29
[*MGH,* 289–90;
Reydellet, vol. 3, 161–62; DB, 662–63]

App. 29 recollects a trip to an island, perhaps Cordouan, a possibility strengthened by the holy figures to whom Fortunatus refers in v. 10, for Cordouan was known to be inhabited by men who repaired to it in order to further their sanctity.[86] Moreover, its harsh terrain and exposed location, lying at the mouth of the Gironde as it empties into the Atlantic, would make it, as Fortunatus describes it in v. 9, infertile. Its infertility, wherever it may lie, makes it unlikely that the three gifts mentioned in v. 8 were grown there. Reydellet thinks the gifts in question are water, earth, and sky,[87] but they could just as easily be Radegund, Agnes, and Fortunatus, each a gift to the other in the friendship they share. The isolation of the setting, in any case, seems to lead to a moment of clarity that friendship sustains. No matter how crowded a city Fortunatus might inhabit, it is a lonely place absent his friends (vv. 11–12).

> We forge ahead—and make out an island in foam,
> where the errant ocean flows, fades,
> and rises to the sky with a regimen of waves
> barking, swayed by their own ferocity;
> where the sandy shore turns away, taking the turbulence   5
> until the sea swells, while the crumpling coast hides its decline.
> The cold has withdrawn; heat once more is upon the land[88]
> and three gifts, God-given, are in this place;
> infertile, though it harbors blessed fruits,
> since its sands feed men worthy for heaven.   10
> If I were holed up in some city, but without you,
> amidst a sea of humanity I'd be alone all the same.
> Mother and sister, let me deserve to see you dine with God,
> happy when his blessed, high feast appears.
> If brother Simplicius returns quickly, as I hope,   15
> to him, for me, say *hello;*
> and I ask: commend me through your sisters;
> let Christ's love make us his own.

App. 30
[*MGH,* 290;
Reydellet, vol. 3, 162; DB, 662–63]

George reads in App. 30 "fear and gloom," and senses in the lack of references to Agnes or Radegund an indication that "lengthy absence, or death itself, is [the poem's] subject."[89] If my less sinister understanding is correct, the poem develops familiar themes: Fortunatus has heard that he may not get an accustomed meal at Holy Cross and, since he seems to be planning an ascetic retreat of some kind (v. 5), will not allow himself to be deprived of food. If fasting is for the moment only (v. 7), then the poet will have nothing to fear. If, on the

other hand, some longer fast is planned, then the poet demurs, though what
he might do is hard to know.

> I've heard—I confess it—that longs fasts are planned:
> if they come to me I won't stand for them.
> I grow pale in the face of hunger; already I hear its whispering
> > approach:
> don't perish in its grip; let it pass quickly by.
> Soon I'll be gone, holed up in a cave,   5
> provided I'm not conquered by a fasting gut.
> But if others feed on piety and grace just now
> I will have nothing to fear.

App. 31
[*MGH,* 290–91;
Reydellet, vol. 3, 163; DB, 664–65; George, *Poems,* 120–21]

App. 31 seems to have been written while Fortunatus was still separated from
Holy Cross for reasons suggested in App. 24. Poetic contact remains a given
and, in this instance, the poet speaks of poems sent to him by Radegund
(*matrem,* v. 10). The description of her in the poem's opening verses is consis-
tent with what Fortunatus has said elsewhere, not least that she continues to
work in the kitchen and to prepare sometimes lavish meals. But the poet is fed
by the words Radegund has sent, which become for him a meal unto them-
selves, their sweetness making them honey-like, a description that playfully
suggests the wax on which they were inscribed (vv. 1–5). But the sweetness of
Radegund's meals, though enough for the rest, is not enough for Fortunatus,
who wants something "sincere" (*sinceros,* v. 8) from Radegund's lips, presum-
ably the "sweet" words that would allow the poet to return to Holy Cross. If
this reading is correct, then the subsequent verses of the poem imagine the
longed-for outcome. Fortunatus prays that Radegund love him again (v. 9)
and that his prayers for forgiveness be answered, thus proving Radegund more
truly a mother (v. 10). He can only return on Radegund's recommendation
(v. 11), but he wants what he deserves, whatever that might be (v. 12).

> You sent great poems to me on little wax tablets,
> sweet enough to fill empty honeycombs (you can do it).
> You tender festive meals in many courses,
> but to me, who long for them more, your words are food
> that you send, little lines polished in a soothing style   5
> whose meanings bind our hearts.
> You traffic in a sweetness all-satisfying to the rest,

but I want your words to be sincerely sweet.
Amidst the prayers of the sisters, I long for you to love
                                        me again,
that my prayers might prove you to be more truly a mother.   10
Let me return to the fold on your good word,
so that through you I might get what I deserve.

Endnotes

1. To Placidina

1. *Leontii:* Duchesne (vol. 2, 61, s.v. *Leontius* II); *PLRE* (774, s.v. *Leontius* 3, *Leontius* 4); *Ruricii* and *Anicii:* Stroheker (no. 218).

2. *Carm.* 1.15.1–92 provides biographical detail contextualized by Prinz, Wood, and Brennan ("Image").

3. Stroheker (no. 58); *PLRE* (1042, s.v. *Placidina*).

4. See de Maillé (85–87) and Reydellet (vol. 1, 43–45, nn. 84, 85, 88), who contextualize these villas.

5. On *carm.* 1.15 see also Brennan ("Image," 121–24) and George (70–73). On *carm.* 1.8 and 1.9 see deG. d'Hestroy; de Maillé (91); George (108 with n. 15); and Reydellet (vol. 1, 170–72). On *carm.* 1.10 and 1.11 see de Maillé (75) and George (108–109); on *carm.* 1.12 see Vieillard-Troiekouroff (284–85, s.v. *Saint-Vivien,* no. 283).

6. *PL* (col. 45).

7. Nisard (62, xvii).

8. Meyer (75); Reydellet (vol. 1, 177–78, n. 83).

9. On Placidina, see also Brennan ("Episcopae") and Griffe; and on Leontius, see Brennan ("Image," 121–28).

10. *Prosperitas . . . plena* = "rich bounty"; *carm* 8.10.14, *omnia plena* = "everything bursts" on Radegund's return from Lenten retreat.

2. To Felix

1. For Eumerius see Stroheker (nos. 125, 148). For Felix see Duchesne (vol. 2, 366–67, s.v. *Felix*); Stroheker (no. 148); *PLRE* (481–82, s.v. *Felix* 5); with George (77, 113–23).

2. *HF* 5.5, 5.49, with Reydellet (vol. 1, 193, n. 86).

3. *HF* 6.15, with George (115).

4. *Carm.* 3.8: George (77–79) and Roberts (51–53); *carm.* 3.4: George (117); *carm.* 3.6, 3.7: George (118–20); *carm.* 3.9: George (120–23).

5. George (114).

6. See also Chadwick; Musset (112–15); Geary (124–27).

7. Corroborated at *HF* 4.4, 5.29, 5.31.

8. See *carm.* 8.5, p. 80, *carm.* 2.4, 2.5, with 1.16, an abecedarian piece.

9. See also Aupest-Conduché, and McDermott.

10. *PL* (col. 134, n. j); Aupest-Conduché.

11. Reydellet (vol. 1, 104, n. 64; 105, n. 65).

12. Reydellet (xxviii).

13. Meyer (87); Reydellet (vol. 2, 34, n. 102).

14. Virgil, *Ecl.* 5.14, 10.51; Calpurnius, *Ecl.* 3.46.

15. *PL* (col. 137, n.d.); Reydellet (vol. 2, 173, n. 104).

16. *Carm.* 6.9.1, *Expecto te* ("I'm waiting for you") is similarly abrupt; see p. 48.

3. To Vilicus

1. *Ep. Aust.* 15, 17 (*MGH,* Epist., 129–30).

2. DB (217, n. 58; 218, n. 59).

4. To Hilary

1. Thus Luchi (*PL,* col. 141–42, n. g).

2. *Glor. Conf.* 42 (*MGH,* SRM, vol. 1, 744–820); Van Dam (*Confessors*), with Stroheker (no. 194) and *PLRE* (598, s.v. *Hilarius* 1).

3. *PLRE* (598–99, s.v. *Hilarius* 3).

4. Stroheker (no. 195) and Reydellet (vol. 1, 115, n. 104); Koebner (72) says only that the poet wrote "to a Hilary."

5. To Bertrand

1. Meyer (83) with Koebner (75 and n. 2), and Reydellet (vol. 1., 197–98, n. 105); this is the husband of Placidina (No. 1).

2. Death: *HF* 8.22, with *PLRE* (227, s.v. *Bertchramnus*); Duchesne (vol. 2, 61–62, s.v. *Bertechramnus*); other appearances: *HF* 5.18, 5.47, 5.49, 7.31, 7.36, 8.2, 8.7, 8.18, 8.22, 9.33.

3. *HF* 8.2 with Meyer (83) and Reydellet (vol. 1, 197–98, n. 105).

4. *HF* 5.47, 5.49, 7.31, 7.36, 8.7, 8.18.

5. The last of the imperial *fora,* or public squares, built in Rome between the time of Caesar and the emperor Trajan, this forum is the largest, constructed in 112/113 C.E. on the occasion of the Roman conquest of Dacia.

6. To Agricola

1. *PLRE* (31, s.v. *Agricola* 1) with *HF* 5.45 and 8.5; Stroheker (no. 143); mentioned by Fortunatus in his *Life of Germanus* (*MGH,* SRM, vol. 7, 372–418).

2. Duchesne (vol. 2, 193, s.v. *Agricola*).

3. Duchesne (vol. 2, 483–84, s.v. *Agricola*) with *HF* 9.41.

4. *PL* (col. 144, n. g); Nisard (109, xix).

5. Reydellet (vol. 1, 198, n. 111) and DB (225, n. 71) offer fuller explanations of this intriguing argument.

6. Verse 1 = epithets of one, two, and three words; v. 2 = two three-word epithets: *praesul, honoris apex, generis fideique cacumen,* / *cultor agri pollens, pastor opime gregis.*

7. *HF* 5.45.

7. To Avitus

1. *HF* 4.35 with *Vit. Pat.* 2 (*MGH, SRM,* vol. 1, 661–744); McDermott and Peters (180–95); Duchesne (vol. 2, 36, s.v. *Avitus*); Reydellet (vol. 1, 119, n. 117).

2. *HF* 4.12, 4.35, 5.11, with George (127–28 and n. 121).

3. See also Brennan ("Conversion") on *carm.* 5.5.

9. To Paternus

1. Corrected by Luchi, *PL* (col. 149, n. d.); Nisard (109, xxv); Reydellet (vol. 1, 125, n. 131). Fortunatus wrote a life of the more famous Paternus (*MGH,* AA, 33–37).

10. To Rucco

1. *HF* 6.27, 7.4, 7.16, 10.14, 10.26, with Duchesne (vol. 2, 471, s.v. *Ragnemodus* [*Rucco*]); Faramod may be the addressee of *carm.* 9.12.

11. To the Archdeacon of Meaux

1. Duchesne (vol. 2, 477, s.v. *Medovechus,* with 476–78).

12. To John

1. *Glor. Mart.* 1.19, 1.88 (*MGH, SRM,* vol. 1, 484–561); Van Dam (*Martyrs*), with Reydellet (vol. 1, 127, n. 135).

15. To Gregory

1. Listed by Gregory at *HF* 10.31; two works are now lost: a commentary on the Psalms that survives only in its incipit and table of contents, and a book of the Masses of the poet Sidonius Apollinaris.

2. See also Van Dam (*Saints,* 52–81).

3. See also George (48–57) on this complex poem.

4. Meyer (47) and, on *carm.* 5.3, Roberts (106–22).

5. Meyer (46) and Brennan ("Image," 131–32), argue for a public function, but Roberts (121–22) dissents while contextualizing the poem's composition.

6. Reydellet (vol. 2, 167, n. 51).

7. Brennan ("Being Martin," 127 with n. 46).

8. Brennan ("Being Martin," 127).

9. Roberts (217, 271, n. 70) notices that the final four letters of *sacer*, "holy," when scrambled, spell *arce*, "citadel," a word that is also an anagram of *care*, "dear."

10. Isidore (*Etymologiae* 15.16.8) with *MGH* (107) and Reydellet (vol. 2, 173, n. 105).

11. But Roberts (271) notes, "the language of love and friendship is undeveloped . . . [while both men] see the relationship as one between unequals, akin to that between patron and client."

12. *PL* (cols. 197–98, n. j), but this runs counter to the idea that a book has been sent.

13. Reydellet (vol. 2, 173, n. 107), with DB (318, n. 67).

14. Roberts (279–80).

15. Roberts (280).

16. Reydellet (vol. 2, 173, n. 107).

17. Nisard (142, b).

18. Reydellet (vol. 2, 173, n. 107).

19. Reydellet (vol. 2, 173, n. 109).

20. *Veneranter . . . salutant* = "their double dignity venerates you with *hellos*"; *carm.* 5.9.13, *venerande, salutant* = "Reverend, [your own daughters] say *hello.*"

21. *Culmen honore tuo, lumen amore meo* = "towering in your honor, a beacon in my love"; *carm.* 5.8.1, *culmen honoratum . . . lumen opimum* = "tower of honor . . . rich beacon."

22. *Pignore amicitiae* = "by friendship's pledge"; *carm.* 3.28.1, *pignus amicitiae . . . nostrae* = "our friendship . . . is pledged."

23. *Officiis generose piis* = "nobly doing piety's duties"; *carm.* 5.12.3, *officiis venerande sacris* = "revered for duties sacredly done."

24. *Sacer arce* = "sacredly strong"; *carm.* 5.8.3, "like a sacred fortress."

25. *Summe pater* = "father on high"; *carm.* 5.7.1, to Felix, "father, Godlike."

26. Brennan ("Being Martin," 133–34), translating vv. 16–22, with DB (323, n. 75).

27. Roberts (275–78), with a translation of the poem.

28. *Summe sacerdos* = "eminence," but at *carm.* 5.12.1 *summe sacerdotum* = "highest of priests."

29. Thus Reydellet (vol. 2, 40) and Roberts (272).

30. Where, at v. 10, Fortunatus also calls himself a "foreigner," *peregrinus* (translated as "wander").

31. *HF* 4.35.

32. *Summe sacerdos* = "eminence" and at *carm.* 5.14.19; *carm.* 5.12.1 *summe sacerdotum* = "highest of priests."

33. Attaining heaven: Roberts (271–72); Reydellet (vol. 2, 40).

34. *Pastor honoris apex* = "the flock cranes its neck to your honor"; *carm.* 5.10.2, *religionis apex* = "holy to the hilt"; *carm.* 5.15.5 *humilis apex* = "poor poem."

35. *Venerabilis arce sacerdos* = "priest of revered strength"; *carm.* 5.8.3, 5.13.1, *sacer arce* = "sacred fortress," "sacredly strong."

36. *Decus alme patrum* = "your kindness glorifies the Fathers"; *carm.* 5.8.1, *decus almum* = "kindly glorious."

37. *Religionis amor* = "the reverent love you"; *carm.* 5.10.2, *religionis apex* = "holy to the hilt."

38. *Virt. Mart.* 4.25 (*MGH,* SRM, vol. 1, 584–661; Van Dam (*Saints,* 199–307).

39. "Health—hello" attempts the Latin pun, *redditus ergo isti, pater alme,* **saluto saluti***.

40. *Lumen generale* = "beacon to the people"; *carm.* 5.7.1, to Felix, *lumen venerabile cunctis* = "revered, beacon to all."

41. *Culminis* = "towering"; *carm.* 5.8.1, *culmen honoratum* = "tower of honor"; *carm.* 5.12.2, *culmen honore* = "towering in [your] honor"; *carm.* 5.15.1, *culmen honoris* = "towering honor."

42. *Arce* = "strength"; *carm.* 5.8.3, 5.13.1, *sacer arce* = "sacred fortress," "sacredly strong"; *carm.* 5.16.1, *venerabilis arce sacerdos* = "priest of revered strength."

43. Roberts (273–74), with a translation of vv. 1–8.

44. *Summe pater patriae* = "father, no one higher to home or hearth"; also *carm.* 5.10.1, 8.16.3, to Gregory, and 9.10.1, to Rucco; *carm.* 5.7.1, to Felix, *summe pater* = "father, Godlike"; *carm.* 5.8b.9, 5.14.19, 5.15.7, *summe sacerdos* = "priest, highness," "eminence"; 5.12.1, *summe sacerdotum* = "highest of priests."

45. *Celsum et generale cacumen* = "Heavenly summit open to all"; *carm.* 8.14.1, *lumen generale* = "beacon to the people."

46. *Toronicensis apex* = "Touraine cranes it neck"; *carm.* 5.10.2, *religionis apex* = "holy to the hilt"; 5.16.1, *pastor honoris apex* = "the flock cranes its neck to your honor."

47. One for every line except v. 3: "to me" (*mihi,* v. 1); "my" (*meo,* v. 2); "to me" (*mihi,* v. 4); "me" (*me,* v. 5; translated there as "I"); "I beg" (*quaeso,* v. 6).

48. *Sacer arce Gregori* = "sacredly strong; Gregory"; *carm.* 5.8.3, "like a sacred fortress, Gregory"; *carm.* 5.13.1, "Gregory, . . . sacredly strong."

49. See also Roberts (255–56 with nn. 35, 37, 38).

50. Roberts (279), with brief analysis, translates vv. 1–4.

51. Also at *carm.* 8.18.5.

52. Brennan ("Being Martin," 135) and Roberts (282–83) analyze the poem and translate vv. 1–8.

53. Verse 11: *rector* = "leader"; v. 13: *praesul* = "bishop"; both are rarely used of Gregory.

54. Not the robe of the papacy, as Nisard (43) thinks; Reydellet (vol. 2, 161, n. 108) notes the scriptural precedents: Rev. 6.11: "Each of them was given a white robe and they were told to be patient"; Rev. 7.9: "They stood before the throne and the Lamb, wearing white robes"; Rev. 7.13: "Who are these wearing white robes?"

16. To Aredius

1. *HF* 8.14, 8.27, 10.9; *PLRE* (106–107, s.v. *Aredius* [*St. Yrieix*]); Vieillard-Troiekouroff (277–78).

2. *HF* 10.29.

3. Reydellet (vol. 2, 77, n. 89) with Longnon (497).

4. Nisard (172, vii) also reports Brower's view, but Reydellet (vol. 2, 77, n. 89) remains skeptical.

5. *Felici tramite* = "happy path"; *carm.* 8.19.1, *tramite munifico* = "generous path."

17. To Ultrogotha

1. The present St.-Germain-des-Prés stands on the site of Childebert's original church.

2. See also Reydellet (*La Royauté,* 326–27) with George (101–105).

3. See also George ("Variations," 60–66).

4. George (103): v. 1, *hic ver purpureum* = "Here crimson spring," is owed, without change, to Virgil, *Ecl.* 9.40.

18. To Dynamius

1. Reydellet (vol. 2, 180–81, n. 104); he eventually added *patricius* to his title.

2. See also *HF* 4.43, 6.11, 6.33, 8.12, with George (141).

3. George (142 with n. 56): one verse of Dynamius' poetry survives.

4. *PLRE* (430, s.v. *Dynamius 1*); two letters presumed to be from Dynamius' hand also survive, on which see George (141–42 with nn. 54 and 57) and *Ep. Aust.* 12, 17 (*MGH,* Epist., 127, 130–31).

5. Koebner (17–20); Stroheker (164, no. 108); *PLRE* (429–31, s.v. *Dynamius 1*).

6. *HF* 7.11.

7. *PLRE* (430, s.v. *Dynamius 1*).

8. George (142, n. 59).

9. *HF* 10.2.

10. Bertrand = *carm.* 3.18.17; Anfion = 3.24.5; John = 3.28.4; Gregory = 5.8.4, 5.9.13, 5.12.3.

19. To Gogo

1. *PLRE* (541–42, s.v. *Gogo*); George (136–40); Roberts (257–60).

2. *Carm.* 7.1.35 and 7.1.41–42, with George (136, n. 20).

3. *HF* 5.46.

4. *Ep. Aust.* 13, 16, 22, 48 (*MGH,* Epist., 127–28, 130, 134–35, 152–53), with George (136–37 and nn. 22 and 27).

5. *HF* 6.1 reports the death; Fredegar 3.59 reports the execution (*MGH,* SRM, vol. 2), but *PLRE* (542, s.v. *Gogo*) and George (136, n. 24) are unconvinced.

6. George (139–40); Roberts (260), with a translation of vv. 1–30 (256–57).

7. Reydellet (vol. 2, 87, n. 7).

8. Nisard (176, ii).

20. To Lupus

1. Military exploits: *carm.* 7.7.49–60; diplomacy: *carm.* 7.7.25; with *HF* 4.46 and George (79).

2. *PLRE* (798–99, s.v. *Lupus 1*); George (80, n. 80); Reydellet (vol. 2, 184, n. 28), with *carm.* 7.7.45–46.

3. *HF* 4.46.

4. *HF* 6.4, 9.12, 9.13, with George (132–33); *HF* 10.20.

5. George (80–81) with Roberts (57–59), who translates vv. 51–60.

6. Consolino (1363–64) discusses the elegiac background of this poem.

21. To Magnulf

1. *PL* (col. 246, n. k); *HF* 7.27.

2. Reydellet (vol. 2, 185, n. 54).

3. Leo (*MGH,* 164, ad loc.) glosses: "since my poem is not able to say everything, for this reason it will remain silent"; but the line seems to say the opposite: "since it can't sing it all, nor does it desire to be quiet."

22. To Jovinus

1. Koebner (17); Stroheker (no. 205); George (141); *PLRE* (715–16, s.v. *Jovinus* 1).

2. *HF* 4.43.

3. *HF* 6.7, 6.11.

4. Roberts (265–69) and translations of vv. 59–64, 89–96, and 109–16.

5. George (146).

23. To Felix

1. *PL* (cols. 250–51, n. s).

2. *MGH* (169); Reydellet (vol. 2, 109).

3. Referred to at *Vit. Mart.* 4.665–67 (*MGH,* 293–370); *Virt. Mart.* 1.15 (*MGH,* SRM, vol. 1, 584–661); Van Dam (*Saints,* 199–307).

4. Reydellet (vol. 2, 109, n. 82).

24. To Berulf

1. *HF* 5.49.

2. *HF* 5.49, 6.12, 6.31, 8.26, summarized in *PLRE* (229–30, s.v. *Berulfus*).

25. To Gunduarius

1. *PLRE* (567, s.v. *Gunduarius*) with Reydellet (vol. 2, 115, n. 99).

26. To Flavus

1. *HF* 5.45, 10.28.

2. Meyer (90).

3. Roberts (253).

4. Koebner (67).

5. Reydellet (vol. 2, 115, n. 100).

28. To Sigimund

1. George (28).

2. Reydellet (vol. 2, 118, n. 108).

3. *Requiro, carm.* 6.9.3 and 7.20.2 = "I search," "I'm a busybody"; *requirit,* 7.20.8 = "ordered"; *requirit,* 7.9.4, *requirat,* 7.18.7 = "demands."

29. To Sigimund and Alagisilus

1. George (28), with Reydellet (vol. 2, 117, n. 106).

2. Thus Reydellet (vol. 2, 118, n. 109), though Roberts (253) considers them brothers.

30. To Boso

1. *PLRE* (247, s.v. *Boso 1*).

31. To Galactorius

1. *PLRE* (501, s.v. *Galactorius*).

2. *HF* 8.22; *PLRE* (563, s.v. *Gundegisilus*) with Reydellet (vol. 2, 122, n. 122).

3. Roberts (261–62) translates vv. 13–16 and by way of summary partially translates vv. 1–12.

4. Roberts (262) with Reydellet (vol. 2, 123, n. 125) notices that *pices,* "ink," puns on what is written, *apices,* "poems."

5. DB (545, n. 108): Justinian, Byzantine emperor (re. 527–565) was of humble origins, served as a military aid to his uncle Justin, and then ran the empire in Justin's name when Justin succeeded Anastasius I.

32. To Chilperic I and Fredegund

1. The other surviving sons, Chilperic's half-brothers Charibert (d. 567), Guntram (d. 592), and Sigibert (d. 575) were the issue of Lothar's second marriage, to Ingund.

2. George (96–101), with a translation in George, *Poems* (40–50).

3. *HF* 6.46.

4. *PLRE* (292–96, s.v. *Chilpericus 1*).

5. George, *Poems* (73–80), a translation.

6. The tradition of reading *carm.* 9.10 as a sycophantic sop to Chilperic is resisted by George (48–57), whom I follow here.

7. George (88–91), with George, *Poems* (80–86), a translation.

8. George, *Poems* (88, n. 92), with translation.

9. George, *Poems* (88, n. 96, with 88–89), a translation of *carm.* 9.5.

10. Meyer (127).

11. Koebner (105).

12. *HF* 6.2, with Reydellet (vol. 3, 183, n. 58).

13. George (91–92).

14. DB (481, n. 43).

33. To Droctoveus

1. Reydellet (vol. 3, 33, n. 95) with DB (494–95, n. 84).

2. Bertrand = *carm.* 3.18.17; Anfion = *carm.* 3.24.5; John = *carm.* 3.28.5; Gregory = *carm.* 5.8.4, 5.9.13, 5.12.3; Dynamius = *carm.* 6.9.1.

34. To Faramod

1. Koebner (38, 105) citing Meyer (20), who lacks substantiation, but taken for granted by Reydellet (vol. 3, 34, n. 96), though not *PLRE* (477, s.v. *Faramodus*).

2. *HF* 10.26; Meyer (21).

3. Reydellet (vol. 3, 34, nn. 97, 98).

4. Nisard (229, xii).

35. To Lupus and Waldo

1. *HF* 8.22.

2. Nisard (234, xiii).

3. *HF* 8.39.

4. Reydellet (vol. 3, 183–84, n. 99), who reports Ewig's view.

5. Nisard (234, xiii), with Reydellet (vol. 3, 183–84, n. 99); Meyer (21) also places both men in Paris on the strength of v. 9.

6. *Virt. Mart.* 3.50 (*MGH,* SRM, vol. 1, 584–661); Van Dam (*Saints,* 199–307); this is not, in any case, Lupus of Champagne (No. 20).

7. *HF* 6.35 with Reydellet (vol. 3, 35, n. 100).

36. To Chrodinus

1. *HF* 6.20.

2. Fredegar 3.58–59 (*MGH,* SRM, vol. 2), with *PLRE* (312–13, s.v. *Chrodinus*).

3. Also so styled in the title of the poem and in the contents to Book 9 ("To Duke Chrodinus," *Ad Chrodinum ducem*).

4. Fredegar 3.58 (*MGH,* SRM, vol. 2); *HF* 6.20.

5. DB (499, n. 94).

37. To Armentaria

1. Stroheker (no. 35); *PLRE* (121, s.v. *Armentaria*).

38. To Sigoald

1. *PLRE* (1150–51, s.v. *Sigivaldus* 3); Reydellet (vol. 3, 95, n. 190); DB (540–41, n. 98); presumably he continued in this role throughout Fortunatus' stay in Austrasia.

2. *HF* 7.14.

3. George ("End Game," 39–41).

4. Reydellet (vol. 3, 98, n. 198).

5. Meyer (34–35); DB (543, n. 105).

39. To Agiulfus

1. *PLRE* (30, s.v. *Agiulfus 1*); DB (643, n. 55).

40. To Radegund and/or to Agnes

1. Fortunatus, *De vita S. Radegundis* (*MGH,* SRM, vol. 2, 364–77); McNamara and Halborg (70–94).

2. As Medard died in 560, Fortunatus never met him, though *carm.* 2.16 honors his memory, as does a prose life attributed, but not incontrovertibly, to Fortunatus.

3. Baudonivia, *Vita Radegundis* (*MGH,* SRM, vol. 2, 377–95); McNamara and Halborg (86–104).

4. *HF* 9.42 with *carm.* 8.3.59.

5. *HF* 9.39.

6. A less charitable view of this friendship may be found in Dill (386–91).

7. George (168).

8. *MGH* (193, ad loc.).

9. Reydellet (vol. 2, 149, ad loc.).

10. Reydellet (vol. 2, 70, n. 4) reads the odors of the virtues into the fragrances mentioned here and in *carm.* 8.7.

11. George, *Poems* (70, n. 6) with DB (450, ad loc.).

12. In the word *ordo,* "line" or "row": Reydellet (vol. 2, 150, n. 76).

13. George, *Poems* (71, n. 7).

14. Ibid.

15. But Roberts (289, v. 18) suggests that *plus ornant proprias te redeunte comas* = "their blossoms will be all the finer at your return."

16. Roberts (289, n. 101).

17. Reydellet (vol. 2, 152, n. 84).

18. Roberts (289).

19. George (169).

20. *Carm.* 8.10.14, *omnia plena* = "everything thrives"; *carm.* 1.17.7, *prosperitas plena* = "rich bounty."

21. Consolino (1353–56, but also passim).

22. Roberts (308–309).

23. Reydellet (vol. 3, 114).

24. DB (547).

25. *Vit. Rad.* 24 (*MGH,* SRM, vol. 2, 364–77); McNamara and Halborg (79).

26. George (172).

27. Luchi's view (*PL,* col. 39), repeated by Thierry (381–82), but George (214 with n. 14) and Reydellet (vol. 3, 115, n. 43) demur.

28. Tardi (85) develops the implications of this title, but Brennan ("Career," 69–70) is unconvinced.

29. George (214).

30. Roberts (302) notices "an element of human frailty" here lacking in Fortunatus' biography of Radegund.

31. Reydellet (vol. 3, 115, n. 45).

32. Reydellet (vol. 3, 115, ad loc. with n. 46) follows Luchi (*PL,* col. 352, ad loc.).

33. Expanded in my "Catullus Among the Christians" (27–43).

34. But see also Roberts (301): "Agnes has kept to her bed all day, eating nothing and speaking to neither of them"; George (170): "it is a neat, evocative, gently teasing little poem."

35. Adams (181, 187).

36. Roberts (300–301), with Brennan ("Deathless Marriage," 89).

37. George (173).

38. Thus Roberts (300), who translates vv. 5–12.

39. Leo (*MGH,* 260, ad loc.).

40. Roberts (300 with n. 122).

41. Reydellet (vol. 3, 188, n. 49).

42. Nisard (265, vi).

43. Reydellet (vol. 3, 188, n. 49).

44. Roberts (305).

45. Although if my understanding and translation of App. 30.5–6 (pp. 121–22) is correct, Fortunatus seems about to embark on a retreat that includes fasting.

46. But Roberts (294, vv. 1–2): *iubes cognoscere semper / qualiter hic epulis te tribuente fover* = "you ask to know how I enjoyed the banquet you provided."

47. Roberts (292).

48. Reydellet (vol. 3, 120, n. 53) with D'Angomont.

49. George, *Poems* (105, n. 8).

50. The poem's natural imagery is analyzed by Guillaume-Coirier.

51. So Reydellet (vol. 3, 122, n. 59): Agnes' culinary talents and her spirituality are to be understood as parallel; by spreading his verses the poet is like a satisfied gourmand who distributes what he has left over. George (175) and Roberts (302) wonder if there is a connection between guilt (v. 10) and the difficulties recalled in *carm.* 11.6.

52. Nisard (265, xiv) with Reydellet (vol. 3, 123, n. 60).

53. Roberts (312–13), with translation.

54. Roberts (309).

55. Roberts, where vv. 5–6 = "who could give me any other banquet, when I declare faithfully, you are the delicacies of (i.e., you feed) my soul."

56. George, *Poems* (105, n. 8).

57. So Roberts (294, n. 111): "say something when I take my meal."

58. Reydellet (vol. 3, 127, n. 67).

59. Dronke (vol. 1, 207) makes Radegund the addressee, with difficulty, in my view.

60. Reydellet (vol. 3, 129, n. 70): *conpleta* = "Compline."

61. *PL,* which prints Luchi's 1787 edition, lacks the Appendix, not discovered until 1831.

62. Nisard (285, x), but Reydellet (vol. 3, 193, n. 83) is unconvinced.

63. George (119, n. 42): v. 3, *tabula* = "wax tablets"; but v. 4, *littera,* "letter/epistle," suggests something more permanent than wax.

64. Thus Nisard (285, xii) with Reydellet (vol. 3, 194, n. 88).

65. Thus Reydellet (vol. 3, 195, n. 93), but for Roberts (310, n. 143): "nothing . . . specifies whether Radegund or Agnes is meant."

66. Twenty-two of thirty-one poems in the Appendix are so titled, with Σ providing no contents for purposes of comparison.

67. Dronke (205–206 with n. 1), a translation whose v. 4, *nam quo forma nequit, mens ibi nostra fuit* = "my mind was there where your shape cannot be," Roberts (310, n. 143) rightly challenges with, "my mind can be where my body cannot." But Dronke's v. 3, *amantes* = "lovers," is superior to Roberts (310), *amantes* = "friends."

68. Thus Roberts (311).

69. Blomgren (*Studia,* 1933–1934, 137–39), but Reydellet (vol. 3, 195, n. 93) is unconvinced.

70. Roberts (306), with translation of vv. 1–4.

71. *OLD* (1641, s.v. *retineo,* 1, b).

72. Roberts (306–307), with translation.

73. Thus George, *Poems* (xxii): "a random and unsystematic collection."

74. Roberts (307), who ultimately reserves judgment.

75. Ibid.

76. Thus Leo (*MGH,* 286, ad loc.), with Reydellet (vol. 3, 156, n. 102).

77. Roberts (311–12) contextualizes the literary backdrop of the poem's opening verses.

78. Roberts (309–10 with n. 140) contextualizes the poem's elegiac backdrop.

79. Roberts (298) analyzes the Horatian backdrop of vv. 7–8.

80. Nisard (286–87, xxiv), dismissed by Reydellet (vol. 3, 159, n. 110).

81. Thus Reydellet (vol. 3, 159, n. 112).

82. Roberts (302–303): v. 14, *me neque velle moras* = "I did not want any delay"; v. 15, *citius remeare parabo* = "I'll try to come soon." But the complete thought of v. 14 includes

the second half of the pentameter, *matris in aure feras* = "bear in the ear of mother that I do not wish delays," i.e., "tell mother I want to come home," while the initial words of v. 15, *oret pro famulo* = "plead for a servant," contextualize what follows, i.e., "plead for the servant, and [if you are successful] I will prepare quickly to return."

83. Reydellet (vol. 3, 160, n. 115).

84. George, *Poems* (120): *fano* = "shrine," but Reydellet (vol. 3, 196, n. 116) follows Nisard (37) in distinguishing *fano, fanonis*, "wrapper," from *fanum, -i*, "temple."

85. Thus Reydellet (vol. 3, 196, n. 117).

86. Nisard (287, xxix).

87. Reydellet (vol. 3, 197, n. 124).

88. On this line's corruption see Reydellet (vol. 3, 197, n. 124).

89. George (174).

Works Cited

Adams, J. N. *The Latin Sexual Vocabulary*. Baltimore, 1982.

Aupest-Conduché, D. "Les travaux de saint Félix à Nantes et les communications avec le sud de la Loire." *Actes du 97e Congrès national des Sociétés savants, Nantes, 1972, Les Pays de l'Ouest. Etudes archéologiques*. Paris, 1977, 147–63.

Blomgren, S. "In Venantii Fortunati carmina adnotationes novae." *Eranos* 69 (1971): 104–50.

———. "In Venantii Fortunati carmina adnotationes." *Eranos* 42 (1944): 100–34.

———. *Studia Fortunatiana*. 2 vols. Upsala, 1933–1934.

———. *Studia Fortunatiana*. Upsala, 1933.

Brennan, B. "Deathless Marriage and Spiritual Fecundity in Venantius Fortunatus' *De virginitate*." *Traditio* 51 (1996): 73–97.

———. "Episcopae: Bishops' Wives Viewed in Sixth-Century Gaul." *Church History* 54 (1985): 311–23.

———. "The Career of Venantius Fortunatus." *Traditio* 41 (1985): 49–78.

———. "The Conversion of the Jews of Clermont in A.D. 576." *Journal of Theological Studies*, n.s. 36 (1985): 321–37.

———. "The Image of the Merovingian Bishop in the Poetry of Venantius Fortunatus." *Journal of Medieval History* 18 (1992): 115–39.

———. "'Being Martin': Saint and Successor in Sixth-Century Tours." *The Journal of Religious History* 21 (1997): 121–35.

Cartellier, W. "Die Römischen Alpenstrassen über den Brenner, Reschen-Scheideck und Plöckenpass." *Philologus*, supp. 18.1 (1926): 1–186.

Chadwick, N. "The Colonisation of Brittany from Celtic Britain." *Proceedings of the British Academy* 51 (1965): 225–99.

Consolino, F. E. "*Amor Spiritualis* e linguaggio elegiaco nei *carmina* di Venanzio Fortunato." *Annali della Scuola normale superiore di Pisa, classe di lettere e filosofia* 7 (1977): 1351–68.

Conte, G. B. *Latin Literature: A History*. Translated by J. B. Solodow, revised by D. Fowler and G. W. Most. Baltimore and London, 1994.

Cook, G. trans. *From the Miscellanea of Venantius Fortunatus: A Basket of Chestnuts*. Rhinebeck, New York, 1981.

D'Angomont, T. "'Les viandes en sauce au miel' chez Fortunat (*Carm.* XI, 10)?" *Revue du Moyen Âge Latin* 23 (1967): 55–63.

de Maillé, G. *Recherches sur les origines chrétiennes de Bordeaux*. Paris, 1959.

deG. d'Hestroy, B. "Les Deux Poèmes de Fortunat en l'honneur de Saint Vincent." *Études mérovingiennes: Actes des journées de Poitiers, 3 Mai 1952*. Paris, 1953, 127–34.

Dill, S. *Roman Society and Gaul in the Merovingian Age*. London, 1926.

Dronke, P. Medieval Latin and the Rise of European Love Lyric. 2 vols. Oxford, 1968.

Gauthier, N. *L'Evangélisme des pays de la Moselle: La province romaine de Première Belgique entre Antiquité et Moyen-Age (IIIe-VIII siècles)*, Paris, 1980.

Geary, P. *Before France and Germany: The Creation and Transformation of the Merovingian World*. Oxford, 1988.

George, J. "Variations on Themes of Consolation in the Poetry of Venantius Fortunatus." *Eranos* 86 (1988): 53–66.

———. "Venantius Fortunatus: The End Game." *Eranos* 96 (1998): 32–43.

Griffe, E. "Un évêque de Bordeaux au vie siècle: Léonce le Jeune." *Bulletin de littérature ecclésiastique* 64 (1963): 63–71.

Guillaume-Coirier, G. "A propos du décor vegetal d'un repas: Réalité, culture et spiritualité chez Fortunat (*Carm*. XI, 11)." *Revue de philologie* 74 (2000): 115–22.

Halporn, J. W., M. Ostwald, and T. G. Rosenmeyer. *The Meters of Greek and Latin Poetry*. Norman, Okla., 1980.

James, E. *The Franks*. New York, 1988.

Konstan, D. *Friendship in the Classical World*. Cambridge, 1997.

Longnon, A. *Géographie de la Gaule au Vie siècle*. Paris, 1878.

Luck, G. *The Latin Love Elegy*. New York, 1959.

Macchiarulo, L. "The Life and Times of Venantius Fortunatus." Ph.D. diss., Fordham University, 1986. McDermott, W. C. "Felix of Nantes: A Merovingian Bishop." *Traditio* 31 (1975): 1–24.

McDermott, W. C. "Felix of Nantes: A Merovingian Bishop." *Traditio* 31 (1975): 1–24.

McDermott, W. C., and E. Peters, eds. *Monks, Bishops, and Pagans: Christian Culture in Gaul and Italy, 500–700*. Philadelphia, 1975.

McKitterick, R., ed. *New Cambridge Medieval History*. Vol. 1. Cambridge, 1995.

McNamara, J. A., and J. E. Halborg, with E. G. Whatley, eds. and transs. *Sainted Women of the Dark Ages*. Durham, N.C., 1992.

Musset, L. *The Germanic Invasions: The Making of Europe, A.D. 400–600*. Translated by E. James and C. James. University Park, Penn., 1975.

Prinz, F. "Die bischöfliche Stadtherrschaft im Frankenreich von 5. bis zum 7, Jahrhundert." *Historische Zeitschrift* 217 (1973): 1–35.

Pucci, J. "Catullus Among the Christians." In *Through a Classical Eye: Transcultural and Transhistorical Visions in Medieval English, Italian, and Latin Literature in Honour of Winthrop Wetherbee*, edited by A. Galloway and R. F. Yeager. Toronto, 2009.

Quesnal, S., ed. and trans. *Venance Fortunat, Vie de Saint Martin. Venance Fortunat Oeuvres*. Vol. 4. Paris, 1996.

Raby, F. J. E. *A History of Secular Latin Poetry in the Middle Ages.* 2 vols. Oxford, 1957.

Reydellet, M. "Tradition et nouveauté dans les *Carmina* de Fortunat." *Venanzio Fortunato tra Italia e Francia.* Treviso, 1993, 81–98.

———. *La Royauté dans la literature latine de Sidoine Apollinaire à Isidore de Séville.* Rome, 1981.

Rogers, B. "The Poems of Venantius Fortunatus: A Translation and Commentary." Ph.D. diss., Rutgers University, 1969.

Stroheker, K. F. *Der senatorische Adel im spätantiken Gallien.* Tübingen, 1948.

Thierry, A. *Récits des temps merovingiens.* Paris, 1858.

Van Dam, R., trans. *Gregory of Tours: Glory of the Confessors.* Liverpool, 1988.

———. *Gregory of Tours: Glory of the Martyrs.* Liverpool, 1988.

———. *Saints and their Miracles in Late Antique Gaul.* Princeton, 1993.

Vieillard-Troiekouroff, M. *Les monuments religieux de la Gaule d'apres les oeuvres de Grégoire de Tours.* Paris, 1976.

Wood, I. "The Ecclesiastical Politics of Merovingian Clermont." In *Ideal and Reality in Frankish and Anglo-Saxon Society: Studies Presented to J. M. Wallace-Hadrill,* edited by P. Wormald, D. Bullough, and R. Collins. Oxford, 1983, 34–57.

Index of Fortunatus' Poems

References to poems translated in this volume are given in italic type.

General Index

In addition to allowing readers to negotiate content, this index also serves as a glossary of names, dates, figures, places, and events. References to poems translated in this volume are given in italic type.